Directing Forensics:
Debate and Contest Speaking

Directing Forensics:
Debate and Contest Speaking

Compiled by
Don F. Faules
OHIO UNIVERSITY

and

Richard D. Rieke
THE OHIO STATE UNIVERSITY

INTERNATIONAL TEXTBOOK COMPANY
SCRANTON, PENNSYLVANIA

Preface

The need for forensic skill has been recognized in this country from the very outset of secondary and higher education. The continuing belief in forensic education has manifested itself in larger and widespread programs during the space age. However, no one single volume has been written for the individual who wishes to obtain a comprehensive view of the pedagogical and managerial processes involved in forensic education. The authors have experienced the frustration of instructing others without the benefit of one source that would give an overall picture of the philosophy and methodology employed in forensic programs in the high school and college. It was this stimulus that prompted the development of a text that considers past, present, and future development of forensic activities. This text is designed for the high school or college teacher who wishes to gain a perspective of the theory and technique involved in forensic education.

The authors sought to provide theoretical discussion and practical advice necessary to the understanding and teaching of skills. Although the book describes normative behavior, it is not written for the rule-oriented individual or those who search for prescriptions. The emphasis is placed on why certain procedures may or may not be fruitful. In addition, it was the intent of the authors that the reader view *some* of the ways that concepts are taught and not *the* method of teaching. The book was written for those individuals who wish to have their thinking stimulated rather than supplied.

Don. F. Faules
Richard D. Rieke

Contributors

Don F. Faules, Ph.D., The Ohio State University, is former Director of Debate at Colorado State College, Greeley, and Ohio University. Dr. Faules is currently Associate Professor of Speech and Associate Director of the Center for Communication Studies, Ohio University, Athens.

Richard D. Rieke, Ph.D., The Ohio State University, is former Director of Forensics at Ohio State University. Dr. Rieke is currently Associate Professor of Speech, The Ohio State University, Columbus.

George Ziegelmueller, Ph.D., Northwestern University, is Associate Professor of Speech and Director of Forensics at Wayne State University, Detroit.

Robert E. Dunham, Ph.D., The Ohio State University, is former Director of the Ohio High School Speech League and the Pennsylvania High School Speech League. Dr. Dunham is currently Associate Professor of Speech and Assistant to the Vice President for Resident Instruction, Pennsylvania State University, University Park.

Edward L. McGlone, Ph.D., Ohio University, is Assistant Professor of Speech and Supervisor of Forensics, Northern Illinois University, DeKalb.

Contents

CHAPTER 1

The Development of Forensic Activities

Don F. Faules

At some time during a teacher's career he will be asked to explain why he is asking students to perform in a certain way or to carry out a particular task. His answer will determine whether he is an educator or a trainer, whether he himself is educated, and whether he has considered the reasons for his beliefs. The educator knows the "why" of what he does, and to him theory and conceptual knowledge take precedence over conditioned responses. It is not enough for the teacher to say, "It's always been done that way." A student, peer, or even a superior will still want to know why. Pedagogy is generated by theory, and theory comes from a philosophy which is grounded in certain values. When one wants to know what influences account for the present state of affairs, he cannot ignore the past. Knowledge of the past helps the teacher formulate both answers and questions for the future, as well as the present. So it is with forensic education.

It is necessary for the forensics instructor to understand just what forensic education is designed to do. Although the following discussion will not ignore theoretical considerations, the main emphasis will be placed on pedagogical movements. (It would be fallacious to attempt to cover the scope and development of forensic education in anything less than a several-volume work. Nevertheless, we cannot disregard a rich heritage that has had an impact on what we have come to know as forensics. And it should be remembered that forensic speaking refers to courtroom speaking or legal speaking. Since its origin, the term "forensics" has been applied to discussion, debate, and a number of other types of speaking. (In Chapter 2 there is an extensive discussion of the term "forensics.")

The following is a brief history of some of the major developments in forensic education which have set patterns of methodology and philosophy for the present day. This does not mean that the patterns presented are right, nor does it mean that they will not change.

ANTECEDENTS OF FORENSIC EDUCATION

The Classical and Medieval periods provide a contrast in pedagogy because of the differing conditions and philosophies. The concept of the function of speaking differs considerably when one examines the subjects and the purposes of speaking exercises. The Classical period emphasizes the notion of probability, while the Medieval period stresses demonstration of truths. The subject matter of speaking exercises during the Classical period deals with social and political problems; that of the Medieval period is more concerned with academic questions.

The Classical Period

In ancient Greece speaking was stimulated by a democratic society that allowed citizens to participate in social decisions. Because oratory was linked with statesmanship and because defendants in the courts acted as their own lawyers, speaking ability was not only necessary but highly prized.[1] It is little wonder that such a highly prized skill soon attracted those who viewed it as a marketable commodity.

Contributions of the Sophists

The sophists recognized that in courts of law, the legislative assembly, and in practical affairs it was most difficult to determine the truth or the "right" answer to questions of justice or policy. In these matters men were convinced by arguments that held the greatest likelihood of truth. Corax and Tisias have been given

[1] W. Rhys Roberts, *Greek Rhetoric and Literary Criticism* (New York: Longmans, Green and Co., 1928), 1–30.

credit for formulating principles that were applicable to these situations.[2] The concepts of probability and "relative truth" were the bases for the teaching by the sophists.

Protagoras (481-411 B.C.), who has been called the "father of debate," invented themes on which his pupils argued the pros and cons. He believed that this practical exercise was a way to train men to participate in Greek society.[3]

Although the sophists contributed to citizen-participation in legal and political matters, their teaching tended to be shallow because of confusion between technique and knowledge. The sophist was concerned primarily with the effect of an argument upon an audience, and sometimes the validity of that argument left much to be desired.

Indictments Against the Sophists

The excesses of the sophists were assailed by those who realized that this kind of philosophy promoted the efforts of those who would take advantage of the weak. If truth or justice in a controversy was decided by what people would accept, then trickery and deceit became the determinants. The most severe indictments against the sophists were issued by Plato, who satirized the teaching of the sophists to demonstrate that they were more interested in teaching likelihood than truth. He also claimed that the only good discourse would have to come from true knowledge.[4]

The Emergence of Rhetoric

Aristotle recognized the shortcomings of the sophists, but he also acknowledged the limitations of man in his struggle for truth and justice. To Aristotle, public speaking was a significant instrument of popular government. Rather than deny persuasion, he sought to elevate its use by stressing logical analysis and the rational use of persuasion. Principles that are absolutely essential to free debate and debate training were stated by Aristotle. He be-

---

[2] Lester Thonssen and A. Craig Baird, *Speech Criticism* (New York: The Ronald Press Co., 1948), 34–35.

[3] *Ibid.*, 37.

[4] See Plato's *Gorgias*, trans. W. C. Helmbold and Plato's *Meno*, trans. Benjamin Jowett (New York: The Liberal Arts Press, Inc., 1952 and 1949). Also see Irwin Edman, ed., *The Works of Plato* (New York: Random House, 1956).

lieved that truth—by its very nature—was stronger than evil and that if a decision in a controversy was not as it should be, the fault did not lie with the judge but with the speaker. Therefore, it was important that every man should be able to defend the truth by acquiring knowledge and skill. Aristotle also gave good reason for examining the various sides of a question. In this way facts could not be obscured by prejudgment and thorough analysis would prevent trickery.[5]

Although the influence of Aristotle has been felt to the present day, forensic training has varied with the influence of the conditions that impinged on forensic activity—government, religion, and educational philosophies. What Aristotle conceived of as free debate has been perverted by dictatorship and dogmatism—which manifest themselves in mere exhibition, topics divorced from political and social reality, and premature closure of inquiry. But there have always been teachers who have been willing to recognize the standards set by Aristotle. Quintilian,[6] the Roman educator, followed the precepts of Aristotle and gave his students rigorous training that was not typical of his day. Students engaged in the practice of writing and delivering speeches as part of adversary debate, in persuasive public speaking, and in speeches of praise and blame. It was common for students to study the great speeches of others, as well.

Several important inferences for forensic training can be drawn from a brief view of antiquity. Speaking is a democratic tool, and speech training flourishes best where citizens have a right to participate in a free government. The art of speaking is a necessary and practical tool wherever citizens are called upon to make decisions. The Greek tradition carries with it a body of speech theory, a democratic philosophy, and a respect for excellence.

Medieval and Renaissance Education

The summit of Classical education was to become an orator, and this ideal, though changed in form, continued into Medieval

---

[5] Lane Cooper, *The Rhetoric of Aristotle* (New York: Appleton-Century-Crofts, Inc., 1932), Book I, 1–7.

[6] See *The Institutio Oratoria of Marcus Fabius Quintilianus,* trans. Charles Edgar Little (Nashville: George Peabody Coll' ge for Teachers, 1951).

and Renaissance education. Subject matter was studied not simply to know and retain information, but primarily to be able to use this knowledge in the development of ideas and in the articulate defense of the ideas in the face of contrasting opinion. Thus it was that between the eleventh and seventeenth centuries education was largely a series of disputations in which students practiced presenting and defending their own ideas and criticizing others.[7] But this was neither oratory in the Classical sense, nor adversary debate as described above.

A disputation involved subject matter likely to be called academic today. The topics were related to studies; disputation did not seek to build a basis for decision but rather simply to allow discussion of an appealing point at issue. In the typical disputation, the proposition or thesis was presented and defended by a single person called the "respondent." He was opposed, usually, by four "opponents." A sixth member participated as a moderator who maintained order, acted as chairman, and summed up the argument.[8] Such disputations could last for hours, and did not follow the orderly adherence to time limits and speaker formality that we tend to associate with modern debate. Not only did the disputation constitute the major student activity in Medieval and Renaissance education, but it also was a popular form of student display on festive occasions. When Queen Elizabeth I made a trip to Cambridge, she was entertained during the day with a series of disputations representing the various disciplines. The nights had been reserved for dramatic presentations, but on at least one occasion the disputations had been so long and tiring that the Queen was unwilling to attend the plays.[9]

Even as English became more and more a respectable language for the scholarly, disputations continued in Latin. Although the citizens of England obtained increasing rights to democratic participation in public affairs, the students continued to dispute over academic questions quite unrelated to the politics of the day.

---

[7] Angelo M. Pelligrini, "Renaissance and Medieval Antecedents of Debate," *Quarterly Journal of Speech*, XXVIII (February 1942), 15.

[8] *Ibid.*, 17.

[9] Bromley Smith, "Queen Elizabeth at the Cambridge Disputations," *Quarterly Journal of Speech*, XV (November 1929), 495–503.

EARLY FORENSIC TRAINING IN AMERICAN COLLEGES

Oral discourse during the Colonial period was in the form of prescribed original speeches, declamations, disputations, dramatic dialogues, and essays and poems read aloud. Students had the opportunity to speak in public college exercises, which included monthly and quarterly exercises, senior examinations, commencements, and special academic occasions. Student-orators chosen to speak at special occasions were those who were outstanding in speaking ability. Oral exercises were used as tools for testing and instruction.[10]

David Potter has stated that the earliest direct reference we have to the practice of debating in the American colleges is a passage in *New Englands First Fruits* which lists syllogistic disputes. He points out that it is probable that syllogistic disputations were held in the Harvard classrooms even before 1642, for they were one of the major oral exercises in the parent British universities, and were a featured study in the continental universities from Medieval times.[11] This exercise was common from 1642 until the late 1700's.

The Syllogistic Disputation

This exercise, which was conducted in Latin, adhered to the strict rules of syllogistic logic. Latin was the language of the educated, and this form of debate served as protection for the scholar and cleric. In other words, this type of exercise gave students an opportunity to demonstrate the truth which was predetermined. It was hardly free-and-open debate on significant social and political issues because of the restrictive format and the large portion of subject matter that revolved around logic and the defense of logic. When audiences viewed the disputations, scripts were examined by the faculty, printed, and distributed to the audience. As further

---

[10] George V. Bohman, "Rhetorical Practice in Colonial America," *History of Speech Education in America*, ed. Karl R. Wallace (New York: Appleton-Century-Crofts, Inc., 1954), 60–79.

[11] David Potter, *Debating In The Colonial Chartered Colleges* (New York: Bureau of Publications, Teachers College, Columbia University, 1944), 3.

insurance that truth would prevail, the moderator clarified the conception of truth at the end of the debate.[12]

In time the rigid nature of the syllogism proved at variance with changing conditions in the colonies. Among the factors that contributed to the decline of the syllogistic dispute were: (a) protestations of the students, (b) changing emphasis in American education, (c) the Revolution and the resultant need of forensic talent, and (d) a new conception that college studies should contribute to commercial and civic usefulness. The foregoing paved the way for a new type of dispute that was more flexible and adaptable.[13]

The Forensic Disputation

Because of the political crises of the pre-Revolutionary period, there was a need for more flexible training to prepare students who planned secular as well as religious careers. Leaders were sought for the pulpit, courtroom, legislative hall, and town meeting. Students seemed to adjust to the demands of the times better than the educators. They were responsible for removing the yoke of the syllogism and substituting English language for the traditional Latin. Members of the Spy Club, a society at Harvard, featured a disputation on two or more questions at every meeting. The forensic disputation flourished from 1747 to the beginning of the nineteenth century; however, it was not recognized by the school administration until the middle of the eighteenth century.[14]

The new flexible format allowed for the use of various forms of reasoning and a range of classical speaking skills. Although the antecedents of the forensic disputation can be traced to the argumentative declamations stressed by Quintilian, there was no set academic form. Generally, members of a class alternately affirmed or denied a question, and speeches were written and read to a tutor who gave his opinion concerning the question. The subject matter for the disputes was largely theological at first, but then interest shifted to literary questions, secular problems, and particularly to the conflict between America and England. Some of the factors involved in the decline of the forensic disputation were ex-

---

12 *Ibid.*, 4–25.
13 *Ibid.*, 25–31.
14 *Ibid.*, 38.

tension of the curriculum, growth of the elective system, and a growing heterogeneous student body.[15]

The Literary and Debating Societies

The primary reasons for the formation of literary and debating societies were the lack of entertainment and the rigid supervision that existed in the early colleges. The first societies, which were of a religious nature and which were in existence early in the eighteenth century, offered fellowship, library facilities, and participation. They flourished from 1719 until the early decades of the nineteenth century.[16]

The societies were free from faculty interference and as a result provided a seedbed for innovation. The students experimented with various debate forms, spoke extemporaneously, and held open discussion after the debates. Debaters were appointed and chose a question from those submitted by a question committee. Participants had their choice of side, but if there was disagreement the president of the organization designated affirmative and negative members. The order of speeches varied from society to society, as did the time limits and format.[17]

It is important to note that these student organizations provided education that was not available in the curriculum. The members provided a critical audience that gave a decision based on content and presentation. The subject matter dealt with contemporary social problems, and truth was not predetermined before a debate. Although such societies may have had their shortcomings, there is little doubt that they contributed to the intellectual growth of their members and provided training in a valuable skill. The basic causes for the decline of the societies were changing national ideals, intellectual interests, and educational purposes.[18]

---

[15] *Ibid.*, 37–63.
[16] *Ibid.*, 66–67.
[17] *Ibid.*, 67–76.
[18] *Ibid.*, 93.

DEVELOPMENT OF INTERCOLLEGIATE DEBATING

Ralph Curtis Ringwalt, one of the first writers to take an interest in debate and to publish aids for debaters, has pointed out that intercollegiate debating arose as a natural reaction against the lax conditions of the literary societies and against the lack of genuine interest in any form of public speaking that for many years existed at Harvard and Yale.[19]

Egbert Ray Nichols has asserted that the history of intercollegiate debate divides easily and naturally into decades: the first, a matter of foundations; the second, dealing with rising interest and technical developments; the third, concerned with rapid growth and expansion; the fourth, agitated by unrest and reform, by controversy over purpose, value, and method; and the fifth, confronted by maturity.[20]

Early Debates and Their Format

According to Ringwalt one of the first organized intercollegiate debates was between Harvard and Yale in 1892. Thomas C. Trueblood states that intercollegiate debating began the next year in the Middle West between Michigan and Wisconsin universities. The following year, Stanford and California adopted this type of contest.[21]

Format of the Early Debates

L. Leroy Cowperthwaite and A. Craig Baird list the following in regard to procedure:

> . . . Usually each speaker was allowed twenty minutes for constructive argument and the "leader" of each three-man team an additional ten minutes for summing up the arguments, with the

---

[19] L. Leroy Cowperthwaite and A. Craig Baird, "Intercollegiate Debating," *History of Speech Education in America,* ed. Karl R. Wallace (New York: Appleton-Century-Crofts, Inc., 1954), 259.

[20] Egbert Ray Nichols, "A Historical Sketch of Intercollegiate Debating, II," *Quarterly Journal of Speech,* XXII (April 1936), 213.

[21] Cowperthwaite and Baird, *op. cit.,* 259–60.

affirmative speaking last. Another variation allotted the first and
second speakers on each side twenty minutes; the third affirmative, twenty-two minutes, the third negative, twenty-three
minutes; and finally, the affirmative a four-minute rejoinder. Still
a third variation, used particularly in the Middle West, allowed
affirmative speakers twenty, twenty-two and twenty-six minutes.
By about the turn of the century most colleges had adopted the
plan then in use among Eastern leagues of permitting fifteen-
minute constructive speeches and five-minute rebuttals for each
speaker.[22]

Thus it is evident that the early debates lasted for a period of at
least two hours; and the first decade of intercollegiate debating
witnessed the evolution of the rebuttal speech and a format that
was used for some time.

According to Cowperthwaite and Baird, many of the earliest
intercollegiate contests had little of the adaptation that is expected
today. They state:

> . . . The general practice was for each speaker to write his speech
> in full, commit it to memory, and, at the proper time, recite it
> much as he would an oration. . . . Even the rebuttal speeches
> were "canned." To correct these defects, the coaches instituted
> what came to be popularly known as the "block system" of
> speech preparation. With this method, all debaters, except the
> first affirmative speakers, were directed to prepare paragraphs or
> "blocks" of arguments on all the conceivably important issues
> that might arise during a debate.[23]

During the period 1904–1913, the debate coach, as such,
emerged. The chief characteristic of this period was the effort to
improve the quality of intercollegiate debating. Thus the "coach"
was deemed necessary. At first the coach was an outside faculty
member, but with the rapid increase in the number of contests
came a demand for academic credit. The inevitable result was the
organization of courses in argumentation and debate taught by
the coaches.[24]

---

[22] *Ibid.*, 262.
[23] *Ibid.*, 266–67.
[24] *Ibid.*, 266.

Contract Debating

According to Potter, the Peithessophian of Rutgers was the first society to engage in a debate with an association from a rival institution. Rutgers gained the decision over New York University in this debate on May 6, 1881. The winner was on the negative side of the proposition "Resolved, That the only limitations on suffrage in the United States should be those of age and sex."[25]

During this period, the early debates were conducted on the basis of the single-debate contract-arrangement. One college challenged another, the second accepted, and a contract setting forth the rules and regulations of the contest was drawn up and signed by both parties. The rules generally set forth the methods of selecting the question and the judges, criteria for judging, number and length of speeches, and order of speaking.[26]

The length and order of speeches varied, but from a Cornell-Pennsylvania debate contract it can be noted that there were three-man teams. Each debater was allowed a first speech of ten minutes and a second of five minutes. The first series of speeches was opened by the affirmative and closed by the negative. The second series was opened by the negative and closed by the affirmative. Except for the three-man team this seems to approach modern debating in terms of order and length of speeches. However, this form seems to have been the exception rather than the rule. In the first Harvard-Yale debate no rebuttals at all were allowed. Each team delivered three fifteen-minute speeches. In 1896 a Harvard-Princeton contest used three rebuttals in affirmative-negative order.[27]

After judges had been selected, there was the problem of deciding what criteria should be set up to decide who was the winner. Nichols states that sometimes a basis of 50 per cent was suggested for argument and the same for delivery; sometimes it was 60 per cent for argument and 40 for delivery, or even 75 and 25 per cent.[28]

---

[25] Potter, *op. cit.*, 96.
[26] *Ibid.*, 102–103.
[27] *Ibid.*, 102–103.
[28] Nichols, *op. cit.*, 213.

Formation of Leagues and Honor Societies

During this period (1904–1913) many new leagues were developed. Triangular leagues (for example, Chicago-Michigan-Northwestern and Iowa-Minnesota-Illinois) sprang up across the country; quadrangular and pentangular leagues were also formed. A significant departure from the single-debate contract plan was the preparation of teams to debate on both sides of the question.[29]

It was during this era, too, that national forensic honor societies were founded. In April of 1906, eight midwestern universities met to organize a college honorary forensic society. This society, Delta Sigma Rho, has as its main object the pursuit of high standards of proficiency among college orators and debaters. It seeks to reward excellence on the forensic platform. Although the "student congress" idea was not originated by Delta Sigma Rho, the organization is closely identified with this movement. The General Council of 1911 moved to publish a quarterly magazine called the *Gavel*. Its purpose was to furnish the members with information about the society.[30]

Tau Kappa Alpha was formed May 13, 1908. In the late 1930's this organization instituted a student council and a yearly tournament conference. This society gained recognition for its "Speaker of the Year Awards." A national board composed of the members made an award each year to a superior public speaker who had distinguished himself for effective, responsible, and intelligent speaking on significant public questions. The official publication of the society was *The Speaker*, which was begun March 21, 1914.[31] Another honor society, Pi Kappa Delta, was organized in 1912–13. Pi Kappa Delta divided the nation into nine provinces, and named governors in each province. It has orders of debate, oratory, and, also, instruction. Its award of degrees of merit in the various orders include: Fraternity, for membership; Proficiency, Honor, Special Distinction, and, since 1936, Grand Distinction, for national tournament winners. Its organ is *The Forensic*, which was

---

[29] Cowperthwaite and Baird, *op. cit.*, 264–65.

[30] E. C. Buehler, "History of Delta Sigma Rho," *Speaker and Gavel*, I (November 1963), 12–18.

[31] Charles R. Layton, "Fifty Years of Tau Kappa Alpha," *Speaker and Gavel*, I (November 1963), 10–11.

first published in 1915.[32] Phi Rho Pi, the National Honorary Forensic Society for Junior Colleges, was founded in 1928 for the purpose of promoting forensic activities and rewarding its members for achievement.[33]

Honor societies have served the purpose of upgrading forensic activity and encouraging participation. The organizations also play a role in deciding the philosophy of the activity. Rarig and Greaves point to this when they report:

> In 1950 the executive council of SAA (Speech Association of America) revised the organization and procedure of its Committee on Intercollegiate Discussion and Debate to provide a representative from each of the four co-operating forensic fraternities—Delta Sigma Rho, Tau Kappa Alpha, Pi Kappa Delta, and Phi Rho Pi—and one member to represent unaffiliated colleges. One purpose was to enable these representatives to select a national question for college debate and also topics for discussion. More significant for the cause of speech education was a second purpose, namely, to provide a meeting place for the evaluation of intercollegiate debate and discussion standards, methods and materials. "The intention," so SAA stated, "was to bring debate and discussion into co-ordination with educational and ethical standards discussed in conferences of teachers since 1910."[34]

On August 18, 1963, the organizations of Delta Sigma Rho and Tau Kappa Alpha were merged into one. The new organization was called Delta Sigma Rho–Tau Kappa Alpha and their publication was named the *Speaker and Gavel*.[35]

The period 1913–23 witnessed several dramatic changes in intercollegiate debate. According to Cowperthwaite and Baird, the University of Denver was the first school to have more than one debate on a trip into other states. In 1913 a Denver team debated Ottawa University in Kansas and then went on to Missouri to debate William Jewell College. Other colleges and universities

[32] Frank M. Rarig and Halbert S. Greaves, "National Speech Organizations and Speech Education," *History of Speech Education in America,* ed. Karl R. Wallace (New York: Appleton-Century-Crofts, Inc., 1954), 510.

[33] *Ibid.,* 510–11.

[34] *Ibid.,* 511.

[35] Annabel Hagood, "The Merger," *Speaker and Gavel,* I (November 1963), 3.

began sending teams on cross-country tours until by 1916 the debate tour had become common.[36]

In 1921 the first international debate took place in England between Bates College of Lewiston, Maine, and Oxford University. About this time, women began to appear on the intercollegiate platform.[37]

Nondecision Debating

During the period 1914–23 criticism grew as debate activity increased. Such persons as Theodore Roosevelt and William Jennings Bryan questioned the moral soundness of requiring college debaters to argue both sides of a question. Educators thought that too much stress was being put upon winning the judges' decisions. Nondecision contests, first held in Ohio in 1914–15, were designed partly to meet this criticism. They were popular until 1923. However, many debaters and debate directors believed that a decision was essential to effective debating. As an alternative to the old three-judge panel, the expert critic-judge was utilized. International debating continued to expand, and cross-examination, direct-clash, and heckling debates were introduced.[38]

Tournament Debating

One of the most significant events in intercollegiate debating was the origination of the debate tournament in 1923 at Southwestern College in Winfield, Kansas. The first tournaments were sponsored by a host college that invited a number of schools to send participants and, usually, judges.[39]

Tournament debating brought several changes in terms of methods and techniques. In order to hold several rounds of debate in one or two days, the length of speeches was limited to ten minutes for constructive speeches and five minutes for the rebuttals. Early tournaments used the three-speaker team but later tournaments were greatly responsible for the invention of the two-

---

[36] Cowperthwaite and Baird, *op. cit.*, 269.
[37] *Ibid.*, 269.
[38] *Ibid.*, 269–73.
[39] *Ibid.*, 274.

speaker system. The tournament brought a renewed emphasis on contest debating. There was also a loss of the popular audience. The real audience became the critic-judge.

The Audience in Early Intercollegiate Debates

On the evening of May 5, 1881, Illinois College and Knox College tangled in one of America's earliest intercollegiate literary and debate contests. President Charles Henry Rammelkamp, of Illinois College, describes the affair as follows:

> The oratorical contest took place that evening in the opera house, and brought out, in spite of the rain, "such an audience . . . as even the 'Athens of the West' itself has seldom, if ever, seen" . . . one wonders whether it would be possible in these later days, when athletics have become the main interest of our American undergraduates, to arouse such interest in oratory in any college or university of the land.[40]

Although Rammelkamp suggests that forensics would have a difficult time competing with athletics, Potter explains that the rivalry encouraged by intercollegiate athletics was largely responsible for emphasizing competition in debate. Rutgers, the reputed site of the first intercollegiate football game, was also the location of one of the first intercollegiate debates in the East. Rutgers defeated New York University before a partisan audience at old Kirkpatrick Chapel.[41]

The first Harvard-Yale debates attracted a great deal of attention at other colleges. Although the editors of the Princetonian were somewhat critical, they add the following:

> The idea, however, of a joint debate between the large colleges undoubtedly puts a keener stimulus in such contests and arouses more enthusiasm from a mixed college audience. A joint debate and oratorical association is a possibility of the future, and none would be more glad to see such a league in existence than Princeton.[42]

---

[40] C. H. Rammelkamp, *Illinois College, Century History 1829–1929* (New Haven: Yale University Press, 1928), 278–79.

[41] Potter, *op. cit.*, 13.

[42] *Ibid.*, 14.

It becomes apparent that the audiences that gathered to hear these lengthy verbal battles were inspired by a spirit of rivalry. Many of those who were enthusiastic and partisan probably knew little of the debate technique involved.

Cowperthwaite and Baird explain:

> Little doubt exists that intercollegiate debating was accepted with enthusiasm by both the participants and the audiences. The annual contest evoked wide public interest and a rousing display of school spirit. The general public and the average university student viewed the debate as primarily a contest of "intellectual sport" characterized by rules and regulations and motivated by the desire for victory.[43]

Because of the rivalry involved, this type of contest became a big event in the school year. Public interest was aroused through advertising in newspapers, on billboards, and the staging of pep rallies. It was not uncommon for students to hold torchlight parades through the city streets. Sometimes the audiences were so large that a local theater or civic opera house had to be rented. When the Oberlin-Adelbert College debate took place on May 5, 1897, about 150 Oberlin students and teachers traveled on a specially chartered train to Cleveland to hear the debate.[44]

Other added attractions for the audience during the course of a debate were musical selections. The Oberlin-Adelbert debate of 1897 was described by Auer as follows:

> . . . While the Mather Glee Club and the Adelbert Mandolin Club offered selections between the speeches, the Oberlin debaters upheld the negative side of the question, "Resolved, That Trusts or Combinations which tend to monopolize any industry should be prohibited by law."[45]

This entertainment was probably introduced to keep the audience in a mood to follow the proceedings of the debate. Since the listeners comprised something of a cheering section, they probably felt that they were a part of the debate.

It is interesting to note that freshman debaters at Yale and

---

[43] Cowperthwaite and Baird, *op. cit.*, 263.

[44] *Ibid.*, 263.

[45] J. Jeffery Auer, "Debate Goes to Town," *Oberlin Alumni Magazine*, XXXV (May 1939), 8.

Harvard were allowed to take part in intercollegiate debate, while at Princeton they were not. The *Daily Princetonian* on March 24, 1899, gives us some insight into the stand taken by that school.

> The faculty considers that the members of the Freshman class are not mature enough intellectually, to be able to take part in a debate that will be a credit to the Universities concerned without an amount of preliminary work altogether disproportionate to the benefit received, or else without faculty coaching to an extent that would make the debate not representative and an artificial production.[46]

During the period of nondecision debates, the audience played another role. Members of the audience were invited to express opinions on the issue under discussion at the close of the formal debate. Thus was born the "open forum discussion." By the spring of 1920 open-forum, nondecision debating had spread through the Middle West.[47]

In 1923, the audience again played an important role in debating. Cowperthwaite and Baird state:

> In the last years of the third decade, American debaters were influenced by the English style of debating. Characterized by its conversational mode, wittiness, and its stress upon audience persuasion, the Oxford, or British, style of debating had a significant and profound effect in tempering the legalistic formalism of American debating. Also the Oxford "split team" system—each team of two members made up of one debater from each of the participating institutions—probably helped to minimize the "sport" aspect of American debating sometimes evident in a "support the home team" attitude among audiences. The British debaters, stressing the importance of audience persuasion and unfamiliar with the American custom of awarding a decision on the merits of the debating, usually requested that audiences be permitted to vote on the merits of the question instead. Hence, the close of the third decade of intercollegiate debating saw the appearance of the "audience decision" debate. In some instances, audiences were asked to vote on the question both before and after the formal debate with a "shift-of-opinion" ballot replacing the judges formal decisions.[48]

---

[46] Potter, *op. cit.*, 14.
[47] Cowperthwaite and Baird, *op. cit.*, 270.
[48] *Ibid.*, 263–70.

The emphasis was on the techniques of persuasion and although the audience did not help debate standards, they did play an important part in the debates. Cowperthwaite and Baird point out that:

> . . . audience participation, while not generally thought to be a prime motive for increased student interest, nevertheless materially transformed traditional debating from an intellectual sport characterized by a legalistic formality designed to win victories over opponents, to a more realistic means of presenting live issues to interest listeners and of helping college youth to speak well.[49]

Therefore, although some of the formality was taken from debate, it became more of a realistic speaking situation.

The widespread use of the radio brought still another audience. Institutions that were near radio stations experimented with educational programs which included debates. It is difficult to determine just what influence radio exerted upon debate. There is little doubt, however, that such an audience necessitated more adaptation and improved techniques of delivery.[50]

FORENSIC EDUCATION IN THE SECONDARY SCHOOL

Education in the seventeenth and eighteenth centuries was characterized by an effort to train young men for the ministry and for membership in a sect. The academies, which started about 1750, were the forerunners of the secondary school system. Oratory, declamation and forensic exercises were offered at the academies.[51]

Borchers and Wagner report that during the period 1800–1825, almost all schools employed some kind of extracurricular performances which had their place in speech training. The perform-

---

[49] *Ibid.*, 270–71.
[50] *Ibid.*, 273.
[51] Gladys L. Borchers and Lillian R. Wagner, "Speech Education in Nineteenth-Century Schools," *History of Speech Education in America,* ed. Karl R. Wallace (New York: Appleton-Century-Crofts, Inc., 1954), 277–79.

ances included declamations, debating, dialogues, and plays. Many of the academies had debating and rhetorical societies.[52]

During the 1825–55 period, students participated in a number of extracurricular speaking activities. These exhibitions varied, but a great deal of emphasis on declamation events was common. Academies and secondary schools encouraged the growth of lyceums and literary societies in the local communities. Some of these societies furnished training in parliamentary procedure. Although the lyceums and literary societies were community projects, student participation was encouraged.[53]

Debate was one of the more popular forms of intellectual entertainment during the 1855–80 period. The debating societies in these years were seldom directly connected with secondary schools or colleges; however, they were encouraged by institutions, and some educators felt that the school should assume more direct responsibility.[54]

Formation of Leagues

The latter part of the nineteenth century and the beginning of the twentieth century witnessed a desire for organization and management of interschool activities. The influence of these organizations structured the speaking events and set standards for their members. Ralph E. Blount reports:

> For many years there has been among the Chicago high schools a literary league called the Chicago Literary Union. Its function has been to manage each year a series of contests in debate, extemporaneous speaking, declamation and reading. About half of Chicago's high schools are members of the league.[55]

The leagues were instrumental in bringing about realistic debate procedure. Blount states of the old system:

> The debates were written out, committed to memory and practiced under the direction of a faculty coach. After the set

---

52 *Ibid.*, 284.
53 *Ibid.*, 284–91.
54 *Ibid.*, 291–94.
55 Ralph E. Blount, "The Chicago High School Literary Union," *Quarterly Journal of Speech*, VII (June 1921), 258.

speeches were delivered each speaker was given a few minutes for rebuttal.[56]

In the new plan,

> About thirty hours before each debate an umpire chooses which of the questions studied and practiced shall be used, and assigns the sides. The design is to have the investigation and library work done during the months of study and practice. The few hours of preparation after the assignment of the question are to be spent in arranging the data and planning the campaign. It is not intended that the pupils shall write out their debates.[57]

The Wisconsin High School Forensic Association was an outgrowth of the Wisconsin High School Lyceum which was organized in 1895. The High School Lyceum Association of Wisconsin sponsored three contest events: (1) declamation, (2) oratory, and (3) debate. The Lyceum Association set forth a body of rules for all participants. Some events were open only to girls and some only to boys. Contest selections were prescribed for declamations. In 1916, full responsibility for speech contests among the high schools in Wisconsin was assumed by the Wisconsin University Extension Division.[58] Fifty-seven years after the founding of the Wisconsin Lyceum Association, 4,386 entrants from 413 high schools took part in WHSFA league contests.[59]

During the period from 1905–10 state forensic leagues were formed in the states of Oklahoma, Georgia, Iowa, Oregon, North Dakota, Kansas, and Texas. Carmack reported that the most common sponsorship of leagues was the Extension Division of a state university (16 states in 1954). Other sponsors included the state university, the state superintendent of public instruction, the high schools themselves, the state speech association, independent league management, and a state organization that handled all extracurricular activities. The typical management included an

---

[56] *Ibid.*, 258.

[57] *Ibid.*, 259–60.

[58] Herman H. Brockhaus, "The History of The Wisconsin High School Forensic Association," (unpublished Ph.D. dissertation, Department of Speech, University of Wisconsin, 1949), 11–140.

[59] Paul A. Carmack, "The Development of State High School Speech Leagues," *The Speech Teacher*, III (November 1954), 265.

individual director responsible to a board of directors or executive committee.[60]

The typical state contest included: (1) debate, (2) declamation, (3) discussion, (4) extemporaneous speaking, (5) interpretation, (6) one-act play, (7) oratory, and (8) radio. Other activities that appeared in state contests included: (1) after-dinner speaking, (2) choric speech, (3) expository speech, (4) monologues, (5) pantomimes, (6) peace oratory, (7) storytelling, (8) student legislatures, and (9) television.[61]

The state leagues are supported by fees and financial sponsors. The fees are obtained from member schools, individual participants on the basis of the events entered, or rates according to the size of the school. Financial sponsors of the activities include the extension division of the host university, the state activities association, or the local school.[62]

The leagues attempted to set standards for the events and the judging of the events, but they differed in their view of what events should be offered and how they should be judged. The desire for reasoned discourse and adaptation in debate is reflected in the rules of the Texas League. Shurter describes the following rule for judges of debate:

> In deciding which team has done the more effective debating, the judges shall take into consideration argument and delivery in both main and rebuttal speeches. In cases of doubt (that is, where the two teams are about equally balanced) argument shall be stressed relatively more than delivery, and rebuttal work more than the main speeches.[63]

Shurter explained that declamations were not original because students in the schools were not sufficiently mature to compose a creditable speech, and that the declamation contest offered no chance for plagiarism which was the bane of interscholastic oratorical contests.[64]

---

[60] *Ibid.*, 265.
[61] *Ibid.*, 266–67.
[62] *Ibid.*, 266.
[63] Edwin DuBois Shurter, "State Organization for Contests in Public Speaking," *Quarterly Journal of Speech*, I (April 1915), 62–63.
[64] *Ibid.*, 63.

At the present time, the high-school forensic leagues provide management of speaking events, research materials, workshops for coaches, demonstration debates, and newsletters to keep their members informed of activities.

The National Forensic League

In a further effort to upgrade forensic activities and recognize excellence, the National Forensic League was formed in 1925. This high-school honor society holds national tournaments under the sponsorship of universities. The events of the tournament include debate, original oratory, extemporaneous speaking, oratorical, dramatic, and humorous declamations, and radio announcing. *The Rostrum* is the organization's official publication. Awards for achievement are made to students and coaches. In addition, chapters of the organization are given awards for outstanding work.[65]

CURRENT FORENSIC ACTIVITY

The last decades of forensic activity have been characterized by intense tournament activity, utilization of technological advances, mobility, specialization, and professional organization.

Tournament Activity in the College

An examination of the American Forensic Association Intercollegiate Calendar for 1966–67 is most revealing.[66] This calendar of events reports only those that are sent to the Journal of the American Forensic Association—182 forensic meets, most of which are invitational. Lack of growth has not been a problem for forensic activities. There is a trend toward the two-man debate tournament. When this system is used, more schools can participate in a tournament. The rise of student population has had its impact on tournament facilities. Because of a limitation on entries, holidays are being utilized for forensic tournaments.

---

[65] Rarig and Greaves, *op. cit.*, 511–12.

[66] Richard D. Rieke, ed., "AFA Calendar 1966–67," *Journal of the American Forensic Association,* III (May 1966), 66–73.

Although two-man, switch-sides debate is popular, there is still a tendency for some schools to adhere to the practice of the four-man team. Whenever the two types are combined, the four-man debate is typically for the novices. The popularity of debate is indicated by the fact that over half of the schools list tournaments that include debate only. Longer tournaments are on the increase. A number of schools are scheduling eight preliminary rounds of debate, plus elimination rounds. There is little doubt about the emphasis on competition. Seventy-four of those reporting forensic tournaments indicate that there are elimination rounds or power matching.[67] (See Chapter 11 for a description of these procedures.)

A number of tournaments are for varsity only, but there is ample activity for all students. Fifty-six tournaments list varsity and novice divisions. There are twenty-seven tournaments that are for novice debaters only.[68]

The majority of debate tournaments use a traditional format (ten-minute constructive speeches and five-minute rebuttal speeches). Eighteen schools report cross-examination debate in their tournaments; direct-clash debate is reported in one; audience debate, one, heckling debate, one, and parliamentary debate, one. Some of the tournaments employ traditional debate combined with one of the other formats.[69]

Over one-third of the schools reporting tournaments list a combination of events. The most popular seem to be oratory, extemporaneous speaking, and oral interpretation. Others include impromptu, discussion, salesmanship, TV-radio speaking, after-dinner speaking, listening, expository speaking, persuasive speaking, parliamentary speaking, interviewing, and rhetorical criticism. Seven tournaments are reported that are for individual events only.[70]

There has been a definite decline in the discussion event as a competitive activity. Six institutions designate the discussion event as part of their tournament offerings. Three tournaments are for

---

[67] *Ibid.*
[68] *Ibid.*
[69] *Ibid.*
[70] *Ibid.*

discussion only.[71] During recent years attempts have been made to adapt the discussion format so that it can survive as a competitive event.[72]

Today's forensic participant begins tournament activity in early October and probably continues until late May. He may even take part in a summer tournament. It is not unusual for schools to participate in at least twenty tournaments per year. Some of the early meetings are clinics and workshops for students and teachers. A number of the tournaments place an emphasis on critiques. There has been a decline in the tendency to make a distinction between men's debate and women's debate. This trend recognizes the quality of women's debate and also indicates the economy of refraining from such a distinction.

A number of institutions hold national intercollegiate tournaments. Other institutions are highly selective and have participants from all over the nation. However, credit for holding the world series of intercollegiate debate for nineteen years must be given to the United States Military Academy at West Point, New York. The system of selection operated as follows: (1) The United States was divided into eight districts; (2) each district was allotted the number of teams that it could send to the National tournament; (3) each district held a tournament to decide who was sent; and (4) each district operated under its own rules which determined tournament structure. At the national tournament each two-man team debated eight preliminary rounds. Sixteen teams were selected for four elimination rounds. Each preliminary round had three judges, and each elimination round had five except the final debate which had seven judges. Students were able to obtain tapes and manuscripts of the final round.[73] West Point sponsorship originated in 1947 and ended in the spring of 1966. The concept of this tournament has been maintained by the American Forensic Association. The structure of the new national tournament is essentially the same as that of the West Point National with the excep-

---

[71] *Ibid.*

[72] See Wayne E. Brockriede and Kim Giffin, "Discussion Contests Versus Group-Action Tournaments," *Quarterly Journal of Speech*, XLV (February 1959), 59–64.

[73] For final-round debates and critiques of 1949–60, see Russel R. Windes and Arthur N. Kruger, eds., *Championship Debating* (Portland, Maine: J. Weston Walch, 1961).

tion of increasing the size of the tournament by adding eight teams at large for a total of forty-four teams.

Although the day of the torchlight parade, the pep rally, and the mass audience is gone, this does not mean that audience debate is dead. Those schools which are quite active in tournament activity are also typically active in audience debating.[74]

Tournament Activity in the High School

Although no one calendar is available that indicates the scope of forensic activity in the high school, a recent survey by Donald Klopf and Stanley Rives points up the growth that is taking place. This survey which was made in 1964 polled 886 NFL chapter sponsors; 507 sponsors reported the following items:

(1) Years school has been actively engaged in forensics: 1–5 years, 19%; 6–10 years, 29%; 11–15 years, 10%; 16–20 years, 7%; 21–25 years, 6%; over 25 years, 29%.

(2) Estimation of school's forensics growth during the last five years: Expanded, 81%; Remained same, 16%; Decreased, 3%.

(3) Number of students participating in forensics in 1964; 1–5 students, 1%; 6–10 students, 3%; 11–15 students, 5%; 16–20 students, 6%; 21–25 students, 12%; 26–30 students, 17%; Over 30 students, 56%. Average for the "over 30" group is 103 students.

(4) Number of faculty members who coach: One, 62%; more than one, 38%.

(5) Number of faculty members for whom forensics is the primary responsibility: none, 19%; one, 69%; more than one, 12%.

(6) Number of tournaments in which school participates each year: Average for the total sample was 17. The range of responses was from 1 to 75.

(7) Number of tournaments school conducts each year: none, 11%; One, 53%; Two or more, 36%.

---

[74] See Don F. Faules, "Survey and Analysis of College Audience Debating in Three National Honorary Forensic Societies for 1955–56," (unpublished M.A. thesis, Department of Speech, Southern Illinois University, 1957).

(8) Types of contests in which school participates: Debate, 100%; Extemporaneous speaking, 87%; Interpretive reading, 75%; Original oratory, 78%; Discussion, 48%.

(9) Types of debate in which school participates: Cross-examination, 80%; Traditional, 70%; Legislative, 26%; Audience, 23%; Television, 15%; Radio, 11%.[75]

The above findings are only part of the survey; the reader is advised to examine the original source for information concerning current practices in forensic activities. When college practices are contrasted with those of the high school, three conclusions are made: (1) High-school participants attend fewer tournaments. (There are some schools that take part in twenty or more tournaments, but this is not the average amount of participation.) (2) High-school tournaments contain fewer rounds of participation. (The typical schedule contains from three to five rounds of competition. In Ohio the student will usually not compete in more than forty debates for the year, while the typical student in Indiana and Ohio will take part in twenty debates for the year.) (3) Cross-examination is the most common form of high-school debate.

The major high-school tournament is the National Speech Tournament and National Student Congress that has been sponsored by the National Forensic League since 1931. This annual affair is open to students who win a state championship or place first in NFL district tournaments. National tournament participation is an exclusive privilege of NFL members. Contests are held in debate, extemporaneous speaking, original oratory, and dramatic interpretation. Each contestant may enter the event in which he qualified as a state or NFL district winner and one other event of his choice. In the 1966 tournament, held at the University of New Mexico, students from thirty-eight states participated which indicates the prestige of this event.

The Role of Technology

The development of media has played an important part in the

---

[75] Donald W. Klopf and Stanley Rives, "More About NFL Coaches," *Rostrum*, XXXIX (January 1965), 4–5.

training of students and also in giving forensic activity public exposure. There have been a number of regional and local experiments with TV-debate.[76] However, the most extensive which took place in 1962, is described by James H. McBath as follows:

> . . . In December, 1961 the NBC Public Affairs Department agreed to launch a sixteen-week series beginning in February, 1962. The series, featuring sixteen teams selected by AFA, pyramided to a final event, and included one non-tournament debate on the topic, "No woman should ever be President of the United States." Later in July, NBC produced a one hour special program on prime evening time between the tournament champions and a team from Oxford University.[77]

The show which was called "Championship Debate" was carried by approximately 160 stations of the NBC network. The weekly audience was estimated at 4.5 million viewers. Over 7 million viewers were reached during the international program when North Texas State University opposed Oxford University. These debates served as a means of instruction for thousands of high school and college students. Although the series was not a commercial hit, it rated high as an educational series.[78]

On April 26, 1964, National Educational Television launched "Championship Debate 1964." The eight best collegiate teams in the United States, as determined by the American Forensic Association, participated in a seven-round elimination contest. The cross-examination format was used and each team was given a two-week period prior to its debate to prepare arguments. Each debate was judged by a three-man panel that gave its reason for the decision. This particular series was especially useful for the

---

[76] See Wayne E. Brockriede and David B. Strother, "Televised Forensics," *The Speech Teacher*, VI (January 1957), 30–35. H. Charles Kline and Donald L. Holley, "A Contest Workshop in Television Speaking," *The Speech Teacher*, XII (March 1963), 119–122. S. Clay Willmington and Linda A. Swanson, "A Televised High School Debate Tournament," *The Speech Teacher*, XV (November 1966), 299–302.
[77] James H. McBath, "Debating on Television," *Quarterly Journal of Speech*, L (April 1964), 147.
[78] *Ibid.*, 151.

teacher who could obtain the video tapes and use them for class-room instruction.[79]

The Bell System has supplied another stimulating innovation. The "telelecture" provides a system whereby a debate can be carried on between schools by telephone. Specially equipped rooms allow an audience to hear the debate. Such a system is particularly helpful when interschool travel is impossible. This technique has been used during summer high school institutes.[80]

All tournament directors face the task of racing against time in their effort to set up tournaments and report results. Computerized tournaments have made their way into the forensic scene. The computer is being used to power-match teams on a round-by-round basis. IBM has been utilized for rapid reporting of results and the walkie-talkie has served as an invaluable aid on the sprawling campus.

A negative dividend from our technological society in the promotion of forensics concerns mobility. In the early part of the twentieth century a cross-country tour was particularly appealing to the participant because most likely he had not traveled much. Today the college student has usually traveled all over the United States, hence the activity must be more appealing than the trip. A student is also faced by heavy academic demands and only so much time to meet those demands. In order to accommodate the students' accelerated schedules, train and plane travel have become commonplace. This in turn has meant a need for more expenditure. The extent of travel for the high-school student will depend largely on the rules that govern his particular state.

Specialization

If a coach of forensics wishes to maintain a program that meets a variety of student needs, he will need a staff that can coach a variety of events and also serve as competent judges. The larger intercollegiate programs have debate coaches, individual-

---

[79] For further details contact your local educational TV network or National Educational Television, 10 Columbus Circle, New York 19, New York.

[80] In the summer of 1965, Ohio State University and Northwestern University conducted such a debate.

events coaches, and those who can help manage tournaments. No one coach can expect to do all of these things on a large scale without detriment to himself and his classes.

Summer institutes and annual workshops for high-school students have aided the high-school coach in his efforts to meet the needs of today's students. The first such institute was held at Northwestern University in 1931. The 1966 directory of institutions conducting summer-high-school speech institutes reveals that there are sixty-one such workshops. This list, which describes each institute, can be obtained from the Speech Association of America.

Professional Organizations

In addition to the national honoraries, state, and regional organizations, certain national organizations have had considerable impact on standardizing forensic activity. (See Chapter 4 for description of forensic organizations.) The Committee on Debate and Discussion Materials of the National University Extension Association selects topics for high-school debate and discussion. This organization, which first became interested in forensic activities in 1928, also supplies debate and discussion materials to high schools.

The Inter-State Oratorical Association conducts a national contest for the winners of state contests. This organization also publishes the orations of those who participate in the national contest. This booklet, *Winning Orations*, can be purchased from the Association.

The American Forensic Association has been instrumental in promoting forensic activities, and improving standards and procedures. Its official publication, the *Journal of the American Forensic Association*, reports calendars of high-school and college forensic events, convention proceedings, and articles concerning forensic activities. This organization has developed a standardized debate ballot, a code for conducting oratory contests, and a survey of college debate budgets. At the present time, the AFA is supporting experimental research in forensics. The tradition of forensic training is well illustrated in the AFA's statement of principles:

Recognizing that the free interchange and objective evaluation of ideas through such forensic activities as public speaking, discussion, and debate are essential to the maintenance of a democratic society, the American Forensic Association herewith records this statement of principles which it believes should govern academic training in these disciplines.

We believe that forensic activity should increase opportunities for intensive investigation of significant contemporary problems.

We believe that forensic activity should promote the use of logical reasoning and the use of the best available evidence in dealing with these problems.

We believe that forensic activity should develop the ability to select, arrange, and compose material clearly and effectively.

We believe that forensic activity should train students in the sincere and persuasive presentation of this material to the appropriate audience.

We believe that forensic activity should stimulate students to honest and original effort.

We believe that interscholastic and intercollegiate competition should be used to motivate students to their best efforts in attaining these objectives.

We further believe that forensic activities should be under the responsible direction of a qualified faculty member, whose duty it should be to maintain and support the above principles.[81]

ISSUES CONCERNING FORENSIC ACTIVITIES

The reasons for training students in forensics have not changed but this can also be said of the criticisms that are aimed at the activity. It may seem amusing that during the days of the Colonial Chartered College the faculty made sure that the truth of a question was presented. Yet, during the 1954–55 debate season, there were those who refused to believe that the topic, "Resolved, That the United States Should Extend Diplomatic Recognition to the

---

[81] *Journal of The American Forensic Association,* III (May 1966), 73.

Government of Red China," had two sides. E. Raymond Platig described the situation as follows:

> . . . the United States Military Academy at West Point and the Naval Academy at Annapolis, along with a smattering of private and state-supported schools, have refused to allow their debaters to debate the question . . . Already self-appointed vigilantes are collecting names of debaters taking the affirmative side and turning them over to the F.B.I. This is the most foolish of the arguments because it is based on the assumption that one cannot agree with a particular stated objective of Communist policy and at the same time be anti-Communist.[82]

This type of criticism has been rare and the major portion of complaints are aimed at method rather than at philosophy. The more common questions include the following:

(1) Is the training realistic?

(2) Who should receive this training?

(3) How much emphasis should be placed on such activity?

(4) How much of the training should an individual receive?

(5) Is the competitive element overemphasized?

(6) Should debaters debate both sides of a question?

(7) Is the expenditure of time and money worth the results?

(8) What does this activity do that cannot be done in the class-room situation?

(9) Does such training make individuals argumentative and obnoxious?

(10) Does such training implant false values and encourage unethical activities?

When one views the development of forensic activities, it is clear that there has been consistent growth and refinement. Growth does not determine the worth of the activities, however. The basic question is simply—are such activities educationally sound? The next chapter considers this question.

---

[82] E. Raymond Platig, "To Debate or Not To Debate," *The Denver Post*, "Roundup," December 5, 1954, p. 4.

SUGGESTED READINGS

Carmack, Paul A. "The Development of State High School Speech Leagues," *Speech Teacher,* III (November 1954), 264–68.

Kruger, Arthur. *A Classified Bibliography of Argumentation and Debate.* New York: The Scarecrow Press, Inc., 1964. (Examine pages 39–45 for specific studies of forensic history.)

Nichols, Egbert R. "A Historical Sketch of Intercollegiate Debating," *Quarterly Journal of Speech,* XXII (April 1936), 213–20; XXII (December 1936), 591–602; XXIII (April 1937), 259–78.

Pelligrini, Angelo M. "Renaissance and Medieval Antecedents of Debate," *Quarterly Journal of Speech,* XXVIII (February 1942), 14–19.

Potter, David. *Debating in the Colonial Chartered Colleges.* New York: Bureau of Publications, Columbia University, 1944.

Thonssen, Lester, and A. Craig Baird. *Speech Criticism.* New York: The Ronald Press Co., 1948.

Wallace, Karl R. *History of Speech Education in America.* New York: Appleton-Century-Crofts, Inc., 1954.

CHAPTER 2

A Philosophy of Forensics
Richard D. Rieke

Too frequently subjects and activities in education are retained not because they reflect a clearly articulated philosophy, but because they have existed in the past and still *seem* to be the right thing to do. This may not be so bad if one assumes that a philosophy could be found should anyone take the time to look for it. But it has its dangers. For instance, an educational activity may have arisen from a philosophy which is no longer relevant today. While there may still be a valid reason to continue the activity, its character and constituents may require modification to reflect more clearly a modern philosophy. Failure to make such modifications may lead to student behavior which is of little value and may even be detrimental.

Philosophical re-examination seems particularly important to activities which are intended to be practical laboratory supplements to class material. Imagine the folly of continuing traditional mathematical drills in a school which has adopted the new math procedures in classes! Or consider the folly of maintaining elocutionary drills in a modern speech program!

Hopefully, no teacher would today insist that elocution should be included in a forensics program. Why? Because scholars in speech communication are largely agreed that the theory or philosophy underlying elocution is in error in assuming that a "correct" way of producing sound, gesture, etc., can be found. Thus, it would be useless and even adverse to drill speech students in correct tones, gestures, and movements. Accordingly, the activities in forensics programs have changed to move away from gesture drills to concentration on the content of the speech—the meaning to be communicated. This chapter aims at a thorough examination of forensic practices and values so as to expose areas in need of study and, possibly, correction.

Forensic programs suffer from some special problems in relation to philosophical re-examination. Probably the most significant one is this: directors of forensic programs are not necessarily teachers of the speech theories their forensic activities are intended to reflect. The minimum requirement to direct forensics is often only the willingness to do so when asked by a principal or chairman. Commonly, directors of forensics are considered qualified by virtue of their own participation in some phase of forensics when in high school or college. Also, teachers of related disciplines, such as English and political science, are often felt to have the background to supervise speech activities. Without questioning the qualifications of such persons, it can still be noted that there is likely to be some problem in communicating modern theories of speech to persons not professionally associated with speech.

Another problem lies in the character of forensic activities themselves. Each teacher is relatively unfree to select those activities which seem best able to reflect the theories he wants to teach. Rather, the teacher finds local customs within his school and among schools nearby; he finds regional customs standardized by tradition as well as by speech associations; and he finds state and national associations which specify the various activities and rules to be used in forensic contests. The need to standardize procedures so that students from several schools can come together to compete necessarily creates a certain rigidity in each program. The need to limit forensic activities to a format conducive to efficient operation of contests also creates rigidity in the program.

A final problem lies in the character of the students inclined to participate in forensic programs. It is noted below that speech contests are excellent means of motivating students to learn. Similarly, speech contests tend to emphasize those activities toward which students are most motivated. It is, therefore, misleading to assume that a student who eagerly pursues a year or so in one forensic activity is generally interested in the field of speech. Colleges which offer debate scholarships with the provision that the recipient major in speech have discovered this. Students are not necessarily inclined toward that speech activity which will help them the most nor are they necessarily eager to participate in a variety of activities to broaden their experience. Consequently, speech programs come to reflect student inclination as much or more than any particular philosophy.

Perhaps still another problem should be added to this list: directors of forensics are usually so busy working with their programs that they have little or no time left for philosophizing. With the exception of an occasional article on a specific point, the teacher of speech activities is so occupied with his work that he has no time left to consider why he does what he does. There is certainly no lack of interest in philosophy by such teachers. When they meet at a tournament or festival they spend long hours talking with each other about such problems as the value of forensics and the ethical responsibilities involved. But before a set of conclusions suitable for publication emerges, the teachers are back working with their students. The new teacher, anxious to examine the philosophy of forensic programs before going to work, becomes obliged to search it out from all the individual articles published over the last half-century or so. While this would probably be a valuable experience, it would also seem useful to seek to summarize, in one place, the leading philosophical considerations in forensics and advance a point of view concerning them. Such is the purpose of this chapter.

A word of reservation is necessary in view of the problems just stated. Nothing said here will change the fact that many teachers of forensics are not professionally related to speech; that the activities are often prescribed and relatively out of the control of a single teacher; that contest efficiency often dictates the choice of activity; or that a certain type of student chooses to engage in forensics. Neither will what is said here necessarily reflect the majority of opinion of practicing directors of forensics, for few have published their opinions. Therefore, it is not unexpected that the views and value judgments presented here will irritate some who consider the suggestions unreasonable, or unrealistic, or simply undesirable. If this in any way provokes increased concern for the philosophical rationale of forensics, it will have been successful.

If, in addition, this discussion inspires some improvements in speech activities, so much the better.

DEFINITION OF THE CONCEPT "FORENSICS"

The term "forensic" is derived from the Greek language and refers to courts of law. Aristotle, in dividing speech into three categories, contrasted forensic speaking (in a court of law) with deliberative speaking (in the legislative assembly), and epideictic speaking (in a ceremony or other special occasion). The term is still used today in such a restricted sense. For example, a physician who specializes in the study of medicine in relation to the determination of legal questions is said to practice forensic medicine.

Using Aristotle's *Rhetoric* for reference, the student of speech is inclined to think of forensic speaking as primarily suggesting adversary debate. That is, a debate in which advocates are assigned to defend opposite sides of a question so as to expose an outside judge to all the available means of persuasion. This is contrasted with the discussion which occurs in a legislative assembly. In the latter, the speakers are both advocates and judges, and they seek to persuade each other through speech.

In common usage today, the term has developed a broader meaning. A modern dictionary defines *forensic* as an adjective meaning "suitable for public speaking or debate." In many parts of the United States, the plural *forensics* is used to refer to any extracurricular speech activity in both high school and college. In developing a concept of forensic programs as a first step to discussing the philosophy of them, it might be useful to discuss briefly the kinds of activities to which the term refers.

Chapter 1 indicates how, in the development of practical speech activities, debate in some form or other has occupied a prominent position; this is still true today. To most persons in the field, the concept "forensics" suggests primarily student debating. In fact, it is still common in some parts of the United States to separate forensics (debate) from individual speaking activities such as oratory. More and more, however, the term *forensics* has come to include all extraclass speech activities with the assumption that debate will involve the largest share of students' time. As the directors of forensics of the Western Conference Universities said:

> We believe that tournament debating is and shall continue to be the heart of most forensic programs. . . . Although debate must be the core of the total forensic program, enrichment of rhetorical skills should be enhanced by the inclusion in the program of other forms of competitive activities.[1]

The other activities mentioned earlier include a variety of speaking events, competitive for the most part, in which a single student performs alone. Most common of these are delivering an oration and speaking extemporaneously. In practice, many other events have been tried such as oral interpretation, declamation, group discussion, after-dinner speaking, radio-TV speaking, expository speaking, salesmanship, student congress, group action, folktale telling, Bible reading, and listening.

A final subject must be discussed in establishing a meaning for *forensics:* Is competition an inherent part of the forensic concept? The values and problems surrounding competition will be examined later; for now, it is important to examine the strength of its association with forensic activities. By definition, debate involves competition although even this is subject to discussion. One author defined academic debating as a ". . . generic term for oral contests in argumentation, held according to established rules . . . academic debating is gamesmanship applied to argumentation. . . ."[2] Other writers stress that debate is essentially cooperative in that it rests upon a commitment to rationality and operates within a mutually agreed upon set of rules.[3] Virtually all authors agree that competition is essential to decision by debate though not all agree that competition is essential to decisions which are rational.

In any event, interscholastic or intercollegiate competition is a

[1] Robert L. Scott and others, "Objectives and Programs of the Western Conference Universities," unpublished report submitted to the Executive Directors of the Departments of Speech of the Western Conference, February, 1964.

[2] Russel R. Windes, Jr., "Competitive Debating: The Speech Program, The Individual, and Society," *The Speech Teacher,* IX, No. 2 (March 1960), 100.

[3] For a full statement of this philosophy see Douglas Ehninger and Wayne Brockriede, *Decision by Debate* (New York: Dodd, Mead & Company, 1963).

relative latecomer in the field of speech activity. It was not until the 1880's that the first intercollegiate debates were held.[4] It was only at the beginning of this century that debate leagues and school debate rivalries came into being.[5] The tournament was initiated as recently as 1923[6] (see Chapter 1). So, competition has not been necessarily associated with forensics to the extent that it should be considered inevitable.

On the other hand, in the period which has followed the development of the tournament for both debate and other speech events, including the ease of transportation which makes it economical to transport students from one school to another, competition has assumed the role of a prime constituent of forensics. Although some forensic programs remain primarily devoted to noncompetitive activities, and some forensic events do not involve competition, it is true that the mention of the concept forensics implies to most people in the field a *competitive* speech activity.

FORENSICS AND GENERAL EDUCATION

In the next section, an examination will be made of the various goals which have been advanced for forensic programs. Here, a similar but not the same question is posed: How should extracurricular speech activities be viewed in relation to an overall program of education at the high-school and college levels? The concentration on practice at the expense of philosophy by the director of forensics has already been mentioned. Added to this, and perhaps a product of this, is the lack of a clearly defined concept of the forensic programs in the total educational structure. Sometimes, as was suggested earlier, speech activities are considered a clear laboratory extension of classroom work. Changing the term from "extracurricular" to "co-curricular," the program may even be set up so that students receive academic credit only for

---

[4] David Potter, *Debating in the Colonial Chartered Colleges* (New York: Bureau of Publications, Teachers College, Columbia University, 1944), 94–101.

[5] E. R. Nichols, "A Historical Sketch of Inter-Collegiate Debating: I," *Quarterly Journal of Speech*, XXII, No. 2 (April 1936), 217.

[6] Winston L. Brembeck, "Correct the Evils," *The Gavel*, XXIII, No. 4 (May 1950).

participation in the forensic program. Although the unique characteristics of forensics could still be recognized, the co-curricular
plan would also presume that the forensic program would benefit
from administrative recognition in terms of load reduction for the
teacher in charge, adequate budget from school curriculum funds,
professional qualifications for the teacher, and so forth. This plan,
if clearly defined, would also help in determining the proper goals
to be sought in a forensics program. That is, if forensic activities
were viewed as a laboratory for the speech class, the goals of the
activity would be dictated by the content of the class.

Sometimes forensics programs are seen in even broader terms—
similar to the rationale of the old disputation—wherein they are
expected to serve an integrative function bringing together all the
knowledge a student gains in classes in the solution of practical
problems. Even here, the role is exclusively an educational one,
with goals determined by the content of the curriculum.

But not all administrators, or faculty members, or even directors
of forensics take this broad view. Many would discount it altogether. In practice, forensic programs often take the form of a student club or after-school activity; an opportunity for students to
pursue interests and hobbies which are both self-fulfilling and socially useful. The teacher in charge plays the role not of educator
but of adviser or moderator. In this function, it becomes acceptable for the administrator to assign the task of meeting with the
forensic students to the teacher who still has a free period in his
schedule. Or, as is the case in some of the leading universities, it
becomes acceptable for the administrator to hire, on a part-time
basis, a young graduate student or law student to spend some time
with the debaters and drive them to tournaments.

Consistent with the concept of forensics as a student activity is
that of it being another varsity sport suitable for students more
inclined to brain than brawn, and providing another medium to
bring honor to the school. (Reference to the teacher in charge of
the forensics program as a coach suggests that this view is held by
many persons.) This concept philosophically supports the notion
that the chief function of forensics is to provide high-level activity for those few students capable and interested. The coach
would be inclined to hold tryouts for the team, eliminating those
who do not qualify or for whom there is simply not enough

coaching time available or enough contests to enter. Such a concept would also philosophically support the practice of what is negatively called a star system, or the expenditure of a disproportionate amount of teacher-time and institutional funds for those few students most capable, and most likely to win the contests.

In itemizing the various concepts of forensics, there is no intent to suggest that they are the only possibilities or that they are mutually exclusive. On the contrary, a single program will probably incorporate each of these concepts at one time or another, at least in the eyes of some observers. Nor is it necessarily so that the various concepts are given here ranked from worst to best, even though there is a strong tendency to find the first one more socially acceptable or respectable.

The problem under scrutiny here is the very ambiguity and instability of the concepts themselves. Quite frequently, forensic programs owe their existence not to an emergent educational need but to the enrollment of students who participated in debate in high school and who would like to continue it in college, or to the appearance of a teacher who had debate in college and would like to institute a program in the high school.[7] Such a forensics program, at least as seen in the minds of these students and teachers, is not necessarily institutionalized for permanence and stability, and this can lead both types of participators to develop an insecurity (often valid) and a defensiveness when required to explain the existence of the program.

Associated with this result is an inclination to talk about the goals and values of forensics in an argumentative way, leading not to statements of educational purposes but to an apology. Teachers of debate succumb to the temptation of *post hoc* reasoning in their effort to prove themselves to the educational world, tending to assume values for their programs for which only questionable support exists. "Once we formulate a defensible educational philosophy," says one author, "and objectively test our pedagogical devices, such as tournaments and decisionless audience debates, we can determine with greater confidence whether some teachers have overemphasized one or both of these teaching devices." Until such a philosophy and testing occurs, however, this author cau-

---

[7] For illustrations of this tendency, see Potter and Nichols in the works already cited.

tions advocates of forensics to be ". . . less dogmatic in our pronouncements."[8]

Such a nationwide professional organization as the American Forensic Association, with its ability to attract to its membership teachers of forensics both in high school and college, both in the field of speech and out, has the capacity to help develop a clear concept of forensics and communicate it throughout the country. If this organization can avoid the very defensiveness and ambiguity of purpose which has beset teachers of forensics and instead prove capable of setting up clear goals understood and respected by all in education, then it will be possible to measure the contribution of forensics to education and adjust it as needed. Regardless of who does it, such a statement of philosophy is needed. Otherwise, as will be seen in the following section, efforts to set goals and measure contributions of forensics will remain confused.

THE GOALS OF FORENSICS PROGRAMS

Faculty members are amused by administrators who boast about the large number of students in the university, the number of new buildings, the size of their budget, and even the total number of flowers planted on the campus. The faculty man is likely to ask about the quality of ideas being exchanged and whether or not anything of value is being accomplished. The administrator replies that ideas are hard to quantify and values are illusive, but everyone understands physical size and cost in dollars. In a way, directors of forensics are under the same pressure as administrators—or at least many think they are. It is not difficult to substitute the pedagogical device for the educational goal and come up with an evaluation of a forensics program solely in terms of total numbers of students involved, contests entered, miles traveled, victories secured, and total per cent of wins over losses. "Those who are motivated by these values," says Glen E. Mills of Northwestern University,

> should realize that size and amount can be either good or bad,
> depending upon the educational ends which are served. They

---

[8] Glen E. Mills, "Audiences and Tournaments: Two Forms of Overemphasis," *The Speech Teacher*, IX (March 1960), 98.

should also consider the probability that something resembling the economists' law of diminishing returns may apply somewhere along the line.[9]

Directors of forensics can be likened to fishermen when it comes to describing the size of their programs. One young teacher, upon assuming responsibility for a program, was told that one hundred students participated in the previous year's program even though only ten were then participating and students from last year could not recall ever seeing more than ten. It appears that the previous teacher counted any and every student who entered the forensics office. Other teachers seem to be inclined to enter a student in every imaginable kind of speaking situation or contest, even if the student has no time to prepare, does not particularly want to participate, and probably will not learn anything from the experience. Why should a teacher do this? The answer would seem to be that the teacher believes the greater the variety in the program the better it is.

The Value of Diversity

Of continuing philosophical interest to students of forensics is the question of the value in increasing the variety of activities taught in a single program. Should it be the goal of a program to concentrate on one or a few activities and move toward perfection, or should the director seek to provide a wide variety of activities to students and broaden their experience? Of course, it is conceivable that one program could accomplish both tasks, but a question of goal remains. First, if a program is to be concentrated, it must be asked how the limited activities were selected and what such concentration will do for the students. If a program is designed for wide experience, the experiences offered and the purpose involved must be defined. As indicated above, it is possible to reach a diminishing return and begin to increase experiences simply for the sake of increasing experiences.

Consider the question of concentration. The first issue is easily answered—the activity selected for emphasis is, typically, debate.

---

[9] *Ibid.*, 95.

Why it is selected requires a longer answer. Speaking in practical terms, debate is probably chosen for emphasis because it has traditionally been the core of forensic activities and more students seem to be motivated to engage in debate. This, obviously, is not a satisfactory answer to a question concerning educational goals. More relevant is the following statement by the Western Conference directors:

> We believe that forensics can provide intensive training in the rational analysis of controversial public problems and in the act of presenting coherent reasoned discourse in defense of a rational analysis. The *unique* value of forensic activity lies in its capability of imparting, as no other curricular or extra-curricular program can, a mastery of processes which may be labeled "dialectical" and "subject-matter oriented." It shares with other speech activities and courses, the value of training students in processes which may be labeled "rhetorical" and "audience oriented." We believe it should be emphasized that training in the former is logically prior to the latter, and that the former arts—the logical, dialectical, and subject-matter oriented—are the peculiar emphasis of intercollegiate forensics.
>
> . . . Forensics will not necessarily lead students to experience richly every possible aspect of rhetorical potentiality. Forensics will probably always stress direct modes of discourse, not the indirect; its emphasis will be on rational analysis. Hence, intercollegiate debating will continue to be the heart of a forensics program.[10]

The directors go on to claim that tournament debating is best able to teach "basic analytical skills," and conclude by saying: "We believe that in the past we have often done too little because we expected too much." The argument is that debate is able both to teach fundamental and prior concepts while at the same time being able to teach a wide variety of skills and concepts. In addition to those already mentioned, those values claimed for debate include research technique; use of clear, concise, colorful language; development of attitudes of fairness, cooperation, honesty and integrity; and the ability to speak well.[11] If even some of these

---

[10] Scott, *op. cit.*, 1–2.
[11] Windes, *loc. cit.*

goals are realistically within the scope of academic debate, then debate merits concentration.

Consider next the question of diversity. Into what activities are programs likely to expand? The expansion tends to be in two key directions: first, an expansion into noncompetitive activities such as audience debates, forum discussions, special interpretation programs for community audiences, and so forth; second, an expansion into a variety of individual speaking contests as already discussed. What is the educational goal of such expansion? One writer makes the following claims: that concentration on tournament debate tends to reduce the total number of students who participate in a forensics program; and that ". . . concentration exclusively on competitive debate also limits personnel qualitatively—for there does appear to be a 'personality type' that is magnetically attracted to competitive debate—and I am not entirely sure I like the type."[12] The writer also suggests that the claims made for competitive debate cannot be proved to an extent necessary to warrant concentration. Probably the type the author mentions is the student who is more concerned with the argument than with communicating it; the student who develops in debate a capacity to argue before a critic judge in such a way that an ordinary audience member would be unable to comprehend. The type probably also includes the characteristic frequently found in tournament debaters to value competition and victory highly. (Chapter 11 discusses this topic further.)

In other words, efforts to diversify a forensics program can be justified in terms of these goals: tournament debate fails to teach effectively communication to an audience in a public speaking situation; it is not attractive to all kinds of students who might benefit from forensic experience, and it may foster values which can usefully be moderated through experience in other activities. It might be added, to the extent a forensics program seeks to duplicate actual communication situations for student practice, diversity is called for. There is some confusion concerning the role of interpretative reading and acting in forensics programs. Some would say such activities seek to teach skills of reading so as to serve the public speaker who is called upon for that task, while

---

[12] Gerald M. Phillips, "Total Forensics Programming at Washington State University," *The Gavel*, XLIII, No. 4 (May 1961).

others simply seek to teach literary appreciation and the interpretation of literature.

There seems to be no philosophical reason to resist diversification of a forensics program if there are students desiring it and teachers and funds to provide it. A model forensics program in this regard is the one at Wayne State University which combines an extensive program in tournament debate with wide student participation in on-campus and audience debating, individual speaking, and community-speaking services.[13] The University provides a staff and budget large enough to accommodate such a program. A school with a small staff and limited budget may choose to begin selectively with a few activities, and then increase the diversity as a need is demonstrated and as administrative support becomes available.

While there may be no reason against diversification, there must be a constant search for an answer to the question, "What activities best serve useful goals and which ones, if any, are superfluous?" It is difficult to escape the conclusion that some individual activities remain in practice because of tradition alone. As a report of the North Central Association and the Speech Association of America asked in 1951, "Are all these events as appropriate today as they may have been 20 years ago? Does declamation (the memorized reading), for example, find a place among communicative situations today?"[14] While the answer to this question could hardly have been in the affirmative, declamation remains a part of many forensic contests. Clearly, the devising of a new contest which differs from others only in superficial ways does not advance the educational goals of forensics.

On the other hand, it is probably not possible to devise a speech contest activity to teach every imaginable rhetorical goal. It seems reasonable to assume that some aspects of communication and persuasion will have to be taught in the classroom alone or through student projects other than those suitable for forensics

---

[13] Robert Cowles, "A View of Forensics and Wayne State University" *The Register*, IX, No. 1 (Winter 1961), and personal interviews with the Wayne director of forensics, George Ziegelmeuller.

[14] "A Program of Speech Education," Recommendations of the Contest Committee of the North Central Association with Respect to Speech as Submitted by the Speech Association of America, *Quarterly Journal of Speech*, XXXVII (October 1951), 357.

programs. Simply because somewhere in the world people actually do engage in salesmanship, folktale telling, Bible reading, or listening, it does not necessarily follow that the best or even mediocre way to teach them is through forensic activities. Some study needs to be made to find those skills and concepts which *can* usefully be taught in forensics. Only then can a meaningful answer be found to such questions as these: "What skills and concepts can best be taught through debate?" "What limits are there to the increasing value of continued experience in debate—when is the point of diminishing return reached?" "What non-debate forensic activities actually provide a unique service to the student?" Little serious effort has been made to answer these questions, and most of the commentary that does exist tends to be highly speculative and partisan.

Duplicating Communicative Situations

With reference to the goals of forensics programs, there is a divergence of opinion with regard to the selection of basic factors of communication as opposed to the duplication of communicative situations found in actual practice. Should it be the goal of forensics to observe problem-solving and policy-making in the world and devise student activities along the same lines, or should forensics determine certain basic factors found in various actual situations and devise the most convenient activity format to teach them? As usual, the two choices are not mutually exclusive, but they do tend to compete with each other for attention.

The most prominent media through which forensics directors have sought to duplicate real decision-making situations are the student congress and group discussion. The purpose has been to develop

> . . . a Congress idea that would bring together in a context of thoughtful deliberations some of the skills of oratory, debate, discussion, extempore speaking, etc. along with the practical and useful interaction of young men and women struggling with some of the intricacies of legislative decision-making. This was not a repetition of the contests that had been going on all during the forensic year. It was not a renewal of the unctuous repetition of charge and counter-charge that had reverberated in empty class-

rooms across the country during the year. It was a design for an educational experience that would merge the skills presumed to develop from the academic exercises of the forensic year. And, while still another exercise, it had an aura of reality to it that made the Congress an exciting and challenging affair.[15]

Probably the most important addition in terms of reality possible in the congress or discussion idea is the practical interaction of human beings. Neither debate nor individual speaking contests teach students to behave in the context of human relations. Group discussion either taken alone or put in a context of committee deliberations in a congressional setting emphasizes the application of content to a consensus situation. Advocates of this forensic activity claim that rarely in human affairs is policy-making done exclusively or even primarily in terms of reason alone. On the contrary, it is claimed, decisions are made jointly by groups of people ranging from two to two hundred or more interacting both intellectually and socially. "I hold," says one author, "that the experience of debate, of oratory, of extempore speaking, and so forth, is a vital experience in the growth of responsible citizenship." But this is the additional view in defense of the congress idea: "I also hold that until that experience and the skill developed therein is translated, at least in part, into the context of the practical interactions of citizens seeking solutions to common problems we have not completed our educational responsibility."[16]

Certainly there has been considerable development of student deliberative assemblies. The traditional Unions of Oxford and Cambridge are set up as student parliaments and operated so as to provide practical parliamentary experience. In the United States, the student congress movement began about 1927 with a Model League of Nations Assembly founded by the School of Citizenship and Public Affairs of Syracuse University.[17] Little expansion occurred until after 1932, but then similar projects were established both in Ohio and at George Washington University. In 1935 the Rocky Mountain Speech Conference included a senate,

---

[15] John Keltner, "Backward or Forward?" *Speaker and Gavel*, II, No. 4 (May 1965), 109.

[16] *Ibid.*, 110.

[17] Lyman Spicer Judson, *The Student Congress Movement* (New York: The H. W. Wilson Company, 1940), 9–10.

as did the University of Iowa Invitational Debate Tournament. The college forensic honoraries Delta Sigma Rho and Pi Kappa Delta decided to hold a National Student Congress in 1938–39. The National Forensic League for high-school students established a permanent student congress as a part of its annual tournament, during the same time.[18] By 1939 it could be claimed that the movement had swept the country and that of fifteen permanent student legislatures, eleven were sponsored by speech departments or forensic groups.[19] As a result the following conclusion was drawn:

> In view of the foregoing evidence, it seems safe to conclude that the student legislative assembly is with us to stay, and that its remarkable growth between 1933 and 1939 has resulted from its active promotion by the speech departments of the United States.[20]

There is, in 1968, some doubt as to whether the movement is as permanent as was believed in 1939, either as a student activity or, more particularly, as a forensic activity. Certainly there are continued model United Nations, Congresses, nominating conventions, and so forth, and some of the speech or forensic sponsored activities continue. But with the combination of two national college forensic honorary associations, Delta Sigma Rho and Tau Kappa Alpha, the emphasis on debate has risen and the student congress has suffered and may disappear.[21] Many of the other such activities continue under the direction of teachers in political science or international relations, but the emphasis and guidance toward communication plays a small role.

The important question to be asked here is not whether such student behavior is of value. Research in small group behavior and decision-making is strong in its emphasis upon the importance of human interaction, and the social constituents of policy-making. Rather the question to be asked here is whether this activity should play a key role in forensics programs either because of efficacy as a teaching method or efficiency of operation. Most critical

---

[18] *Ibid.*, 15, 17, 18–19.
[19] *Ibid.*, 21.
[20] *Ibid.*
[21] Charles Goetzinger, "Death Comes to an Old Friend?" *Speaker and Gavel*, II, No. 4 (May 1965), 103.

in answering this question is the factor of competition. Previously it has been observed that competition may not be an inherent part of forensics but it is certainly common. The focus in forensics is on competition and the tendency is to cast activities in competitive form. This has led to group-discussion and student-congress competitions. There is considerable doubt whether any lasting value is to be derived from the study of social decision-making when each individual is motivated to impress a critic-judge watching the process. It was observed in 1939 that the activity emulated too effectively state legislatures and ". . . thereby introduces too much of the pernicious politics and horseplay."[22] The same author saw, even then, what has proved to be the dilemma of this activity: without the element of competition ". . . there is no chance to ballyhoo and emphasize the 'I won!' [and] . . . it may fall by the wayside."[23] But with competition, the ballyhoo may assume too much importance. One director of forensics, somewhat bitter over the recent fate of congresses, said:

> . . . it is asking a lot of people committed to the philosophy of "one more debate tournament" to get very excited about something *educational* in nature. . . . The winning debate team can take home a nice big trophy to show what they have learned. The congress member takes home only something intangible which may even be more frustrating than warm and comforting.

> .   .   .   .

> The impossibility of rating a student congress should be obvious to even the most naïve person, but evidently it seems to have been suggested by somebody and used. The reaction was as one could have expected. For every student who was taken with the admonition that a student congress was a special affair and take care of yourself as best you can, there seems to have been one who was brought by his coach and told that while not good enough for debate he just might pick up a piece of hardware in the student congress. Somewhere, we've lost the values of creating and feeling the success of working a bill through, or running for office and winning. What better evaluation can you find in life?[24]

---

22 Judson, *op. cit.*, 17.
23 *Ibid.*
24 Goetzinger, *op. cit.*, 103–104.

It has already been observed that the chief goal of debate (and some of the individual events as well, it might be added) is the teaching of the *content* variables of communication, persuasion, and decision-making: analysis, critical thinking, logic, and so forth. As long as it is true, or generally assumed to be true, that competition is essential to forensic activities as a form of motivation, then it is probably unrealistic and unwise to expect the teaching of the human elements in communication and decision-making to be a major goal of forensics. The decline of group discussion and student congresses in forensic programs probably is not only a sign of intense concentration on debate but also of a general lack of enthusiasm for such an activity on the part of students and teachers. Nevertheless, to the extent forensic activities continue to devote themselves to events which deal exclusively with content variables to the exclusion of the social variables, forensics will become more and more divorced from reality and it may in the long run become more and more difficult to account for its presence in a modern educational system in any capacity other than a sport or hobby for aggressive and verbally oriented students.

Public Speaking as a Goal

Since Classical times, the ultimate goal of practice in speaking has been the public occasion in which a speaker rises to address an audience. Theories of rhetoric, classes in speech, and activities in forensics have been aimed at the final task of adapting to the particular audience at hand and moving it in a desired direction. The student was prepared accordingly: if he was inclined toward politics, he addressed a legislative assembly or a group of voters; if his aim was law, he spoke to a jury or a group of citizens on a public question; if he was generally concerned with preparing for citizenship, he prepared to speak to the city council, the town meeting, the P.T.A., or a similar audience. The forensic activity in which a student addressed a single critic judge was and is justified on the ground that useful learning could take place in such a situation that would transfer to the large audience situation. It is pointed out that such skills as analysis, reasoning, and organization, can be efficiently and effectively taught by a critic judge without the difficulty and expense of finding an audience for each student. But it is generally assumed that if a forensic activity is failing to prepare students for audience situations and is even training them in skills which are unsuitable for the general audience, then forensics is failing seriously. This is expressed in the statement of policy by the North Central Association and the Speech Association of America:

> [The end of debate is] . . . the teaching of advocacy. In all school debates greater emphasis should be placed on the speakers' talking to an audience. Possibly desirable or necessary as an exercise or as a rehearsal, tournament debating can not be justified as an end in itself. Does not every student of debating have the right to speak before a genuine audience at least as often as he speaks in a tournament rehearsal?[25]

Thus, critic-judged forensic activities are viewed as a rehearsal, not for a real-life situation, but a rehearsal for the final student practice activity of speaking before a live audience.

There can be no doubt that most forensic activities now occur in a critic-judge situation. There is considerable doubt, as will be discussed later, whether such practice inculcates good habits of audience speaking. It is traditional in the United States to observe that British debaters charm audiences and to regret that American students do not develop the same ability. In contrast, American debaters tend to develop habits of fast-talking, emphasis of the reading of quotations for documentation, and talking in a content-code that can only be understood by one who is well informed on the topic and willing to listen carefully and take notes. Former debaters and speech teachers who were active in forensics twenty or more years ago remember a time when all debating and oratory took place before enthusiastic audiences, and they criticize the current tendency to intersperse an occasional audience appearance between regular tournament activities.

The issue here is not the capacity of critic-judged activities to teach effective public speaking, but rather whether effective public speaking is the only legitimate goal of forensics! It should first be stressed that the question is not one of debating before a judge *or* an audience; it is a question of learning to speak to one kind of audience—the critic-judge—or another kind of audience—a large

---

[25] "A Program of Speech Education," *op. cit.*, 357.

group. If one were to consider the various roles played by students after graduation, he would undoubtedly realize that most people rarely find themselves standing before a large audience with a need to communicate. Even those who frequently engage in public speaking probably expend more of their communicative efforts in semipublic and private situations involving from two to ten people freely interacting and behaving not at all like the so-called "audience."

Recall the politician: certainly he addresses the legislature and his constituents; but he spends long and important hours in committee discussions, party caucus, and with lobbyists. Or the attorney: certainly he will address juries and citizens' groups, but most of his work is in an office informing and convincing clients, negotiating with other attorneys, and interviewing and persuading individuals. Consider the ordinary citizen: certainly he may occasionally address town meetings, city councils, and PTA groups, but his day-by-day challenges will probably be in business conferences, planning sessions, social meetings of an informal, small group nature, and so forth. As one observer has said:

> Before anyone dichotomizes tournament debating and audience debating and declares that only the latter is realistic, he should face the facts that many important debates in real life are not presented for audiences in the popular sense, and that the rival advocates *do* compete for decisions.[26]

In more forceful words, another has said: "If we remember what academic debating is and is not, then we should concern ourselves less with entertaining a large audience through a program of 'audience debates' and more with teaching sound and thorough research, good case analysis and construction, and good attack and defense."[27] He goes on to say that, "Academic debating in its true perspective does not have as one of its purposes the conviction of the masses; it is not for the purpose of entertainment or amusement. Nor is its chief function the teaching of oratorical delivery."[28]

To assume that the true perspective of academic debate is

---

[26] Mills, *op. cit.*, 96.
[27] Windes, *op. cit.*, 101.
[28] *Ibid.*

totally apart from speaking to audiences (either ordinary or specialized) is probably extreme and may be a reaction to the equally
extreme assumption that audience speaking is the only goal of academic debate. Although a great proportion of the speaking that
people do is not public, it does not necessarily follow that public
speaking is less important than it once was, even though values
have changed in terms of oratorical delivery. But there is a need
for a re-evaluation of priorities. It can no longer be assumed that
public speaking is unequivocally the most important goal of forensic programs. Student behavior which results in increased
capacity to communicate, persuade, solve problems and make
decisions in the less publicized (but no less important) small
conferences, negotiations, and interviews is equally important to
education.

If this thesis is accepted, some modifications of immediate goals
of forensics programs will result. It does not necessarily follow,
then, that failure to provide as many audience debates as tournament debates is a failure in education itself. Under this thesis it is
possible to conclude that students would be cheated educationally
if they experienced only audience speaking. While this may seem
heretical, one need only refer to the same British debaters mentioned before (and call attention to their penchant for humor and
articulate—but highly speculative—opinion at the expense of rigorous analysis and documentation of ideas) to illustrate the value of
speaking before a critic judge. If this revision of goals is accepted,
the assumption that four full years of tournament debate is educationally fallacious or even useless cannot be held. While it may
still be valuable to spend the senior year speaking exclusively for
audiences, it is also valuable to continue critic-judge debate as
long as learning takes place; nonaudience activities need not be
considered a rehearsal for a rehearsal—they can be held as an
educational end in themselves.

Decision-Making as a Goal

While the preceding discussion has stressed such goals of forensics as critical thinking, effective research and analysis, and
logical organization, the purpose of these ends requires some

attention. That is to say, the generic term usually used to suggest such talents as these (including public speaking) is advocacy or persuasion. The attention is directed toward the function of influencing opinion and decision. Debaters and persuasive speakers in forensics programs devote themselves almost exclusively to the preparation of partisan statements designed to express a single point of view in a debatable controversy. While most debaters today receive experience defending both sides of the proposition, they perceive themselves as advocates, even though they may be defending a position they do not personally choose to believe. The judging function in forensics is typically left to teachers or other adults with various qualifications. Even then, the judge is defined as the selector of that individual or team doing the best job of advocation, regardless of the substantive decision the judge might be inclined to make. Chapter 10 is a discussion of how a critic judge may vote in favor of a team defending a position which he, himself, does not accept. At almost no time is the student of forensics directly confronted with the task of making a substantive decision on the problem under debate. In fact, many people are anxious to assume that all debaters automatically have a belief regarding the topic either inherently or from the moment of its announcement. From there it requires little effort, for instance, to assume it is unethical to force a student to advocate a position in which he does not believe.

However, when students are asked what their belief is regarding the topic, and apart from the contest, debaters are apt to answer that they had a feeling about it at first which has proved to be hasty, and that now they can see merit in both sides. Some are glad that they do not have to make a real decision; or if they did, they would probably include material and issues which have not been part of the specific proposition.

It seems common to conclude that extensive experience in advocacy is adequate preparation for decision-making in general. Anyone who can do the research and critical thinking necessary to prepare a good case or persuasive speech, it is reasoned, can certainly go on to make a rational decision when called upon. Curiously, students are rarely, if ever, called upon while still in school to make such a decision. Thus it is difficult to tell whether the assumption holds. It is true that sometimes students who are older do judge junior debates, but this is only occasionally and usually not a formal part of the forensics program. Their decisions are certainly not scrutinized or questioned by anyone who might be able to offer advice. Moreover, students who have only recently graduated from college and who turn to the task of judging (for which they are now presumed qualified) often report what an extraordinary experience it is and how difficult it is to feel confident about the matter.

It is, perhaps, paradoxical that in law schools until quite recently it was assumed that anyone who was thoroughly familiar with the judicial processes (as learned through the study of judicial opinions) was able to assume the role of advocate upon graduation. Testimony of practicing attorneys overwhelmingly rejects this notion, and law schools have responded, however reluctantly, with increased attention to the functions and perspectives of the advocate.[29] While there has been no similar outcry from practicing decision-makers over the failure of forensics programs to teach judging, it seems reasonable that high-school and college forensic programs should at least abandon the assumption that a good advocate is necessarily a good decision-maker. From this point, it is likely that some modification of forensics programs from typical procedure would emerge.

Social and Personal Goals in Forensics

It might seem that little would be accomplished from a listing of goals for forensics programs which was no more than the general goals of all formal education. Such ends as (1) clear and rational thinking, (2) ability to utilize effectively the library and other research facilities, (3) capacity to engage in intensive intellectual activity, (4) ability to avoid uncritical acceptance of ideas, (5) social adjustment, (6) commitment to ethical behavior, (7) effective use of language whether written or oral, (8) ability to organize and synthesize diverse bits of information into a meaningful whole, and so forth, are considered to be the objects (either direct or indirect—major or minor) of virtually all formal educa-

---

[29] For a detailed discussion of this see Richard D. Rieke, *Rhetorical Theory in American Legal Practice* (unpublished Doctoral Dissertation, Columbus: The Ohio State University, 1964), 90–134.

tion. Nevertheless, teachers in forensics have come to believe—
with considerable pragmatic support—that most of these goals are
realistically within the scope of forensics and, more important, not
as actively sought by other disciplines as is desirable. Because of
this, more must be said about such goals than simply that forensics joins with all education in seeking them.

At the grave risk of overgeneralization, the following charge is
directed toward educators at large: too many teachers concern
themselves with lecturing and testing their subject matter and only
become aware of the aforementioned goals by crying out over the
failure of someone else to teach them. It is not altogether uncommon for students to reach their senior year of college with no
broader experience with the library than the *Readers' Guide,* and
with the idea that material in textbooks and lectures is not to be
critically examined but simply written down for recall during
examinations. In many of the larger schools, seniors who need a
recommendation from a faculty member have difficulty finding
one who will remember their name.

Without suggesting that forensics is the only, or even the best,
method of approaching these problems, it can be said that forensic
activities can make a singular contribution. In the first place, few
student-teacher relationships are as close as that in forensics, and
probably few are as personally and intellectually rewarding. The
relationship approaches a tutorial situation. In the second place,

> The combination of superior students, close student-teacher re-
> lationship, and high motivation all combine to . . . require the
> student to develop habits of sustained mental discipline and a
> commitment to excellence. Relatively few undergraduate students
> ever experience the intensity of intellectual concentration and
> production which become the common experience of the partici-
> pant in forensics.[30]

While many feel that the intensity of the concentration and the
commitment to excellence may be excessive (as will be discussed
later), it cannot be denied that it is an extraordinary personal and
intellectual experience for the high-school student and college
undergraduate.

A final, social, goal which has emerged indirectly in forensic

---

[30] Scott, *op. cit.,* 4.

activities, can now be considered a legitimate purpose. As a product of the development of regional and national tournaments, considerable travel to other schools and colleges is an inevitable part of the program. During the course of four years in college, for example, it would not be unusual for a student to visit the campuses of more than thirty institutions and become acquainted to some extent with students selected from among those attending over two hundred colleges or universities. The opportunity to share and compare cultures and ideas is extensive. While still not common, it does occur that within one year a student may visit colleges from coast to coast. Such a student's concepts of excellence and appreciation of varying values are necessarily broader than those of students whose forensic experience is limited to intramural or local activities.

Serving Students in Forensics

In comparison to the total enrollment of a school, the number of students served in any forensics program is usually small. The reasons for this vary, according to the observer. Many claim that there is a limited number of students who are interested in forensic activities and who would benefit from the experience. Others indicate that the tutorial nature of the teaching task limits the number of students that a teacher can serve, and that furthermore it is a rare school, indeed, that is willing to allocate funds to hire more than one full-time director of forensics in either high school or college. Still other observers assert that the competitive nature of the activity leads teachers to focus attention on the best students and let the others fall by the wayside.

Whatever the reason or combination of reasons responsible for the actual size of forensic groups, the question here is "What *should* be the goal of forensics in terms of serving students?" Often, the issue is stated thus: assuming a single teacher can only do so much, should he seek to devote his attention to as many students as possible, trying to help everyone a little, or should he discover those students who can benefit most from forensic experience and give them the full attention required to develop excellence? While it is conceivable that one could help many students a little and a few students much, this is an issue which does tend to be either-or. The teaching of forensics is a very expensive proposition in terms of time. The bright and eager students can absorb as much attention as a teacher is willing to give and still be unsatisfied. One of the truly unique characteristics of forensic activities is the attitude of the students. Rather than the typical attitude of doing only what is asked and not volunteering, the student in forensics tends to complain when he does not have enough practice, attention, competition, or opportunity for research. It is frequently the teacher—not the student—who says, "That's enough; we must stop now." No matter when the statement is made, he will probably realize that the student could benefit from further work. This knowledge is more painful when a student is intellectually superior and the denial of further attention will prevent his achievement of superior potential. While it is popular in the United States to believe in the democracy of education and make it available to all who can benefit—no matter how little—there is at least a sentimental attraction to those situations which allow the setting of high aspirations for superior students and the provision of resources necessary for their fulfillment. Forensic activities, by virtue of the tutorial teaching relationship and the integrative character of the subject, are particularly suited to working in this way with superior students.

For good or ill, many teachers of forensics dodge this philosophical conundrum by declaring they serve as best they can all students who *come* to the program. In this there is a selection only in the sense that the students are left to choose for themselves. Particularly in college, it is often only those students who have already found themselves to be capable in speech who choose to participate in forensics. There is no effort to guarantee that these are either superior students or well distributed among all who could benefit from forensic experience. Additionally, even teachers who proclaim their willingness to work with all students may, by casting their programs either in the direction of superior or average students, cause one group or the other to leave the activity voluntarily. To serve *all* students requires a *positive* effort to maintain motivation in all students and probably does not fulfill the goal to let all the initiative come from students themselves.

This is a problem which cannot be easily solved. Forensics probably will continue to serve a small number of students, proportionately, and forensic directors probably will continue to exploit the unique quality of the activity to work with superior students. But to the extent the teacher believes in the value of his subject, he cannot rest knowing that many who could benefit are being passed by. As one individual states:

> This is clearly an age of oral communication. All of us talk a great deal. . . . Conferences, committees, meetings, even telephone conversations, put us all into the scene as active oral communicators. As teachers of speech, then, we should seek to provide training in the skills of speaking for as many as possible. I would not have debate coaches neglect the bright, the able debater, but I would certainly hope that their efforts would not be concentrated exclusively on him.[31]

The most difficult challenge of all to the teacher of forensics is this: to realize that to succeed as an educational endeavor, forensics must serve not only the student who comes voluntarily; not only the student who sounds as if he could be a winner; but forensics must seek out the students who are capable and potentially effective who have never heard of debate, and who do not appear in a speech class. As long as forensics remains virtually anonymous on the campus, or is generally perceived as a program for those who are specialists, it will fail to grow in a true sense.

AN EVALUATION OF FORENSICS

Once goals have been discussed, it is possible to inquire about the outcome: Is the activity accomplishing what it intends? Is the activity, in the words of the debater, creating any disadvantages? A word concerning the frame of mind in which this evaluation should take place is appropriate. Mention has already been made of the defensiveness of people in forensics. Criticisms are frequently regarded as a life or death matter, and to admit any inadequacy or disadvantage might result in the elimination of forensics altogether. One would think that the existence of interscholastic and intercollegiate forensic activities in the United

---

[31] N. Edd Miller, "The Status of Debating: 1958," *The Register*, VII, No. 2 (Spring 1959).

States since colonial times would lead to a greater feeling of security. To be sure, changes have taken place and interest and enthusiasm have fluctuated, but forensic activities as a concept in education have been consistent. Rather than flexibility and willingness to adjust to criticism, it is probably rigidity that may do permanent damage to the strength of the activity. Thus, it is with the frame of mind of the strong and secure that a discussion of values follows. It is not to *prove* itself but to *improve* itself that forensics engages in such introspection!

A Question of Causal Relation

When the ancient sophist took money for teaching, philosophers were upset. To be paid suggested that the teacher was fairly sure he could supply the desired goods. Certainly all teachers today should be grateful that they are not paid on a sliding scale according to what each student learns. One cannot help but wonder whether it is useful to spend so much time trying to prove which concept or talent was learned in a particular educational endeavor. The attorney has a concept of "proximate cause" which suggests that among innumerable relevant factors, one stimulus was closer to the outcome than the others, either in time, space, or importance. By being the proximate cause, the one stimulus may be given credit for the outcome not because anyone believes that it alone was capable of effecting the outcome but because it is convenient to do so. There may well be a danger of overvaluing a given educational effort when it is the proximate cause of a given skill or concept that is particularly valuable or noteworthy. While pleasing to hear, one must be a bit skeptical when a college president says, "If I were to choose any single activity in college which has contributed most to my career, I would certainly choose debating."[32] Fortunately, people do not gather together anthologies of statements by people who believe debate to be the most useless part of their education. If there are such persons they would perhaps be too busy recalling how math, or history, or driver-training had been their most valuable experience to remember debate.

---

[32] Austin Freeley, "An Anthology of Commentary on Debate," *The Gavel*, XLI, No. 3 (March 1959), quoting a statement by Samuel B. Gould, President of Antioch College, printed in the *Bates College Bulletin*.

While teachers of forensics can certainly point with pride to many former students who have achieved success, almost no worthwhile research has been done to establish the extent of the importance of forensic experience in the success.[33] It cannot be said, presently, whether successful people come to debate or whether debate makes people successful, or whether (as is probably nearer reality) a bit of each is involved. Perhaps it is enough to note that forensic activities and very capable people continue to get together, and if such people find the activity worthwhile and enjoyable, it is fulfilling its goal. On the other hand, it would also be worthwhile if some empirical research were conducted to learn more clearly what are the effects of forensic experience.

The Value of Faculty Direction

The role of a coach is discussed at length in Chapter 3 and need not occupy too much space here. However, the influence of the faculty member in charge of forensics is so interwoven with the values and weaknesses of forensics that some observations must be made. First, there can be no question but that students who have been guided by a teacher will do better than students who have worked on their own no matter what criterion is used to define "better." This is no different from saying that students who have studied physics under a faculty member will learn physics better than those who did not. Exceptions do occur, but if this were not a generally true proposition teachers would be losing their jobs. Years ago, it was charged by Harvard students that Yale played unfairly by having faculty members who could furnish references, criticize speeches, change and amend arguments, and even argue in practice against the students.[34] Such help apparently improved the Yale debating ability—certainly the educational end sought—and the only apparent reason for Harvard to complain was their lack of faculty help. The answer to this should be for Harvard to get help too; but that had been banned

---

[33] Sister M. Annerose, O.S.B., "Wastelands in the Field of Debate," *The Register*, IX, No. 3 (1961); see also Chapter 12.

[34] David Potter, ed. "The Debate Tradition," *Argumentation and Debate*, Chapter I, quoting the *Harvard Crimson* of November 27, 1896 (Henry Holt and Company, Inc., 1954), 20.

by the Harvard Advisory Committee on Debating because the students had become more concerned with victory than self-improvement.[35]

This seems to be a typical reaction: as soon as one has made improvement he begins to think about winning! It seems inconsistent to believe that the Harvard students, when so concerned about losing, were operating on other than a victory–defeat plane. When an educational program seeks to accomplish its goals through a contest situation, it follows that students will be concerned with victory. If the contest is indeed relevant to the subject being learned, then it is to be expected that victory will derive from effective teaching. The question to be asked is whether anything is wrong with this.

It is not too surprising or regrettable that in situations such as this students conceptualize self-improvement in terms of victory, *so long as genuine self-improvement is positively correlated with victory!* What probably concerned the Harvard Advisory group— and what is still of concern today—was the possibility that self-improvement (or education in whatever form) is either not significantly correlated or is even negatively correlated with victory. In this event, the contest situation is failing to warrant its existence and a change is called for.

More to the present point, is there any reason to expect a relationship between faculty help, victory, and education? It hardly seems reasonable to picture students without faculty guidance operating in a more educational atmosphere. If the students are motivated to enter the contest, they presumably want to win; if they want to win, denying them help will probably not lessen their desire for victory nor increase their interest in self-improvement. It may lead them to seek help from persons not concerned with the educational goal (which was precisely what the Harvard debaters did[36]) and in so doing increase the likelihood of interest in victory over education! It might be added that former debaters and law students are still coaching at Harvard, that Harvard debaters are still interested in winning. But the use of nonprofessional teachers does not mean that the student product will be

---

[35] *Ibid.*, 19.
[36] *Ibid.*, 20.

undesirably competitive; it simply increases that probability by decreasing the teacher's commitment to an *educational* goal.

In the final analysis, though, it is certainly true that a teacher can be instrumental in weakening, or destroying, the correlation between self-improvement and victory. He can do this, quite simply, by finding short cuts around education to victory. When the coach does everything for the student except giving the speech himself to assure victory, he is short-cutting the basic process and short-changing the student. It is pointed out in the chapter on coaching that there is a difficult distinction to be made between helping a student to see a way of improving and simply giving the student an improved product which will help to bring victory without increasing insight or capability. Although the line is narrow, it must be observed. Most teachers at least pay lip service to this philosophy, but for some, once the line is crossed it is simply redrawn to accommodate the situation. But there is no evidence to suggest that this is so common as to indict the value of forensics teachers in general.

The teacher, however, must take positive steps to guard himself against such a violation. It is probably untrue that some teachers are just wrongly committed to victory at all costs while others are driven only by pure motives. In each teacher's career there will no doubt be times of great temptation and even times when he succumbs to it. On the other hand, care must be taken in defining those actions which are short cuts; losers may characterize almost anything as a short cut to explain away the victory. Some have even been known to criticize hard work, great expenditure of time, and extensive experience as unfair short cuts used simply to obtain a cheap victory. Always, there seems to be a group that wants to dabble in an activity rather than to work diligently. Naturally they become angry when they are consistently beaten by hard workers. They want everyone else to hold back to their pace and not become too competent. This is a difficult area in which to label something good or bad.

It must be the teacher himself who asks the question: "Am I asking my students to work at a pace, albeit rapid, that is consistent with the value they derive from the activity, or am I driving and exploiting them—to the exclusion of more valuable endeavor— to increase the winning?" It must be the teacher who asks himself:

"Am I writing this argument to help a student learn to do it himself next time, or am I simply trying to win?" It must be the teacher who asks: "Have I become so anxious for victory that I will justify behavior that I would condemn at other times or which I would be ashamed to admit before respected colleagues?" While it may inspire resentment or envy, the coaching function cannot be condemned because a teacher has set the highest possible levels of aspiration and urged students to come up to them. On the other hand, the person who looks upon forensics as a tool for the gratification of his own unsatisfied need for competition and victory, and who considers the students to be only pieces to be moved in the game, is perverting an educational system and doing a disservice to the students as well.

Such personality traits are easy to recognize, and it would be worthwhile for all teachers of forensics to check themselves for the following symptoms: denying any student the fullest possible opportunity for experience simply because he does not win; an angry public denunciation of a student for failing to win; expressing, and encouraging students to express, the somewhat paranoiac belief that any judge voting against a student must be either an ignoramus or a scoundrel; making a public fool of himself in an effort to learn the outcome of a contest before the public announcement; becoming so personally involved in a student contest that he develops "nerves" while waiting for the results and either weeps in defeat or applauds himself and becomes smug in victory; becoming so concerned with victory that he will take unethical steps to prevent competitors from prevailing legitimately. There are other symptoms, but it is enough to note the characteristics to put the idea across. There should be no inference that desire for victory alone should be criticized—a good teacher striving to improve students as much as possible cannot avoid being interested in victory.[37] The critical question concerns the steps which a teacher

---

[37] For a pointed discussion of this idea see Keith Erickson, "Calling a Spade a Spade," *Speaker and Gavel*, III, No. 3 (March 1966), where it is argued that people in forensics should lose their fear of desiring victory so long as it is sought in proper ways; see also James H. McBath, "Call me Coach," *The Register*, IX, No. 3 (1961), in which the teacher is exhorted to maintain a ". . . sensible attitude toward competition as motivation, and . . . is neither detached from nor does he become the third man on his team."

is willing to take to reach victory, and his own perception of himself as a teacher.

The Value of Competition

Quite clearly, the difficulties mentioned above center around competition. It is probable that such behavior would disappear if practical speech activities were not cast in the form of competition. Either the interest in victory would diminish or, simply, people so obsessed with victory would not be attracted to the job. It is necessary to ask, then, whether competition makes such a valuable contribution to forensics to warrant its retention in the face of such disadvantages. In a practical sense, this debate has been argued already and is, for the time being at least, decided in favor of competition. The trend in recent years has definitely been to increase the interest in contests and decrease the interest in noncompetitive activities. Nevertheless, the issue is more likely dormant than dead, and the points are such that reasonable men can be expected to disagree on them.

It was stated earlier in the chapter that debating has inherently competitive elements, but debate did not assume the character of competition on an intercollegiate level until relatively a short time ago. Even in the 1890's, though, rivalries were intense and the desire to win led students to seek faculty help from which debate coaching emerged.

> The audiences were large, and almost invariably intensely partisan. Their enthusiasms were carefully developed and nurtured, as in athletics, by the cheering section. Debate became from the beginning a type of intercollegiate sport in the mind of many persons who did not inquire very deeply into it. On the face of things, debate was a contest—it was accepted in that spirit and its rules were built upon that assumption. Very conveniently, this idea of debate allowed the audience to support the home team regardless of individual belief upon the question.[38]

Not long after World War II, when the excuses of expense and efficiency involved in debate and speech tournaments were not as

---

[38] Egbert Ray Nichols, "A Historical Sketch of Inter-Collegiate Debating: I," *Quarterly Journal of Speech*, XXII, No. 2 (April 1936), 219.

relevant as they had been during the Depression and the War, many in forensics began to request the elimination of contests, or at least a diminution of emphasis on them. The North Central Association declared its desire to abolish tournaments and later, after consultation with the Speech Association of America, said this:

> To encourage the proper response, interscholastic meetings might well be called *festivals* or *conferences* rather than *contests*.
>
> Interscholastic meetings will attain their greatest value when participants and teachers ask *first* "How can we improve?" not "Who won?"
>
> Extra-class occasions for speaking should be as real and as meaningful as possible.[39]

Among the charges made against competitive debate are these: it tends to narrow the scope of forensics programs to the tournament alone; it tends to narrow the study of topics to one national proposition; it lessens the variety of types of debates in which students engage; it narrows the number of students who are used in a program; and it fosters poor public speaking.[40] Tournament debating is held as the epitome of the evils of competition. The tournament is charged with the intensification of all the wrongs of competition, as well as leading to proselytizing by coaches for winning prospects rather than students. Tournaments are accused of creating or intensifying an ". . . anti-social, predatory philosophy of the strenuous life. While such a philosophy may have had a role in America's pioneer days," it is concluded, "there is considerable evidence that today it creates more harm than good."[41]

The replies to these arguments tend to fall into three categories: competition is indeed realistic and unavoidable; competition is a particularly fine source of motivation; and valuable learning does take place in a tournament situation.

First, it is answered that competition and a strenuous life did not end with the pioneer days, but are an inherent part of living

---

[39] "A Program of Speech Education," *op. cit.*, 358.
[40] N. Edd Miller, "Competitive Debating Should be De-Emphasized," *The Gavel*, XXXVI, No. 4 (May 1954).
[41] Lester L. McCrery, "Tournament Debating *Should* be Abolished," *The Gavel*, XXXVII, No. 3 (March 1955).

in a modern society as well. If the North Central Association and other critics call for forensic speaking to be as "'real and meaningful as possible," then the reply is that the world is full of debate among men competing for decisions, and that student activities which duplicate this are real and meaningful.[42] Decision-debating, it is claimed, teaches students humility and prepares them for a hostile world which contains men capable of irrationality as well as reason.[43]

Second, competition is an excellent form of motivation. No one really denies this point, but rather, criticizes using such a motivation. The reply, in one case, called attention to the fact that while condemning competition in forensics, the North Central Association applauded it in athletics.[44] An impartial observer might comment that competition in athletics has its problems also, and that the inconsistency might be resolved by abolishing both activities. However, the argument continues to claim that while there is something regrettable in the use of extrinsic forms of motivation, no substitute has yet been found that will inspire the students half as well. One coach asked vehemently:

> Have you ever tried to motivate a group of young debaters to become skilled advocates by telling them they will have the opportunity in three months to meet Beatnik High in an audience debate? Have you ever tried to motivate a group of young debaters to spend hours in research, preparation, and practice so that they can engage in four non-decision debates a year? If you have tried, you know of the impossibility of succeeding. I am merely saying this: tournament debating is simply academic debating in a situation which adds the element of competition and excitement and gives students the incentive they need to do competent research, thorough preparation, and to learn the principles of argument.[45]

Third, it is claimed that valuable learning does take place in the tournament situation. A glance at some of the goals discussed

---

[42] Joseph A. Mosher, "Debate and the World We Live In," *Quarterly Journal of Speech*, X (June 1924), 332–39.

[43] Hargis Westerfield, "Decision Debating: A Philosophy," *Quarterly Journal of Speech*, XXVIII (February 1942), 24–27.

[44] Court Peterson, "Student Reaction to NCA Report, *The Gavel*, XXXIII, No. 3 (March 1951).

[45] Windes, *op. cit.*

earlier will be enough to show that most of them can be accomplished without an audience and with an atmosphere of competition but that some cannot be accomplished without a tournament environment.[46] It seems probable that students would be less likely to experience the sustained intellectual intensity and depth of research if competition were removed and that fewer students would participate in forensics if there were no competition. Particularly, those students whose only association with speech is debate and whose field of study would probably never expose them to the theory and practice of advocacy would be less inclined to investigate forensic activities.

Competition, therefore, will probably remain—and *should*. Actually, learning to overcome the excesses and undesirable concomitants of competition is a good preparation for later life where the same struggle prevails with greater intensity. The important thing is that students *do* learn to overcome such evils, and it is the responsibility of the teacher to see that they do. As with the football coach who teaches his players to kick and punch in a pile-up, nothing is so disheartening as a teacher of forensics who coaches students to exploit the evils of competition rather than resist them. In such a case, the teacher should be eliminated—not competition itself.

One persistent attack on competition is the fact that a single national debate proposition is used. This practice does not seem to be inherent to competition or the tournament, but rather is employed more for convenience. Further, it can be argued with merit that students benefit from the *sustained* study of a proposition deep enough to challenge them for a full year, and that such benefit could be accomplished with even more propositions if they derived from a single subject area. An evil to be avoided is this: students become more or less hypnotized by the wording of a proposition and their responses lose flexibility after a few months' study. Often, debaters discover that the most significant area of study is slightly apart from the exact wording of the proposition and thus they fail to develop it into the issues most deserving of their attention. Inasmuch as the topics are worded by teachers of

---

[46] For a full statement of the argument see Robert P. Newman, "Tournament Debating Should *Not* Be Abolished," *The Gavel*, XXXVII, No. 3 (March 1955).

forensics rather than experts in the problem area, such adherence to a given set of words approaches indulging in word-magic similar to that of carrying out a crude mathematical calculation to the fifth decimal place.

The answer to this problem has been sought by teachers of high-school debate through the original selection of three topics within a given problem area and the delay until mid-season of the choice of one proposition. This has largely failed to accomplish its purpose since teachers and students rather quickly settle on the most likely topic and concentrate on it alone as early as June and July. The problem is that they know in advance that one of the three topics will ultimately be chosen as the real proposition. If this is not desirable, some other plan will have to be found.

The answer does not lie in the selection of a series of different topics throughout the year. Students are capable now of doing brief study and debate on various topics, and most of them do. But to do this, exclusively, would deny debate its value in the depth and persistence of research it now enjoys.

ETHICAL RESPONSIBILITIES OF STUDENTS AND TEACHERS

Ethical responsibilities for students and teachers of forensics have been suggested throughout this chapter, but further exploration regarding some specific problems needs to be done. There is recurring interest in forensics over the debating of both sides of a single proposition, the misrepresentation of facts in debate, the use of unoriginal material in contests calling for a student's own work, and the relationship of the teacher to the students.

Debating Both Sides of a Proposition

Evidence in Chapter 12 shows that the problem of debating both sides is a diminishing one in the minds of most teachers and that it has come to be generally accepted. The rationale is clear and philosophically defensible: in an adversary system of debate, the decision-maker assigns advocates to present all the relevant arguments that can legitimately be made in behalf of their assigned position. The point is to assure that the decision-maker is exposed to all the available means of persuasion so that he can select from them the best on which to base his decision. If the proposition were such that one side was clearly superior and *should* win the decision, there would be no need for adversary debate. The debater is not expected to distort or exaggerate a position or to say anything he does not himself believe to be legitimate. Even though all of his arguments do not add up to a decision in favor of the position he is advocating, it should be recognized that it may add up to listeners who have different perspectives and other values.

As indicated earlier, the act of debating both sides of a question generally broadens a student's thinking; at least it gives him a more intelligent understanding of his chosen position, and may cause him to change his mind from a previous, less well-founded, belief. To defend one side effectively requires that a person be prepared to state all the legitimate arguments for the other side.

Many teachers are reluctant to let their students defend, before an audience, a position in which they do not have a strong belief. This is probably a defensible practice in terms of a student's vigor and interest in stating his position publicly, however it is not required of those who believe in the theory of adversary debate. Although it is difficult for many to accept, it follows logically that even in deliberative questions the truth can only be defined in terms of the perceptions of each person. A debater may *reasonably* and *responsibly* convince an observer to decide in favor of his position, even though the debater would not so decide for himself.

The alternative to this philosophical position is one in which a person is justified in taking whatever steps are available to him—including the denial of debate—to see that his chosen policy is adopted. It is in this frame of mind that "good" citizens (including colleges) refused to permit advocates of undesirable policies to speak. Concerning the philosophy of debate, it is preferable to have advocates defend both sides of a proposition rather than to allow a position to go undefended.

Misrepresenting Facts in Debate

There is hardly a philosophical controversy over the value of representing facts accurately in a debate. Only the most unscrupulous debater would openly speak in favor of intentional distortion to win a point. There is, however, a roaring controversy concerning the incidence of misrepresentation in school debates and what should be done about it.

Not long ago, a study conducted at the University of Pittsburgh revealed substantial problems in the use of evidence in the final round of the West Point National Debate Tournament.[47] This created, at least for a time, a feeling that misuse of evidence was rampant in debate, though the evidence was lacking for such a generalization. The real concern, of course, was that students were leaving school having been taught directly or otherwise to believe in the use of trickery to win debates.

In the chapter on attitudes and practices in debate, the conclusion is advanced that debaters have those ethical standards that might be desired, and further, that debaters do not see each other making many transgressions from these standards. With such contrary evidence, and with the lack of positive evidence to prove the frequency of ethical violations in debate, it is not appropriate to call for elaborate systems of punishment. Rather, additional research must be done.

What the research is looking for is another question! In the Pittsburgh study, a transcript of a debate was studied for some time following original presentation to track down references and discover errors or misrepresentations. Three cases of outright fabrication were found, over which there was no dispute. Other errors were exposed which would have a greater or lesser ethical impact depending upon the observer. At least two philosophical questions are presented.

In the first case, the fabrications were admitted to be the work of a member of the debate group, but not one who appeared in the debate. He was simply part of an elaborate system set up to prepare two debaters for a national tournament. Is it proper to

---

[47] Robert P. Newman and Keith Sanders, "A Study in the Integrity of Evidence," *Journal of the American Forensic Association*, II, No. 1 (January 1965).

demand that each debater use only that evidence which he has himself verified and thus avoid this outcome? Certainly such a course has much to recommend itself!

On the other hand, it is likely that many debate groups now work as an organization, sharing information and helping to advise each other. And it is also true that much communication today, whether it be in a court of law, legislature, administrative agency, or business, is organizational in nature to the extent that no one or two men can say they have verified material used. Legal arguments and business presentations are prepared by bits and pieces by various bureaus or departments, and the final speaker may only synthesize. A dilemma emerges: Either the speaker should restrict himself to using only that information which he has personally verified, and risk a mediocre presentation in comparison to an organization's product; or, the speaker can use the work of an organization, and run the risk of suffering because of a single weak link in it.

In the second case, material used has been called an error when reasonable men would differ as to the probative impact or ethical evaluation of the alleged error. That is, what to one man may be a heinous ethical violation, may be a harmless inaccuracy to another, and to a third, the reference may be quite reasonable. Another dilemma emerges: A debater may strive to eliminate from his presentation anything which anyone might see as an ethical violation in fact statements, and run the risk of so inhibiting his speech as to make it sterile and not an adequate defense of his presentation (still at the risk of being censured by someone); or the debater may seek to avoid only those obvious fabrications of fact, leaving his presentation free for persuasively stated points that may exaggerate or even change a word in a quotation, and run the risk of being severely censured. The United States Supreme Court has had occasion to comment on this last point. In the case of *New York Times Co.* v. *Sullivan* the court declared:

> . . . erroneous statement is inevitable in free debate . . . it must be protected if the freedoms of expression are to have the "breathing space" that they need . . . to survive. . . .[48]

---

[48] *New York Times Co.* v. *Sullivan*, 376 US 254, at 271–72.

The court decided that factual errors do not warrant suppressing speech which would otherwise be free. In this decision, the Supreme Court felt that so arranging punishments as to inhibit a debater from freely and fully defending his position was a violation of free speech and a destruction of the principles of debate.

Neither the Supreme Court nor this author is arguing for the free use of lies and distortions in debate. The conclusion advanced is twofold: first, truth inheres not in a set of words but in human perception; and second, no decision of significance is made after a single 60-minute debate. In the first place, to assume a debater could eliminate all misuse of evidence from his speech is to assume that he can accurately predict how any auditor perceives misuse of evidence. As suggested previously, it is possible to think of a continuum of ethical use of evidence, ranging from the most unethical at one end to the most ethical at the other. For behavior at either end of this continuum, there is most likely universal agreement—everyone condemns outright fabrication of evidence. But as behavior moves toward the middle, it is likely that the same use of evidence might be considered as an ethical violation by only *some* observers.

A judge may declare the debater has unethically exaggerated the meaning of some evidence because the conclusion claimed exceeds that which the judge himself drew upon reading the evidence. Another judge may have drawn an even more extensive conclusion in his own reading of the evidence and perceive the debater's position to be restrained. To demand that the debater so restrain himself as to avoid exceeding *anyone's* expectations is probably to deny debate the "breathing space" of which the Supreme Court spoke. It seems inevitable that each debate will contain *some* evidence which *some* person could easily label as unethical.

In the second place, such inevitable excesses are to be regretted only if the system of debate is such that significant decisions might be made on the basis of distorted evidence. In answer to this, it can be said that no decision of importance is made after a single hour of debate. On the contrary, questions of public policy are debated again and again over a period of months or even years. If, in a single debate, a speaker has used evidence which seems to be unethical to some observers, they will have ample time to check it out and expose the distortion before a final decision is made. Even in business decisions, if a question is raised about facts used in some argument, decision will probably be delayed until the point is verified. Although a decision could still be based on bad evidence, responsibility does not rest with a single debater's error, intentional or otherwise; it rests with the entire system.

It could be said, then, that enforcement of rules prohibiting misuse of evidence should be restricted to those areas in which there is almost universal agreement concerning the meaning of the ethical requirement. To condemn debaters for other, questionable, behavior is to tend to put an unreasonable challenge to the debater, diminish the "breathing space" of debate, and to show lack of trust in the system of debate itself.

This discussion of the misrepresentation of fact has presented no solutions. Rather, an effort has been made to define the problem as clearly as possible. Factual error is undesirable in debate; factual error occurs in debate to some extent large or small; students do not seem to be unscrupulous in their moral beliefs and do not see each other making substantial errors; simply increasing the punishments for discovered error creates dilemmas which may— but not necessarily—result in the weakening of the debate process itself, or at least put students in high conflict situations in selecting their behavior.

The Use of Unoriginal Material

Again, there is little ethical controversy over this subject: no one but the most unscrupulous openly defends the practice of using ghost-written material in a contest calling for original work. Nevertheless, occasionally a case occurs that leads a person to believe that it happens more often than suspected. Again, the question of definition is the most important.

At what point does an original oration become the work of the teacher and not the student? At what point does a debate case become the teacher's? How much can a teacher help a student before the teacher is writing the work altogether? As usual, in extremes it is easy to answer questions. On one hand, teachers have been known to give students a manuscript to be memorized for original oratory, or a debate case (sometimes mimeographed to widen use) to be digested for debate. These cases are clear ethical violations for which there is no excuse. On the other hand, some students go off by themselves and do their work from start to finish before showing it to the teacher. Between these extremes, there is much to be questioned.

The teacher need not refrain from making suggestions. If he has an idea that will improve a work, he should mention it to the student. When does the teacher go too far? The best that can be done here is to present a tentative formula: so long as both the teacher and the student—particularly the student—truly believe the work to be the student's, then the teacher has not gone too far. For some students, this will require less help than is customary. It is the teacher, as usual, who must exercise the restraint. While there are many other specific practices which could be discussed under the heading of ethical responsibility, the foregoing are probably sufficient to lead to two conclusions. First, even traditional ethical subjects may be more ambiguous and require more restraint before judgment than is typical. Before casting an ethical judgment, one must think carefully, and realize that others might see the situation a bit differently. Second, it is the teacher who is the first and last line of prevention of unethical behavior. If he is operating from crass motives, the students will likely respond accordingly, and the system of forensics will suffer.

In conclusion, the meaning of the concept "forensics" has been examined, and it has been concluded that contest debate has consistently been the key activity in forensic activities. However, in recent times the term has come to include all contest speech activities—both debate and individual speaking contests—and noncompetitive speech programs operated in an extracurricular, intercollegiate or scholastic format. The relation of forensic programs to general education has been discussed, and it has been observed that a lack of clearly defined educational goals has led to a confused role for forensics in education. This in turn has led to an insecurity and defensiveness on the part of teachers of forensics.

The goals of forensics programs have been itemized, compared, and contrasted. The primary goal discovered is the teaching of content variables in communication and decision-making, for which intercollegiate and interscholastic debate remains the primary vehicle. While public speaking is still an important goal of forensic activities, it has been recently recognized that attention must be paid to nonpublic situations in which decisions are made and attitudes changed—in which communication plays a somewhat different but no less important role.

Diversity in forensic programs has been shown to be a subject for debate. Diversity for the sake of mere size and novelty has been rejected as educationally useless. The diversity of the noncompetitive programs (such as discussion and congresses) has been praised in terms of goal, but some doubt has been raised as to whether such programs can ever be an important part of forensics because of the lack of motivation for student participation. Most important of all, efforts to include the human or social variables of communication in the practical study of speech have been labeled here as essential to the continued meaningfulness of forensic activities, even though their inclusion in competitive programs will remain difficult and largely unpopular with students.

An evaluation of forensic activities has been made. It has first been said that a study of the values must not be turned into a defensive apology. The educational quality of forensics has been firmly established for years; there can be no question that such work has been particularly valuable to many students. Forensic activities have proved particularly effective in education of a tutorial nature toward generally good scholarship and critical thinking, and the capacity to be an effective democratic citizen. The value of using faculty directors and competitive activities has been accepted, although constant check and correction is necessary to avoid excesses that might invalidate the entire program.

Finally, the ethical responsibilities of students and faculty in forensics have been examined. Curiously, such ethical questions as the debating both sides of a question and the misrepresentation of facts in debate are interwoven in the concept of debate itself. It is possible to see two-sides debating as part of the concept of adversary debate and not a question of ethics.

The use of evidence, similarly, apart from obvious fabrications, is involved with the decision-making process. It has been suggested that these ethical questions are best discussed within the context of the decision system itself, and not individually in terms of a single student's commitment to right and wrong. By the same token, the use of unoriginal material is involved with the relation to the practical world of speech and persuasion. While in school it is expected that a student presenting a speech as his own will actually have written it; in everyday life it is common for speeches and persuasive campaigns, articles and briefs, and so forth, to come from an organization or a ghost writer with no apologies made if this is discovered. The ethical question should be considered in terms of the process of speechmaking in the modern world, and not in terms of absolute ideas of right and wrong.

In summary, perhaps the most important message contained in this chapter is the notion that forensic activities should be the product of a clear philosophy of *some* kind. Although it is expected that disagreement with some ideas contained herein will exist, it is hoped that the disagreement itself will foster a better philosophy of forensics.

SUGGESTED READINGS

Buehler, E. C., ed. "A Symposium: Debate Tournaments Appraised," *Gavel*, XXXII (May 1950), 75, 82, 83.

Ehninger, Douglas, and Wayne Brockriede. *Decision by Debate*. New York: Dodd, Mead & Company, 1963.

Ehninger, Douglas. "Six Earmarks of a Sound Forensic Program," *Speech Teacher*, I (November 1952), 237–41.

Freeley, Austin. "An Anthology of Commentary on Debate," *Speech Teacher*, IX (March 1960), 121–26.

Miller, N. Edd. "The Status of Debating: 1958," *American Forensic Association Register*, VII (Spring 1959), 5–11.

Mills, Glen E. "Audience and Tournaments: Two Forms of Overemphasis," *Speech Teacher*, IX (March 1960), 95–98.

Newman, Robert P. "Tournament Debating Should Not Be Abolished," *Gavel*, XXXVII (March 1955), 56–60, 68.

Phillips, Gerald M. "Total Forensics Programming at Washington State University," *Gavel*, XLIII (May 1961), 62–65.

Westerfield, Hargis. "Decision Debating: A Philosophy," *Quarterly Journal of Speech*, XXVIII (February 1942), 24–27.

Windes, Russel R. "Competitive Debating: The Speech Program, The Individual, and Society," *Speech Teacher*, IX (March 1960), 99–108.

CHAPTER 3

The Role of the Coach

George Ziegelmueller

The nature, scope, and success of a forensics program are largely dependent upon the forensic director. His ability and view of his role as a coach will influence the program more than the size of the budget, the students' interest, or any other factor. An interested coach will find ways to extend and expand the budget, while one who is disinterested may extravagantly waste a large budget. An energetic and able coach will create enthusiasm and attract students to the program; a less energetic coach may tend to discourage student participation. Although there are definite limits to what he can accomplish, in most situations the coach is the primary determinant of the forensic program.

The use of the term "coach" to refer to the forensic teacher has frequently led to confusion regarding the nature of his role. Clearly, the approach of the forensic teacher is that of a coach, for he provides a more intensive and personal kind of instruction than that offered in the average classroom. The confusion, therefore, results from a misconception regarding the purpose of coaching. Unfortunately, many people think of coaching only in the context of athletics and in the sports world where the aim of the coach is to create winning teams. Although forensics, like athletics, is a competitive activity, its primary objective is not to entertain or to make money but rather to educate. The forensic coach, like the singing coach or the drama coach, should have as his major purpose the development of his students' individual abilities. Thus, the term "coach" appropriately describes the role of the forensic teacher to the extent that it implies a particular approach to instruction and to the extent that the instruction is directed to the development of individual talents. It is inappropriate to the degree that it suggests a major concern for the winning of contests.

In order to understand clearly the role of the forensic coach the various aspects of that role must be examined in detail. There are three major aspects to the forensic coach's role; they are (1) as a teacher, (2) as a counselor, and (3) as a professional person.

THE COACH AS A TEACHER

As a teacher, the forensic coach is faced with a number of special problems by the very nature of his field of endeavor. The many areas of knowledge associated with coaching debaters, speakers, and readers create problems regarding what to teach and what to emphasize in teaching. The competitive environment in which the activities exist raises the question of how much the teacher should do for the student, and the largely extracurricular nature of the teaching situation results in numerous problems of the teaching method.

What Should be Taught

The major area of controversy regarding what the forensic coach should teach concerns the relative importance of technique as opposed to subject matter. Some forensic coaches believe that their only duty is to teach the techniques of research, analysis, and presentation. These coaches argue that as forensic teachers they are not subject-matter experts and, therefore, are not qualified to advise students regarding specific content. Moreover, they contend that if students are taught the methods of analysis and the skills of presentation they will be adequately prepared to select and evaluate ideas for themselves. In opposition to this, those coaches who favor a content approach argue that ideas are the only things which matter and that a deep knowledge of the debate topic or a thorough understanding of the literature to be interpreted is sufficient to assure adequate presentation.

Each of these positions has some merit, but there can be little doubt that the forensic coach must teach some of both technique and content. Both are essential to student speakers, and often it is impossible to teach the one without teaching the other. It is necessary, for example, for the debate coach to have some knowledge of the debate topic in order for him to help students analyze the issues of the proposition, and the interpretation coach must be familiar with the material to be interpreted by his students so that he can aid them in the development of characterization, mood, and tempo. This obligation to know something about both form and content means that the coach must frequently read and study in content areas along with his students. As long as the coach's reading does not become a substitute for the students' investigation and as long as the coach remembers the limits of his own expertness, his teaching of content will be desirable as well as necessary. While the forensic coach must be prepared to deal with content in at least a limited regard, he should place much greater emphasis in his teaching on rhetorical and logical methods. The academic training of most forensic coaches has better prepared them to teach these methods than to teach in subject-matter areas, and it is these methods which constitute forensics' special contribution to the students' education.

How Much Should be Taught

A second major problem which the forensic coach must resolve concerns the question of how much coaching to give his students. Some coaches do very little by way of directing or teaching their students. These coaches apparently believe that by placing students in a variety of forensic situations they will learn through experience. While an unusually interested or capable student may make progress under this system, most students will not. Without instruction in the principles and standards of forensics, the average student will be unable either to identify or to correct his own weaknesses. Furthermore, to expose certain students to audiences or to competition without adequate guidance may be seriously harmful to them, for an undirected or poorly prepared student is much more likely to find the speech situation to be traumatic than is a well-instructed one.

If too little coaching is undesirable, too much coaching is

equally bad. The coach who is overzealous in his desire to have students perform well and win contests may resort to any of a number of forms of "overcoaching." Thus, he may write the student's orations, rather than constructively criticize them; he may seek to impose analysis, rather than guide in its development; or he may demand imitation of his performance, rather than encourage the use of particular techniques. Such overcoaching not only denies the student the opportunity to learn by doing, but it also discourages his individual investigation and independent thinking.

While it is impossible to establish exact limits as to the degree of coaching which is most desirable, certain minimum and maximum guidelines can be suggested. In general, the forensic coach can be assured that he has provided the necessary minimum amount of coaching when (1) he has thoroughly explained the nature and requirements of the specific activity, (2) he has introduced the student to the techniques of the activity, and (3) he has heard and criticized the student's practice performance. In order to avoid overcoaching, the forensic teacher should (1) never attempt to *impose* ideas or material on his students and (2) never demand that students *parrot* what he has said or *imitate* how he has said it.

What constitutes a desirable amount of coaching within these guidelines depends to a considerable extent on such factors as the teaching method, the nature of what is taught, and the maturity of the students. The more directive the teacher's method the greater is the danger of thwarting the students' initiative and creativity by overcoaching; therefore, indirect methods of teaching such as the asking of questions and the criticism of students' work should be utilized whenever practical. When the material being taught concerns content rather than technique there is a greater possibility of "spoon feeding" students; thus, indirect teaching methods are normally to be preferred when coaching content. Finally, with students who are more mature, more experienced, and more intellectually able, the coach may be more directive in his teaching because these students are better prepared to accept or reject direct suggestions without being unduly influenced.

How to Teach

The teaching methods used in coaching forensics must be adapted to the outside-of-class environment of the activity and to the special nature of forensics, itself. The traditional classroom method of lecturing may be used to explain theory or to present background material on the debate topic. However, because of the more informal atmosphere of the extracurricular setting and because of the need for personal instruction, the lecture method has limited application to coaching.

The two most important means of teaching for the forensic coach are through informal discussions and through the criticism of students' practice performances. Informal conferences may be arranged with small groups of debaters to help them in developing case analyses and in preparing for refutation. Similar conferences may be held with orators and extemporaneous speakers to help them with the analysis and construction of their speeches and with readers and declaimers to aid them in understanding and preparing their materials. Once the students have prepared their speeches or readings they should have repeated opportunities to rehearse their presentations in the presence of the coach. Through the observation and criticism of these practice debates and speech practice sessions the coach can determine the particular difficulties of each student and make constructive suggestions for improvement. Thus, small group discussions and the criticism of practice sessions allow the coach to provide individualized instruction.

It is impossible, of course, for a coach to give as much personal attention to each student as he may require, since the coach's time is limited. This is particularly true if the coach has a large number of interested students with whom to work. One way in which he can provide for some degree of individual instruction to a large number of students is to enlist the aid of experienced upper-class debaters and speakers. These experienced students can assist beginners in collecting, selecting, and analyzing materials and may occasionally be used to criticize constructively novice practice sessions. Both the experienced and the inexperienced students can benefit from such an arrangement. The experienced student will inevitably increase his own understanding of basic techniques and ideas by attempting to explain them to beginning students, and he may gain insight into some of his own performance difficulties by critically listening to novice practice sessions. The inexperienced student will profit from the knowledge and experience of the upperclassman, and if the upperclassman is enthusiastic about the activity, the novice may capture some of that excitement.

As helpful as the system of student coaching is, it must not be overutilized. In the long run, student coaches cannot be expected to provide the same maturity of judgment nor the same depth of understanding as an experienced, professionally trained forensic teacher can provide. Moreover, both students and teachers are limited in the amount of time they can give to the activity, and too much time spent in helping novices may cause the experienced students' preparation to suffer.

No matter what approaches to teaching the forensic coach uses, it is essential that he do everything possible to make participation in the activity attractive. Forensics inevitably requires considerable work on the part of the students, and in most cases, they receive no academic credit for that work. The intellectual challenge of the activity, the excitement of speaking before audiences, and the recognition resulting from competition against other schools usually provide considerable motivation to students. Nevertheless, the forensic teacher should attempt to heighten this motivation by making the learning activities *fun*. Student criticisms can be made more acceptable if they are accompanied by gentle humor or good-natured joking. A full day of group research can be rewarded with a pizza party or some other group social activity. Forensic trips can be arranged so that they take advantage of tourist opportunities along with competitive experiences. In these and similar ways, forensics can be made more interesting to students, and the coach's motivational problems can be lessened.

THE COACH AS A COUNSELOR

In addition to his role as an academic instructor, the forensic coach is frequently called upon to act as a personal counselor. The very nature of the coach's role requires him to be concerned with the ethos of the speaker and to be prepared to offer advice on such matters as appearance and good manners. Moreover, the informal and personal relationship which tends to develop between forensic students and coaches makes it likely that students will turn to their coach when they have personal difficulties or are in any way in need of counsel.

Forensic-Related Counseling

The ancient Greeks and Romans long ago recognized that the education of an orator involves the education of the whole man. Today the training of public speakers and declaimers still requires a concern for more than just rhetoric or logic or any other traditional academic discipline. Appearance, personality, poise, manners, and personal hygiene can all play a part in the ultimate success of a speaker, and the conscientious forensic coach will not hesitate to counsel with his students regarding problems in any of these areas.

The student whose overly aggressive personality manifests itself during the clash of debate will need practice and experience to gain control of his behavior, but in addition, he may also need the personal encouragement and support of the coach. The inappropriately or poorly dressed orator may need advice on styles and colors or he may need financial assistance in order to purchase better clothing. (More than one such student has obtained his first good suit of clothes through the efforts of his forensic coach.) The able debater with whom no other student wants to work may have problems of personal hygiene which need to be brought to his attention. The immature speaker who is ill-mannered in the presence of judges and thoughtlessly discourteous to other contestants will need specific guidance in the development of appropriate standards of conduct.

Problems such as these can be expected to arise regularly, and each one is capable of affecting either the preparation, the performance, or the evaluation of a student.

In order to assist students with these problems, a coach must have good judgment and considerable tact. Further, he must be aware of the limits within which he can counsel effectively. He should recognize, first, that the willingness of students to accept his advice will depend, in part, upon their appreciation of and respect for him as a person. It is necessary, therefore, that the coach have good rapport with his students before he attempts to guide them in any of these matters. Second, he should realize that students are more likely to accept suggestions when they understand the basis for the advice and when the suggested course of action is related to their immediate goal achievement.

Finally, the coach should be specific and realistic in what he asks of students. If his suggestions are unclear, students will have difficulty following them. If the coach asks students to strive for more basic changes in appearance or behavior than they are willing to undertake or are capable of achieving, his suggestions will probably be both rejected and resented.

Personal Counseling

The coach's role as counselor is not limited to strictly forensic related problems, for students will frequently bring such private matters as career choices, interpersonal difficulties, or problems of courtship and marriage to the coach for airing and advice. Although the forensic coach may sometimes wish that these private problems would not be brought to him, he will probably feel both a personal and a professional responsibility to discuss such matters with students.

There are a number of explanations why students so often turn to the forensic coach for counseling. In most cases students have had greater opportunities to get to know the forensic coach on a personal basis than they have other teachers. Through their work with the coach, students may also have learned to respect his ability to examine and analyze problems. In addition, they may feel that the coach is capable of taking a more objective point of view toward their problems because of his relative detachment from their private lives.

If a forensic coach is to be called upon to serve as a counselor for personal problems, it is essential that he understand what kinds of functions he may properly perform and how he may wisely proceed. The professional training of the coach does not qualify him to psychoanalyze his students nor does it prepare him to give advice on specific personal problems. For the coach to attempt to do either of these, therefore, is not only foolish but potentially dangerous.

However, without going beyond the limits of his professional qualifications the coach may perform a number of useful counseling functions. First, by encouraging a student to discuss his problem fully, the coach may help the student gain some perspective on his difficulty. Second, by letting an emotionally overwrought student openly express his feelings, the coach may help the student in achieving a kind of catharsis. Third, when a student has already arrived at a satisfactory solution to his problem, but has hesitated to act, the coach may reinforce the student's decision and motivate him to act on the basis of it.

In order for the coach to accomplish these purposes there are certain principles of counseling to which he should adhere. First, the coach must project an attitude of acceptance. As a counselor, he does not necessarily need to understand the causes of the student's difficulties or to approve or disapprove of his actions. Frequently what a student needs most is to be accepted for what he is, as he is without praise or blame. Unless a student senses such acceptance, he will hesitate to express his true feelings or thinking. Second, the coach should seek to maintain his own detachment from the problem. He must avoid becoming personally involved in the problem if he is to help the student view his difficulties in their proper perspective. Third, the student seeking advice should be encouraged to do most of the talking. The counselor's major functions should be to listen to and to reflect back what the student has said. Through questioning the counselor may also probe unexplained areas of the problem or suggest overlooked facts and values. Fourth, the coach should avoid imposing his values on the situation. Ultimately, the student must make a decision based upon his own needs and his own values. Finally, the coach should recognize the limits of his own abilities and responsibilities. When these limits have been reached, he should refer the student for further assistance to someone more qualified or more responsible.

THE COACH AS A PROFESSIONAL PERSON

The forensic coach's role extends beyond his teaching and counseling activities to include his obligations as a member of a professional group. As a professional person, the coach must be specially trained and qualified. He must conduct himself in a manner which will bring credit to his profession and set a good example for his students. He should also be interested in the activities of his professional organizations, and he should be concerned with his professional future.

Professional Qualifications

Although no specific requirements have been established to determine a forensic coach's professional competence, certain minimum standards can be suggested. Experience over many years indicates that the forensic coach is more likely to be a qualified person (1) if he is a full-time educator, (2) if he has had some formal speech training, and (3) if he possesses certain particular qualities of mind and personality.

Only a full-time educator can provide the long-term direction and planning necessary to establish a truly sound forensic program. While graduate and law-school students may sometimes coach successful debate teams, the short-term nature of their involvement makes it probable that they will be more concerned with achieving immediate recognition in the form of contests won than with establishing a continuing program. Because the full-time forensic teacher has a commitment to education and because he has a long-term interest in the program of his school, he is more likely to be concerned with educational objectives and the long-range reputation of the program.

Some formal speech training is essential for the forensic coach since the skills peculiar to forensics are taught primarily in speech departments. While the English teacher may be qualified to help students analyze literary works or guide them in the organization of arguments, he is not prepared to discuss such topics as vocal variety, character placement, refutation, or burden of proof. While the history or social science teacher may be able to discuss the subject matter of a debate with students, he is normally not qualified to explain the techniques involved in presenting and defending arguments. Some speech training is necessary, therefore, to assure that the coach has a thorough knowledge of the concepts and techniques basic to forensics. Moreover, without an up-to-date knowledge of current theories and research in communication and persuasion, the forensic coach may discover—as, no doubt, many old-fashioned elocution teachers have—that his standards and theories are no longer significant or relevant.

As important as educational commitment and formal speech training are, they alone cannot assure the competence of a forensic coach. Ultimately, how successful the coach is in guiding and inspiring students will depend upon his own personal qualities and upon his ability to maximize his inherent strengths. Ideally, the forensic coach should have an open, genuine personality and a quick, deeply analytical mind. To the extent that he is deficient in these qualities, the coach should endeavor to cultivate them or at least to compensate for them. A coach can, for example, compensate for a reserved personality by conducting squad meetings in an informal, less structured way or by encouraging group social functions. He can compensate for his own weaknesses in analysis by placing greater emphasis on the techniques of analysis in his teaching and by directing advanced students to more specialized experts or sources for additional guidance.

Professional Conduct

The forensic coach has a special obligation to conduct himself in a manner which will set a desirable example for his students. Because students tend to emulate the behavior patterns of those adults with whom they identify and because the forensic coach is frequently such a person, this obligation should not be taken lightly. If the coach is courteous and respectful in all of his associations with others, he may find that his students are more interested in improving their manners. If he continually belittles the efforts of those coaches whose teams do well in forensics, he should not be surprised to find his students depreciating the accomplishments of other teams.

The extent to which the coach's conduct will influence his students' behavior is probably most apparent in the tournament situation. The coach's attitude toward competition and winning will inevitably reflect itself, not only in his own behavior, but also in that of his students. When a coach repeatedly blames poor judging for those losses, he is establishing a pattern of behavior which his students are likely to consider appropriate and acceptable. In the long run, the coach's admonishments against overemphasizing winning will have less effect upon students than will his personal behavior in the competitive situation.

Professional Activities

There are many reasons why the forensic coach should become an active member of his professional organizations. Through their meetings and publications these organizations provide a wide variety of information which can be useful in the everyday teaching and administration of forensics and which can stimulate new thinking and ideas. Professional forensic organizations also frequently carry on public relations programs which are directed at increasing the layman's understanding of and appreciation for forensic training. Furthermore, it is through participation in professional organizations that the coach can hope to be effective in influencing professional standards and ethics and forensic practices and procedures.

Professional organizations in which the forensic coach may wish to become active exist on the national, regional, and state levels. The American Forensic Association is the only national professional organization concerned exclusively with forensics.[1] Membership in the AFA is open to anyone interested in forensic activities and is composed of people from both the high school and college levels.[2] The Association publishes a quarterly magazine, the *Journal of the American Forensic Association* which presents articles and reviews of special interest to forensic people. The programs and meetings of the AFA are held in conjunction with the national conventions of the Speech Association of America.

Membership in the American Forensic Association automatically makes a person a member of one of the four regional forensic associations. Each of these regional associations has its own set of

---

[1] The National Forensic League is not a professional organization for coaches, but rather an honorary organization for high-school students. Each year, the NFL sponsors a national championship forensic tournament. For information, write to the Executive Secretary, National Forensic League, Ripon College, Ripon, Wisconsin.

[2] Information regarding membership in the American Forensic Association may be obtained through William Work, Executive Secretary, Speech Association of America, Statler Hilton Hotel, New York, New York.

officers, and each has its own special projects. The meetings and programs of the regional forensic associations are generally co-ordinated with those of the regional speech associations.

The High School Discussion and Debate Interest Group of the Speech Association of America exists on the national level and is open to all interested members of the SAA.[3] Although this group is a part of the SAA and not an independent, affiliated organization, it does hold its own business and sectional meetings, and these meetings provide an opportunity to discuss problems related to high-school forensics.

Most of the state speech associations exhibit a considerable concern for forensics in their convention programming and project planning. Some state speech organizations have special forensic interest groups which frequently exert major influence on forensic practices within the state.

Professional Future

Sooner or later, every forensic coach must face the question of how much of his professional life to devote to forensics. A teacher can find working in forensics to be a rewarding experience since it allows him to work closely with able and interested students in a worthwhile and stimulating activity. On the other hand, forensics can demand much of the coach's energies and leave him with little time for his family, for writing, or for his other personal and professional activities. Therefore, a coach's decision regarding whether to leave forensics after a few years or to stay with it throughout his professional life often involves a difficult choice.

Whichever choice the coach makes, he is likely to find continuing challenges and opportunities awaiting him. The teacher who chooses to remain active in forensics will continue to enjoy the satisfactions and challenges peculiar to coaching. In addition, once his program is firmly established and he learns how to use his time and energies most effectively, the forensic coach should be able to devote less time to coaching and somewhat more time to other activities.

Certainly, there is an abundance of opportunities for experi-

---

[3] Information concerning the High School Discussion and Debate Interest Group can also be obtained from the SAA Executive Secretary.

enced coaches to assume positions of influence and leadership within the forensic community. Perhaps one of the most neglected areas of research and writing in the field of speech is that concerned with argumentation and debate theory, and forensic leagues and professional forensic organizations are almost continuously seeking active members with leadership interests and potentialities.

The coach who decides to leave forensics after a few years will also have many future opportunities. If he chooses to give some of his time to classroom teaching, he may find other areas of speech education of interest to him. Many former college coaches, for example, have found that instructing graduate students provides some of the same opportunities to work closely with superior students that forensics offers. If the coach is interested in moving into a more attractive teaching situation at another school, he will probably discover that his years in forensics have made such a move easier. Through his forensic trips to other schools, the coach is able to establish employment contacts and to create favorable personal impressions to a greater extent than are most regular classroom teachers. Finally, if the coach desires to move into administrative work, he may find that his experience in managing and directing a forensic program has served to prepare him for a department chairmanship or some similar responsibility.

In summary, there are three major phases to the forensic coach's role. The first phase of his role involves the coach's work as a teacher. The forensic teacher must be prepared to guide students in the understanding of content materials for their speeches and in the use of appropriate rhetorical and logical methods. Methods, rather than content, should be emphasized. The forensic teacher should carefully avoid the extremes of either too little coaching or too much coaching. In order to provide a necessary minimum amount of coaching, he should (1) explain the nature and requirements of the specific activity, (2) introduce students to the techniques of the activity, and (3) constructively criticize student practice performances. In order to avoid overcoaching he should (1) never impose ideas or material and (2) never demand imitation or parroting. Informal discussions and the criticism of students' practice performances are the coach's primary teaching methods. The coach may sometimes utilize experienced varsity students to aid him in working with beginning students. In all of his teaching the coach should strive to make the learning experiences enjoyable.

The second phase of the coach's role concerns his responsibilities as a counselor. The forensic coach must be prepared to counsel with students on a variety of problems related to behavior, appearance, and personality, since these matters can greatly influence their success in forensic activities. The advice of the coach regarding matters in these areas is more likely to be accepted by students if (1) he has good rapport with them, (2) he relates his suggestions to their immediate goals, and (3) he is specific and realistic in what he recommends. In addition to forensic-related counseling, the forensic coach may also be called upon to act as a personal counselor. His role as a personal counselor should be viewed as that of mature friend rather than as a psychologist. In keeping with this view, the coach may legitimately help students gain perspective on their problems, or assist them in achieving a kind of emotional release, or encourage them to act on the basis of a well-thought-out decision. Five principles of counseling can be suggested to aid the coach: (1) he must project an attitude of acceptance; (2) he should remain detached from the problem; (3) the student should be encouraged to do most of the talking; (4) the coach should not impose his values on the situation; and (5) the coach should be aware of the limits of his own abilities and responsibilities.

The third phase of the coach's role involves his obligations as a member of a professional group. As a professional person the coach must be a well-trained and specially qualified person. He should be a full time educator with some formal speech training, and he should have a genuine, open personality and an analytical mind. The coach should be aware of the extent to which his behavior influences students and should pattern his conduct accordingly. Students' attitudes and behavior in the competitive situation are more likely to be influenced by what the coach does than by what he says. It is important for the coach to participate in professional organizations in order for him to keep abreast of new ideas and research and in order for him to be able to influence professional standards and procedures. Whether a coach decides to remain in forensics throughout his teaching career or whether he wishes to leave the activity after several years of experience, he will find important opportunities and challenges awaiting him.

SUGGESTED READINGS

Bennett, Margaret. *Guidance and Counseling in Groups.* New York: McGraw-Hill Book Company, 1963.

Buehler, E. C. "What Constitutes a Superior Director of Forensics?" *Gavel,* XXX (May 1948), 63.

Capp, Glenn R. "Training College Debaters," *Southern Speech Journal,* I (March 1936), 11–15.

Cox, Phillip, and John C. Duff. *Basic Principles of Guidance.* New York: Prentice-Hall, Inc., 1948.

Hess, Maurice A. "How Much Should a Coach Do?" *Gavel,* XIV (March 1932), 10–13.

Lahman, C. P. *Debate Coaching.* New York: H. W. Wilson Co., 1940.

McBath, James H. "Just Call Me Coach," *American Forensic Association Register,* IX (College Calendar Edition, 1961), 1.

Phifer, Gregg. "Organizing Forensic Programs," *Argumentation and Debate,* ed. James H. McBath. New York: Holt, Rinehart & Winston, Inc., 1963, 304–30.

Quimby, Brooks. "Is Directing of Forensics a Profession?" *Speech Teacher,* XII (January 1963), 41–42.

Shaw, W. C. "The Crime Against Public Speaking," *Quarterly Journal of Speech,* VIII (April 1922), 138–44.

Watkins, Lloyd I. "The Social Responsibility of Debate Coaching," *Gavel,* (1957), 3–6.

Woolbert, Charles H. "The Coach versus the Professor," *Quarterly Journal of Speech,* IV (June 1923), 284–85.

CHAPTER 4

Administration of Forensic Programs
Robert E. Dunham

THE FORENSIC COACH

This chapter could properly be subtitled "How Do I *Proceed* as a Forensic Coach," for it deals with procedural problems facing a forensic coach, primarily a beginning forensic coach. It deals with initiating and managing a forensic program, locating help, and philosophies and perspective for the forensic coach. While much of the discussion will reflect normative data, some of it will also be predicated upon what this author feels should be a deviation from present normative behaviors. Here, then, are several suggestions for the forensic coach:

The Coach's Credentials

If you were to examine the background of all the teachers who are coaching forensic events today you will find a varied and peculiar pattern. One would normally expect to find the coach with a background in speech since all of the forensic activities have some base in oral communication. On the college scene most forensic activities are directed in speech departments, although at a few schools the debate coach is hired as a separate person from a department, much like a football coach, with primary duties to coach the debate team. In a few of the New England states there are debate coaches at schools which have no speech departments. In high schools most of the forensic directing is done by English teachers, either because it is expected of them or because there are not enough speech teachers.

In a recent survey conducted through the Department of Public Instruction in Pennsylvania, it was found that 94 per cent of the schools had some form of co-curricular speech activity; however, only 28 per cent of the coaching was done by speech teachers.[1] English teachers comprised 61 per cent of the forensic coaches. In addition, many of the teachers who were called upon to coach forensics did not feel adequately prepared to do this. On occasion you will find a successful coach who is neither a speech teacher nor an English teacher, such as the former debate coach at Louisville, Ohio, who was a mathematics teacher, or the successful all-events coach at a Delaware, Ohio, high school, who was a Latin teacher. The prevalence of non-speech teachers in the field of forensics is not usually because they are more prepared or even as well prepared as the speech teacher, but primarily because the speech teacher is reluctant to coach or—what is more probable— the qualified speech teacher is nonexistent at many schools. The non-speech teacher wins the job by default. After a few years of actual coaching he learns enough about the contest circuit to feel somewhat competent in *coaching*, although probably he never will be too competent in *teaching* the oral communication which is so greatly involved in these forensic events.

While it is not the purpose of this chapter to prescribe a specific course of study which will assure qualified coaches, a coach would be well advised to have at least a strong minor, if not a major, in speech; to have some background in argumentation and debate and oral interpretation of literature; to understand certain basic fundamentals of oral communication; and to keep up with the literature being published in many of the forensic journals. This kind of coach could provide a good strong teaching program for all of his students, and could provide leadership in the forensic circles for non-speech coaches, as well. This would also be in keeping with the recommendation made by the contest committee of the North Central Association in its report on a program of speech education. In their recommendations they included one

[1] Robert E. Dunham, *Speech Education in Pennsylvania High Schools* (Harrisburg: Department of Public Instruction, 1966).

which reads "That extra class speech activities be taught by a person whose qualifications are in every sense equal to those of persons teaching speech in courses."[2] It appears then that the first step in developing any program is to secure a coach whose credentials are proper.

Determining the Needs of Students

It is difficult to ascertain whether some forensic programs are meeting the needs of the students, the teacher, the administrators, or meeting no needs at all. While almost all programs claim to meet student needs, in many cases the needs are never really identified. Particular contest events are perpetuated not because they fulfill a need for students, but because "we have always had them," or because the coach likes to teach these events, or because "we have always done well in these events." The forensic coach should determine the needs of his students, both individual and group, and relate these to the objectives or goals of his program. While the events chosen will probably result from group needs, the assignment of a student to a particular event should depend upon individual needs.

Balcer and Seabury discuss, in their recent book, a method for diagnosing and appraising the speech problems and needs of students:

> . . . likely to be recognized by the teacher as a result of the appraisal and diagnosis are (1) poor adjustment to speech situations; (2) lack of vocal control and vocal flexibility; (3) poor articulation; (4) unacceptable pronunciations; (5) language inadequacies; (6) lack of organizational techniques; (7) inadequate use of developmental and supporting materials; (8) poor choice of basic ideas; (9) failure to adapt to the immediate speaking-listening situation; (10) poor listening habits; and (11) speech defects.

They conclude by saying: "Without such appraisal and diagnosis it is hard to know where to begin, whether any progress is being

---

[2] "A Program of Speech Education—The North Central Association," *Quarterly Journal of Speech*, XXXVII, No. 3 (October 1951), 347–358.

made or whether the objectives of speech education have been accomplished. . . .[3]

Once student needs have been determined, the next step is to begin to set up specific objectives or goals for the program. Benjamin Bloom suggests that there are at least three ways for categorizing objectives. In *The Taxonomy of Educational Objectives: Cognitive Domain* and *Taxonomy of Educational Objectives: Affective Domain* (which he co-authored), he categorizes these goals into cognitive domain, affective domain and behavioral or psychomotor domain. One of the most fruitful and yet frustrating processes a teacher might become involved with is the placing of his specific educational objectives into these three categories or domains. In a recent seminar in directing forensics taught by this author, students were asked to take a specific forensic event, and to set up objectives for that event in accordance with Bloom's taxonomy. Almost to the person they found this exceptionally difficult and frustrating but, when finished, extremely rewarding and helpful to their coaching.

Planning Events and Activities

There are a number of questions facing the forensic director when he chooses specific events and activities. He must decide whether or not to enter interscholastic activities or intramural activites, or whether simply to become involved with community speaking activities having a speakers' bureau. He must also decide what specific events or activities in interscholastic or intramural programs would best serve the needs of his students.

Unfortunately this particular phase in a coach's job is often decided by a national league, a state league, or by tradition of the school. If a school has always had oratorical declamations it may continue to do so whether or not it serves a useful function. To perpetuate a program based solely upon tradition is to ignore the real values of a forensic program. In most cases, a broad program including both interscholastic and intramural activities will best meet the needs of most students. In fact, in a majority of good forensic programs variety both within and among events is the

---

[3] Charles L. Balcer and Hugh F. Seabury, *Teaching Speech in Today's Secondary Schools* (New York: Holt, Rinehart, & Winston, 1965), 74–75.

key to success. In a debate program, for example, it is wise to include not only contest-debating but in many cases—to meet the needs of students to adapt to a particular audience—some parliamentary debate or other form of audience debate. Not all students can tolerate a contest atmosphere and will need to be channeled through other forms.

Although the speakers' bureau has much to offer students, very few schools include it in the program. In a recent survey in Pennsylvania, it was found that only six per cent of the secondary schools in that state have a speakers' bureau. It is interesting to note that at Charleroi Area High School in Western Pennsylvania a number of students, through the speakers' bureau, presented a discussion program to various civic groups about *The Catcher in the Rye;* at the same time several schools in the immediate vicinity had banned the book. Adults hearing these discussions thought they were provocative, mature, and highly commendable. These particular students may never have done well in a contest-speaking or debating event and yet the speakers' bureau provided an outlet to meet their specific needs.

Although it is difficult to say which event or events should be the first to be included in a school forensics program, it does appear wise to begin with noninterscholastic events. With this intramural approach either contest or noncontest activities are possible. In order to stimulate interest in debate, perhaps one of the best things to do is to sponsor a British union-style debate in an assembly period. A unique event, it has the feature of involving an audience with the debaters and becomes a very exciting and challenging activity. This form of debate usually includes three speakers on either side. The topic should be timely and preferably local. For example, a high school might debate such a resolution as, "This house favors the abolition of final examinations." In a union-style debate a few years ago at Pennsylvania State University, the topic "This house favors the term system" was debated. Speakers for debate could include both students and faculty members, although they should be more or less equally balanced on both sides. The rules also state that the house is to be divided: those favoring pro arguments in the debate sit on one side of the auditorium; those favoring con, sit on the other side. If, during the debate a member of the audience changes his mind, he may move to the opposite side of the auditorium. Members of the audience or the opposing team may ask the chairman to interrupt the speaker and address a question to him. Of course, the speaker has the right either to yield to interrogation or complete his debate without any interruptions. This spontaneous activity should create considerable excitement for debate. Once a number of students are aroused, it is possible to direct them into this and other forms of debate, and perhaps eventually interest them in a contest debate on the national topic.

In debate or any other forensics event, the students must enjoy listening to whatever speaking activity they hear in order to be interested enough to participate. If they hear activities or speeches which seem trite, outmoded, or dull they cannot be expected to want to participate in such a program.

Relating Co-curricular Speech Activities to the Speech Program

Edgar Johnston, in an article for the *Bulletin of the National Association of Secondary School Principals,* stated that one of the weaknesses of school activity programs still prevalent was the "failure to keep the program vitally related to the curriculum."[4] In the report of the contest committee of the North Central Association, which was mentioned previously, it was recommended that "The extra class events be regarded as the counterpart of curricular instruction and that extra class events be integrated as closely as possible with class instruction."[5]

If the program of forensics is based upon needs of students and if it is taught by a person qualified to teach speech, then it should be comparable to the curricular program in terms of objectives and purpose—at least it should not be in opposition to the curricular program. If, in the curriculum, a student is taught to prepare himself to speak, to adapt to his audience, and to consider speech as an interpersonal relationship between speaker and listener, it is difficult for him to move next into a co-curricular forensic event which emphasizes highly polished, stilted delivery, has very little

---

[4] Edgar G. Johnston, "Critical Problems in the Administration of Student Activities," *The Bulletin of the National Association of Secondary School Principals,* February, 1952, 1–12.
[5] North Central Association, *loc. cit.*

or no concern about an audience, and lacks regard for preparation. It is equally difficult for a coach to spend many weeks in a classroom setting teaching the fundamental principles of oral communication only to have a student participate in a co-curricular contest where the "critic-judge" may negate and contradict what the student had originally been told.

Now no one assumes that all critics give the same advice nor denies that occasionally there are different viewpoints on speaking; but it is extremely discouraging for a competent teacher to be contradicted by an *incompetent* critic judge whose knowledge about speech is limited and whose viewpoint is educationally unsound.

A high-school coach recently commented about the possibility of dropping out of one of the national organizations because her students were constantly receiving information and criticism contrary to what she was apparently trying to teach in the classroom setting. Here, co-curricular criticisms were violating the basic principles of classroom teaching.

Involving as Many Students as Possible

For some time in the speech journals there has been a running battle about the star system in forensics. The basic issue seems to be whether or not to train a few students exceptionally well over a period of several years so that they become highly polished and capable forensic students, or whether more effort should be devoted to a number of students, even though it would be impossible to give each one enough time to have the end result be as polished as might be desired. If a teacher is fulfilling the needs of coaches or of an administrator, he probably would choose the star system. Or if the budget is unlimited and there are no problems with supporting a small minority of your school population, then he would probably choose the star system, also. But if the teacher is concerned with meeting needs of students, he should try to involve as many students in the program as possible. This means more work for the coach and perhaps a little more money in the budget, but the program would be more educationally and economically defensible.

In Edgar Johnston's article on some of the school activity programs, he cites as one of his criticisms: "Participation limited to too few pupils."[6] Sometimes, however, the budget at a particular high school will limit the interscholastic activities to a few people because it is expensive to travel to the tournaments. Intramural activities, on the other hand, are not at all expensive and can involve a great number of students. Such programs do not win trophies nor bring glory to a coach, but they can provide experience and motivation for students who might eventually want to participate in a contest. It would seem that coaches are obligated to provide forensic programs for as many students as possible.

Securing a Reasonable Budget

One of the greatest complaints of forensic coaches throughout the country is that not enough money is allowed to support an adequate forensics program. Many schools have no support at all. These are usually small high schools in rural areas. Most colleges and universities have some support either from a department of speech or from the student activities fund. Some college budgets are quite elaborate and provide thousands of dollars per year for students to travel around the country debating and speaking. Others colleges are limited to several hundred dollars. Because college and university contests are usually far apart, they involve a great deal of traveling. In high schools, the travel problem is not quite as severe because schools at least in the East and Midwest, are closer together. Only in the western part of the country are great distances involved when going to a tournament. Often a coach will pay out of his own pocket to enter students in contests, or he will drive his own automobile and pay his own expenses to deliver those students to a tournament. While the coach in this case certainly should be commended for his generosity, this kind of financing is incredible and unreasonable.

It is difficult to believe that there is a high school in this country which supports any kind of athletic team or musical organization which cannot provide adequate funds for a wholesome academic forensic program. Most high-school forensic programs have financial support from a variety of sources. Some receive

---

[6] Johnston, *loc. cit.*

from the school boards an outright gift, which is placed in a forensic budget. Others support their forensic programs from receipts of dramatic productions. In some schools the forensic program will receive money from the athletic program. Unfortunately, there are some schools whose forensic financing must resort to bake sales, carnivals, car washes, and similar activities. Usually, the person called upon to lead these financial parades is the forensic coach whose time is already taken up with his teaching and forensic activities. *If the forensic programs are important, then the school system should provide adequate financial support without involving students and coaches in time-consuming money-raising projects.*

For extra kinds of activities, such as a trip to a national tournament, (which is not a usual practice) the school might resort to contributions from various civic and community organizations. It is not at all uncommon for a Kiwanis Club or an Optimist Club to provide funds to send a student to a national tournament or to a summer institute. These requests should not be regular or demanding. Reciprocation in the form of sending members of the speakers' bureau to that organization might be extremely desirable from the financial and public-relations points of view.

Associating with Speech Organizations

There are numerous organizations and leagues throughout the country whose purpose it is to help forensic coaches and forensic programs. In addition there are a few honorary fraternities which honor outstanding students in debate and speaking events and which sometimes sponsor contests or festivals of their own.

While the national picture is not clear, in at least one state a large percentage of schools having co-curricular speech activities belonged to some co-curricular speech organization.[7] It would seem imperative for a school to affiliate with a forensic organization. The following discussion will elaborate on a number of high-school and college forensic organizations with the objective of pointing out the purpose and some of the features of each organization.

---

[7] Dunham, *loc. cit.*

NUEA Committee on Discussion and Debate

One of the strongest committees of the National University Extension Association is the Committee on Discussion and Debate. It is the only committee of the NUEA to have a national director and its own national office, which is located in Eugene, Oregon. This nine-man committee meets twice a year to discuss the problems connected with high-school debate and discussion activities throughout the United States.

The committee has been in operation for more than thirty-five years and has as its prime purpose to distribute worthwhile materials to high-school debaters and discussants; its distribution of debate material is now quite extensive.

When the Committee on Discussion and Debate was first established, however, as the Committee on Debate Materials and Interstate Cooperation, the committee's efforts were limited in scope to· a debaters' handbook. Since that beginning, almost through the single-handed efforts of its former executive secretary, Bower Aly, the committee has prospered until now the national office publishes annually four volumes of the *Forensic Quarterly,* distributes many magazines (such as *Current History* and *Congressional Digest*) at a greatly reduced price for state leagues, and disseminates a wealth of free materials to its members and affiliates.

Reutter wrote in a recent issue of the *Speech Teacher:*

> One aspect of the work of the Committee on Discussion and Debate that receives perhaps too little of notice is the solicitation, acceptance and distribution of the so called free materials. Although the "free" materials are free to the league wishing to distribute them they are not "free" in the sense that they have no cost or value. This year for example the committee had received and expanded the sum of $16,264.29 from foundations and other donors to provide books and pamphlets to the leagues. These grants and cash are used to purchase books in quantity and are in addition to the gifts of many thousands of books and pamphlets still needed by agencies interested in presenting their views on questions for discussion and debate.

> The committee enforces just two rules, but enforces them strictly in the acceptance and distribution of materials through its office: (1) every piece of material must bear the name and address of

the person, publisher or agency responsible. Anonymous materials will not be accepted. (2) The editor of the manual must approve every item distributed.[8]

The handbooks which are now called Volumes I, II, III, and IV of the *Forensic Quarterly*, are unlike many of the debate handbooks in that they do not present the cases or write out complete speeches for the discussion and debate topics for that particular year. Instead they include an excellent series of articles on a variety of viewpoints of the topic area.

In addition to distributing free and low-cost debate materials the other primary purpose of the committee is to select the national high-school debate and discussion topics each year. To do this they have working with them an advisory council made up of a representative from each state which has a speech league or similar organization, plus a representative from the National Forensic League and National Catholic Forensic League. This advisory council meets each year in late December. Prior to this meeting each state has the opportunity to send to the National Office suggested topics for discussion and debate for the following year.

The advisory council considers the various problem areas at its meeting in December and eventually decides upon three problem areas for possible adoption for the following year. Each problem area has a general overall statement plus three discussion questions and three debate propositions. In addition to selecting three problem areas for the following school year, the council also chooses one of the three current debate propositions which shall be selected as the national high-school debate topic for the remainder of the present school year. Council recommendations are referred to the NUEA Committee on Discussion and Debate which normally adopts recommendations by the advisory council. After approval by the NUEA Committee on Discussion and Debate, these three problem areas are submitted to a national referendum for each state to vote on which one problem area they shall use for the following school year. This is normally done in January or February and announced in the spring of the year.

---

[8] D. C. Reutter, "Providing High School Students with Debate and Discussion Topics," *Speech Teacher*, XII, No. 3 (September 1963), 235.

Once the National high-school debate proposition has been decided the state leagues are free to choose it or any other debate proposition. States are under no obligation to select the national topic chosen by the advisory council and the committee. D. C. Reutter in his article in the *Speech Teacher* points up a few interesting facts concerning the choice of the problem area.

(1) Whenever any league chooses a problem other than the one adopted by the majority the committee assists that league in any way possible. Since the resources of the committee are not adequate to develop materials indefinitely on many topics the majority effort of the committee must naturally be placed with the problem area approved by the majority of the leagues.

(2) Since 1928 the committee has never once overruled a substantive recommendation made by the advisory council. On three occasions however, the Committee on Discussion and Debate has been required to authorize changes in wording in order to meet exigencies not foreseen at the time the advisory council met.

(3) For many years the Committee on Discussion and Debate had maintained a subcommittee on wording which serves throughout the year. The duties of this subcommittee are to receive reports from any of the constituent members and to serve as a standby agency to recommend appropriate modification in wording if necessary.[9]

The National Forensic League

One of the most prestigious and influential organizations for high-school forensic students is the National Forensic League. This organization was founded in 1925 by Bruno E. Jacob, and is headquartered at Ripon College, Ripon, Wisconsin.

Unlike the NUEA Committee on Discussion and Debate, the primary emphasis of the National Forensic League is to encourage contest debating and speaking. Today there are 1,041 chapters located in most states of the union totaling some 237,000 members. NFL membership is issued to students and to coaches at the schools which have maintained chapters. There are three advanced degrees of membership: Degree of Honor, Degree of Excellence, and Degree of Distinction. These are based upon the

---

[9] *Ibid.*, 234.

number of points accumulated by a student when he participates in debate or speaking activities.

Under this point system, the coach receives one-tenth the number of points accumulated by all of his students and he too receives membership in degrees of honor, excellence and distinction. A coach receiving 1,000 points receives a diamond pin; there are at present some coaches who have merited at least three diamond pins. This point system with its consequent awards is a very attractive incentive for high-school students to participate in forensic activities; indeed, some schools are attending forensic contests starting in October and running through March.

The NFL chapters are divided into districts. In larger states, the districts may cover the entire state, while in smaller states there may be as many as two or three states included in one district. Ohio, which is one of the larger states in size and population, has three NFL districts within the state border.

The National Forensic League, itself, does not sponsor invitational tournaments at the local schools but encourages each of its member schools to sponsor practice tournaments. The two primary contests supported by the NFL are the District Tournament open to all member schools in that district, and the National Tournament which is open to students of member schools who qualify through winning either the NFL District Tournament or the State Tournament. In recent years, the National Tournament has become so large that efforts are being made to reduce the size through the elimination of some events and declaring winners of district and state tournaments as eligible for competition on a first-come basis.

The contest events open to a student at the district tournament are debate, extemporaneous speaking, original oratory, oratorical declamation, humorous declamation, dramatic declamation, and student congress. At the National Tournament some of these events are eliminated and other events such as radio announcing and oral interpretation of literature are added as second events. Because of the large number of schools wanting to enter the National Forensic League today and because the National Forensic League does not want to increase greatly the number of chapters, there are a number of affiliate memberships. Once the school has maintained a creditable record as an affiliate member, it is then invited to become a full-fledged chapter.

Any organization such as the NFL constantly needs to re-evaluate its program and emphases to make sure that it is not encouraging sophistry but is making each contest a very valuable educational experience. With its prestige and influence, the National Forensic League is in the very enviable position of having a tremendous opportunity to shape the minds of our young people to make them the nation's future leaders.

National Catholic Forensic League

One of the newest and yet most active national high school forensic associations is the National Catholic Forensic League. This league which is approximately fifteen years old, has no permanent national headquarters, but changes every two years. The office resides with the president and is currently in New York City. Over 500 Catholic schools representing most of the states belong to the NCFL. The events offered by the NCFL are debate, original oratory, boys' extemporaneous speaking, girls' extemporaneous speaking, oratorical declamation, and student congress. Each year some five- to six-hundred students participate in the NCFL national tournament which awards scholarships to the winners. While limited to Catholic schools, it nevertheless provides a supplement to the state leagues and to the NFL. Some schools belong to a state league, the NFL and the NCFL.

State High School Speech Leagues

Almost every state in the country has some organization which sponsors debate or other forensic activities. Many of these are called state high-school speech leagues. Some have other names such as the Texas Interscholastic League which administers not only speech, debate and dramatics, but athletics, slide rule, and many other activities. Some states have activity associations which include speech and debate.

While the form and some of the purposes may vary from state to state, usually the strong purpose of each of these particular organizations is to sponsor contests and festivals in debate and other speaking events, to conduct clinics and workshops, and to work with the NUEA National Office to distribute valuable materials. Many of these state organizations have monthly newsletters or newspapers which keep coaches and teachers informed of current happenings and also provide them with some very valuable articles on teaching and coaching. Almost every state has some form of a program in debate. The individual speaking events will vary according to state but usually will include extemporaneous speaking, some form of oral interpretation of literature, and some individual speaking events such as oratory or persuasive speaking. Many state organizations still sponsor declamation contests although these are slowly being eliminated.

Every coach who has a forensic program or wishes to begin a forensic program should affiliate with the state organization and should do this early in the school year. Not only will he receive monthly newsletters and useful debate materials but he will have a central agency to contact when he has questions either on coaching of the forensic program or in teaching of speech in the classroom. This agency usually serves as a clearinghouse for contests and tournaments so that it is possible to know where the contests are being held and who to contact for an invitation.

Most states sponsor a state tournament or festival in nearly every event. Many have district or regional elimination contests before the state tournament.

American Forensic Association

The only national professional forensic association for highschool and college teachers and directors of forensics is the American Forensic Association. While this organization has been known in the past primarily as a college and university organization, there have been great efforts made in recent years to attract highschool forensic people to its membership roles.

Individuals who are members of this organization receive a quarterly publication, *The American Forensic Association Journal,* which has just recently replaced the *AFA Register.* In addition they receive valuable reports, articles of special interest related to the directing of forensic programs, calendars of forensic activities, debate ballots, professional advice, and many other helpful items.

Teachers and coaches should look to this organization for professional development rather than for contests and activities. As one of the five purposes states, this organization wants to "create a means of educating the general and professional publics to the important educational functions of forensics."

Forensic Honorary Organizations

Until a few years ago there were four forensic honorary organizations. At that time two of them combined to make just three extant today.

Delta Sigma Rho, founded in 1906, and Tau Kappa Alpha, founded in 1908, united in 1963 to become Delta Sigma Rho–Tau Kappa Alpha. Thus the two oldest honoraries became the newest organization for college students. At the time of union there were some 170 chapters which were a part of this combined organization. DSR originally had as its publication the *Gavel;* TKA had the *Speaker.* When the two organizations united they formed a new publication entitled *Speaker and Gavel.* Membership in this organization is limited to resident undergraduates or members-at-large at a college or university with a bona fide charter. While primarily honorary in nature, there are national events sponsored by this organization.

Pi Kappa Delta is another similar honorary organization which was founded in 1912 for college and university students. It encourages participation in various forensic activities and also meets nationally. Its quarterly publication is the *Forensic.*

Phi Rho Pi, founded in 1928, is the national honorary society for students in junior colleges. It has no publication but does hold an annual meeting in the form of a speech tournament.

Securing Ample and Worthwhile Materials

Any good forensic coach should make sure that his students have ample materials with which to work. In debate, a student needs to have access to information about the national debate topic or any other topics he may be debating. An economist recently admonished a group of debate coaches to be certain that their debaters understood the topic area if debate was to be anything more than glibness. Many of the handbooks on the market today are including actual debate speeches and briefs to make the job of a debater easier. If a coach is to heed the economist's admonition and help his students practice something other than glibness, he is obligated to disregard many of the handbooks on the market which offer to make the job easier by supplying actual cases and speeches for both the affirmative team and the negative team. His alternative is to motivate the debaters to inquire about the problem in a number of varied sources; sources which are in the problem area, but not necessarily written as a pro or con of the debate question.

For high-school debaters, the National University Extension Association's Committee on Discussion and Debate has for years distributed free and low-cost debate materials on the national topic. These materials include publications such as *Current History, Congressional Digest, Annals of the American Society for Social and Political Sciences, Vital Issues, Public Affairs Pamphlets, Editorial Research Reports, Congressional Quarterly,* plus specially prepared packets of materials distributed by organizations such as the AFL-CIO, The National Association of Manufacturers, The American Enterprise Association, The National Chamber of Commerce, and the Foundation for Economic Education. (See Chapter 6 for a detailed discussion.)

There is an office in every state through which these NUEA materials may be secured. College debaters are not quite so fortunate in having a national clearinghouse for the debate materials, but many of the above-mentioned publications are also available on the college debate topic. It is also wise to read widely in the subject discipline areas in which the debate topic is found. For example, if the debate topic concerns foreign aid or foreign trade, topics which usually reappear on the scene, the debater would be well advised to attempt to understand some of the basic issues in economics. Debaters are sometimes quite naïve on fundamental matters and yet sound very glib in expounding the solutions to the world's problems.

When gathering materials and examining them closely, it would be well for the debaters to work together and share materials and ideas. In some circles there are student librarians who gather and classify material for the debate teams. This is an interesting assignment for a debater who cannot quite manage to do the actual debating; but a coach should guard against the debaters' not knowing the material as well as the librarian. Without this knowledge the debater is only a shallow sophist.

In individual speaking events, a speaker might be well advised to consult a number of sample speeches. *Vital Speeches, Repre-*

sentative American Speeches, Winning Orations, The Speaker's Resource Book, are but a few sources which could be useful. The Wetmore Declamation Bureau, and the Edna Means Dramatic Service for years have supplied declamations, orations, and readings for those who prefer not to do their own selecting and cutting. Of course the coach of an extempore speaker must see to it that his speaker reads constantly in a number of magazines such as *Newsweek, U. S. News and World Report, Time, Saturday Review, The Reporter, Atlantic Monthly, Business Week,* and newspapers such as the *New York Times, The Wall Street Journal,* and perhaps a good foreign paper if one is available.

Up until this time the discussion has centered around reading materials; however, this does not exhaust the possibilities. Television has provided new possibilities in coaching forensic activities. Video tapes may be available showing good model speakers. Some video-tape recorders are so inexpensive now that schools and colleges can well afford to invest in a portable model. This kind of equipment is invaluable in working with student speakers and debaters. In the PHSSL Summer Speech Institute of 1965, the final debate was video taped and simultaneously shown live to an audience of high-school debaters. After a short intermission, the critique began utilizing flash-backs or instant replays of the debate. Students and teachers alike felt that this was a very educational experience. Of course there are numerous other films, recordings, and similar materials, which are available to the forensic coach.

Participating in Contests and Festivals

One of the features which has made forensics exciting and attractive to students is its competitive element. While contests in and of themselves are not an objective, they do provide a tremendous amount of incentive. Without the contest element, it is doubtful that forensics would be nearly as attractive as it currently is. For this reason, then, it should be recommended that every school which has a forensic program should participate in contests and festivals on an interscholastic or intercollegiate basis. It is also recommended that there be an intramural program within the school which provides contest and festival opportunities.

In most parts of the country there are many contests offered on the high-school level. It is wise for a coach to select tournaments which offer a unique experience for his students, so that over a period of a semester or a year students have not repetitiously wasted their time on similar contests but have gained very valuable practice experience.

In some of the stronger state and NFL leagues, schools will begin to travel to practice tournaments as early as late October and continue weekly throughout February or March. This could provide as many as fifteen to twenty different contests or festivals for the students. It is questionable whether or not a student will gain much value from that many tournaments unless he experiences a good variety of activities.

For example, in debate it is highly questionable whether there is sufficient value in a student's attending a regular orthodox or cross-examination-style debate week after week for ten to fifteen weeks. There seems to be a point of diminishing returns after several contest experiences. It would be wise for a coach to attempt to get some direct-clash experiences, audience debates, regular orthodox debates, cross-examination debates and some parliamentary debates as well as student congress experience. If a debate team were able to participate in four or five different kinds of debate activities in the period of a year, it could be a very profitable learning experience. Likewise, in the speaking events excluding extempore, it would be wise for a student to prepare himself to speak on a number of different speech topics throughout a given year. To use the same oration or persuasive or informative speech week after week after week, has its diminishing returns, which usually becomes evident fairly early in the year. In prose and poetry reading events also, it seems wise for students to read as many as ten or twelve selections in contests or festivals in a year's time. On the other hand, a student who reads only one or two selections during the year will probably be highly polished but inexperienced, generally, at the end of that period of time.

Unfortunately, on the high-school scene in most parts of the country there is very little opportunity for variety in debating and speaking contests. In college circles, there is more of an opportunity for a student to participate in a variety of debate experiences. For example, Wayne State University in Detroit has for several years provided an audience type of setting for its debate. Wooster College in Ohio for some years has sponsored a direct-clash tournament. The University of Pittsburgh and many other schools have provided a cross-exam or Oregon-style of debate experience, and there are many student congresses and debaters congresses such as the Joseph O'Brien Debaters Congress at Pennsylvania State University.

In choosing the number and kind of contests to attend, the following criteria may be helpful:

1. Does the contest provide a unique educational experience for students?
2. Is there an opportunity for more than a few students to participate?
3. Will there be valid criticism given at the contest?
4. Is the winning kept in perspective?
5. Is this contest economically reasonable?

For information regarding what collegiate tournaments and festivals are available, one should consult the *American Forensic Association Journal,* May issue. A listing of high-school tournaments may be secured either from the chairman of the NFL district or the NCFL districts, or from the director of the state speech league or activity association.

Sponsoring Contests and Festivals

There is no better way for a new school in an isolated area to begin a program than to sponsor a tournament, contest, or festival. While this takes careful planning, it is not in any sense of the imagination an insurmountable task. If the school is just beginning, the coach probably would want to host some kind of novice tournament or festival. He might choose one or several events and invite a few schools or as many as ten or twenty depending upon purpose and accommodations. (See Chapter 11 for specific details.)

A decade or so ago it was the practice of many high schools to participate in triangular meets. It may be advisable in some sparsely populated areas to reinstitute this former contest pattern.

Keeping Motivation and Winning in Perspective

It was stated earlier in this chapter that the contest element makes forensic activities very attractive to students and provides a great deal of incentive. Like any incentive, winning in contests can get out of line. In competition, the coach must stress the principles of good sportsmanship. It is difficult to be a good loser but the loss *can* provide a valuable teaching opportunity. The coach can use the defeat as a valuable tool in teaching adequate preparation and the principles of oral communication.

According to Ehninger, success is not measured by the number of victories but by the contribution which the program makes toward the intellectual, social, and moral development of the students who participate.[10]

There have been a number of people who have written warnings of what can happen when winning takes over. Abernathy stated: "The debater is changed from a sincere student of speech into a 'debate bum,' trained in the tricks, fair or unfair, of winning, rather than an honest technique of persuasive speaking." [11]

Robert Smith, in an article in *Central States Speech Journal* stated:

> . . . the fact that some student speakers in their understandable desire to "win" become modern sophists with pressure to "win" the coveted trophies, to attain points for a higher degree, or to increase the chapter's chances of winning the leading chapter award. Some students compromise their ethical standards. Some of them manufacture and store evidence, and some often rely on glib delivery to camouflage their deception.[12]

---

[10] Douglas Ehninger, "Six Earmarks of a Sound Forensics Program," *Speech Teacher*, I, No. 4 (November 1952), 237–41.

[11] Elton Abernathy, "The Criticism Against Speech Tournaments," *Quarterly Journal of Speech*, XXVIII, No. 3 (October 1942), 354–56.

[12] Robert Smith, "NFL: A Perversion of Values," *Central State Speech Journal*, XI, No. 1 (Autumn 1959), 9.

Ehninger also pointed out a few years ago that the danger
". . . lies in the fact that it [the large program] may come to replace more fundamental values, or that the uncurbed desire to be
'big' will lead to a compromising of crucial values."[13]

Unless a forensics coach is sincerely dedicated to the task of
providing a valuable educational experience for his students and
of providing contest experiences where winning does not get out
of hand, then we can expect the undesirable attributes of the
winning obsession.

Maintaining a Good Public Relations Program

It is difficult for the average forensic coach to be a man with a
gray flannel P.R. program, but it is extremely important for him
to maintain good public relations. Someone once said that public
relations is 90 per cent doing the right thing and 10 per cent
telling people about it. Nevertheless, the forensic coach needs to
communicate about his program to other students, to administrators, to other faculty members, and to the general public. He
needs to reach other students so as to attract them to become
future forensic speakers and debaters. He needs to sell other
faculty members on the value of his program, and to impress
administrators with the program so that he may secure more
cooperation and financial help. And he needs to sell the general
public, for in many cases it is the general public which provides
the motivation to increase the program or to give it more financial
support.

Ideally, the forensic coach who becomes the public relations
man needs to have a knack of working with people, a journalistic
flare, promotional talent, sense of feature material, and an ability
to build contacts and relationships with the city officials, civic
leaders, school administrators and news outlets. A good public
relations program does not happen by chance; it is well-planned.
Most often the local newspapers can provide one of the greatest
opportunities for publicizing the program. Normally, the coach
must supply them with material. In doing so he must stick to the
facts, avoid "arty" language, and write for the public (not fellow-

---

13 Ehninger, *loc. cit.*

educators). In addition, he should constantly be looking for more ways in which the forensic program can make news. Newspapers are particularly interested in contest results or unusual activities.

There are a number of good manuals on public relations that are available if the coach is interested in obtaining suggestions for preparing press releases for the local newspaper.[14] The coach should always remember to thank the local newspaper editor and his staff for their cooperation and effort. The newsmen's contribution can be recognized with a letter of appreciation or an invitation to a school award banquet at the end of the year. Practice good public relations in daily contact with newsmen and many of the problems that might otherwise appear will be eliminated.

Summer Speech Institutes

One of the most popular ways for high-school students to spend part of the summer is in a summer high-school speech institute. These institutes range from one week to eight weeks and cover subject areas such as debate, speaking, drama and oral interpretation of literature, broadcasting, and speech and hearing science. Normally they are held on a college or university campus. Although these summer institutes are not new (some of them having started thirty-five or forty years ago) they have just reached their popularity peak within the last four or five years.

A new forensic coach can receive a great deal of benefit by sending some of his students to a summer institute. There, in a very intensive program, they will learn a great deal about forensic activities and oral communication. When they return to the high school, they will be able not only to help the coach but to help other students in school. The coach should be careful, however, not to let the summer institutes usurp his responsibility of coaching.

Many of these institutes have conducted some form of an evaluation and students seem to be very pleased with the outstanding instruction, the opportunity to live on a college or a university campus, and to receive a head start on next year's debate topic area.

---

[14] See Suggested Readings at the end of the chapter.

Most of these institutes are well taught and well attended. It is not at all uncommon for a student to attend three different institutes in three summers. While there is danger of a student's becoming somewhat overconfident because he has attended these extra sessions, summer institutes on the whole, provide a very valuable educational experience for high-school students.

Evaluating the Forensics Program

With any program of forensics it is necessary to institute a systematic evaluation program. It is not enough to create goals and objectives. It is not enough to analyze student needs and plan activities appropriately. For in the heat of forensic activity, it is often possible to lose sight of the goals; therefore, periodically the forensic coach needs to evaluate his program objectively. In evaluating his program he might ask these questions: "What are the objectives?" "Are they educationally sound?" and "Is the program accomplishing these objectives?"

The evaluation of a forensic program cannot necessarily be measured in terms of how many trophies or awards are won. Balcer and Seabury in their book propose certain questions which might help direct one's thinking toward an educationally sound philosophy of co-curricular speech activities. These may also be very useful questions for evaluating one's forensic program, and are listed here as a sample of the kind of questions one might use to evaluate.

1. Does my co-curricular activities program teach my students a code of ethics?
2. Does my speech activities program help my students understand and use the reflective process in arriving at conclusions?
3. Does my speech activities program give my students knowledge about the communicative process and understanding of it?
4. Does my speech program result in an opportunity for my students to receive a realistic evaluation of their own speech performances in comparison with others?
5. Does my co-curricular speech program grow out of a curricular speech program? If not, am I working toward the

inclusion of a course in speech education in the school's curriculum?

6. Do I consider thoughtfully suggestions which I seek from my own state and national speech organizations?
7. Do I maintain a sound and proper perspective in winning in relationship to the educational values which can be derived by students in my program?
8. Is my program financed on a sound basis?
9. Do I limit participation in my co-curricular speech program including interscholastic activities to a few students, or am I clearly giving evidence of my desire to help many students in school?
10. Have I adequately taken stock of the students' speech interests, needs, abilities and capacities in my school?
11. Is my program respected in my school and in the community?
12. Does my program succeed in teaching social responsibility?
13. Does my program call for systematic evaluation by me as to what I am accomplishing and to what I want to accomplish?
14. Do I take advantage of enough opportunities in my community to give my students real and meaningful speech experiences?
15. When I present awards do I carefully examine the type of awards, the criteria by which I decide to whom awards will be presented, and the manner of presenting awards in the light of educational and psychological implications of the awards?[15]

SUGGESTED READINGS

Balcer, Charles L., and Hugh F. Seabury. *Teaching Speech in Today's Secondary Schools.* New York: Holt, Rinehart & Winston, Inc., 1965.

Braden, Waldo W. *Speech Methods and Resources.* New York: Harper & Brothers, 1961.

Brockhaus, Herman H. "Summer High School Speech Institutes," *Speech Teacher,* XIII, No. 2 (March 1964), 133–38.

Ehninger, Douglas. "Six Earmarks of a Sound Forensics Program," *Speech Teacher,* I, No. 4 (November 1952), 327–41.

---

[15] Balcer and Seabury, *op. cit.,* 286–87.

Lillywhite, Herold. "The 'Star System' in Forensics," *Western Speech Journal*, XIV, No. 2 (March 1950), 31–33.

McCloskey, Gordon. *Education and Public Understanding*. New York: Harper & Brothers, 1959.

Public Relations for the American High School. The Bulletin of the National Association of Secondary School Principals (September 1960).

Quimby, Brooks. "Is Directing of Forensics a Profession?" *Speech Teacher*, XII, No. 1 (January 1963), 41–42.

The Sight and Sound of Better Public Relations. Harrisburg: Pennsylvania State Education Association.

Robinson, Karl F., and E. J. Kerikas. *Teaching Speech Methods and Materials*. New York: David McKay Co. Inc., 1963.

Walsh, Grace. "Tournaments: For Better or Worse?" *Speech Teacher*, VI, No. 1 (January 1957), 65–67.

CHAPTER 5

Analysis in Debate

Richard D. Rieke

Too often debaters and coaches believe that research and analysis are the same. At the start of the season, the coach sends the debaters out with the assignment to come back with a number of cards which should represent so many books and articles read and understood. It does not take much encouragement for debaters to go on to measure their preparation for debate in terms of the number of cards in their possession. When asked: "Will you be ready to debate by next week?" the reply may well be: "Of course we'll be ready; we have over 200 cards!"

The next step, is to find a "case." Where does a case come from? Often, debaters have in mind the stock issues—need, plan, advantages—and accept the first "need" that is brought to their attention either in a book, article, or handbook. From thence, all efforts are directed toward finding "quotes" which support the *need* and devising a *plan* which will both do something about the need and still conform to the requirements of the resolution. Sometimes it is discovered that the *need* does not relate to the *plan* in anything more than the most indirect way, but since it is "our need," it is not discarded. Rather, efforts are redoubled to find quotes that seem to bring the need and plan together. Social pressure, rather than logic, tends to dictate whether or not a *need* will persist. If many other debaters are using the same or similar need, it will probably persist for a time—if not a full year—no matter how much tortured reason is required to keep the discussion centered on the policy mentioned in the resolution. If, on the other hand, a team's need is being used by no other team it runs a grave risk of being considered as odd and rejected no matter how reasonable it may be in terms of the actual concept of the resolution.

The fundamental problem is that a distinction has not been made between research, case building, and analysis.

What is meant by analysis? In a strict sense, the word means the breaking down of a subject into its constituent parts. In debate, analysis involves essentially two processes: discovering what questions must be asked in considering the resolution; and discovering what basic lines of reasoning are appropriate in setting about to answer the questions.

The typical approach to the teaching of analysis is through the stock issues. At its very best, the concept of stock issues is a mixed blessing. At its worst, the approach so restricts the thinking of debaters and judges as to narrow and distort debate as a system of reasoned discourse and decision-making. Even though the stock issue concept is useful as an educational tool and will be discussed in this chapter, there is reason to believe that much good would come from a universal four-year moratorium on the use of stock issues. But before any further attacks are made it might be useful to make some explanations.

EXAMPLES OF ANALYSIS

It is quite common to explain analysis through an analogy to legal debate, because legal questions can be more highly structured and regular. A frequently used example is the analysis of a charge of burglary. If Mr. X is accused of being a burglar, then his trial involves a debate on the subject, Resolved: That Mr. X is a burglar. Rather than simply calling in all the witnesses and evidence haphazardly, it becomes necessary to ask first what will be required in the form of reasoning and evidence to affirm the resolution. What, in other words, are the *essential elements* of the concept "burglar"? What minimum facts must be found to prove a man to be a burglar? In legal practice, through common usage and sometimes through codification, burglary has come to mean, quite often, breaking and entering a dwelling house in the nighttime with the intent to commit a felony therein. Thus, the prosecutor's analysis is facilitated by knowing he must present argument and evidence to answer the following questions affirmatively:

1. Did Mr. X break and enter?
2. Did Mr. X do so in a dwelling house?
3. Did Mr. X do so in the nighttime?
4. Did Mr. X do so with the intent to commit a felony therein?

These are the essential elements of the concept "burglary." These four questions could also be called the potential issues of the debate, potential in the sense that real issues do not emerge in a debate until assertion and counterassertion have clashed head-on, but to be thought of as issues, nevertheless, because these are the questions from which the clash must almost certainly emerge. If there is to be a debate, the defense or negative must clash on one of these essential elements or introduce other elements equally essential to the final decision on the resolution. For example, the negative could ask this:

5. Did Mr. X do so under circumstances which mitigate the effect of the act to the extent it should not be considered burglary?

But there is understandably a limited number of elements so essential to the resolution that they have the potential to become issues in a debate.

To the lawyer, therefore, the first step in analysis—discovering what questions must be answered to decide the resolution—is aided by the orderliness with which the concept "burglary" is handled in the law.

The prosecutor's next step now becomes clear: taking each of these essential elements or potential issues one at a time, he asks what reasoning and evidence are necessary and available with which to answer the question affirmatively. The defense attorney similarly asks what reasoning and evidence are necessary and available to answer the question negatively, or at least prevent an affirmative answer and thus deny the fulfillment of the burden of proof. Of course, on question No. 5, the negative makes the original assertion and bears the burden of proof, and thus the positions are reversed.

To continue the analogy further, in seeking the answer to question No. 1, the prosecutor or affirmative would begin by asserting his answer:

I. Mr. X did break and enter.

The defense or negative (assuming he wanted to debate the issue at all as is his option) would start with his answer:

I. Mr. X did not break and enter;

or, the negative could take advantage of the affirmative burden of proof and assert no more than this answer:

I. The Prosecutor cannot prove Mr. X did break and enter.

Thus, what had been a potential issue becomes a real issue by virtue of the direct clash of affirmative and negative assertions:

I. Mr. X did break and enter ←———→ I. Mr. X did not break and enter

The question, or issue, which clearly emerges from this clash of assertions or contentions as they are typically called is "Did Mr. X break and enter?" The issue or question is neither affirmative nor negative, it simply describes an essential point of difference between the debaters which must be decided one way or the other if the resolution itself is to be decided.

The full cycle in the first step of analysis is thus described: well in advance of the actual debate affirmative and negative both reasoned that if a judge was to decide whether Mr. X is to be declared guilty of burglary, he would first have to agree that Mr. X did indeed break and enter. For, if he did not agree that Mr. X did break and enter, then he could not agree that Mr. X had satisfied all the essential elements of the concept "burglary"; if Mr. X had not satisfied all the essential elements, he could not be declared guilty of burglary and the decision would go to the negative or defense. Having reasoned thus, both debaters determine to debate the question and devise contentions accordingly. With the actual meeting of these contentions in the debate, an actual issue emerges which then becomes a part of the final decision.

If this issue is an element in the decision, it must be answered.

Therefore, the debaters must prepare themselves to assist the judge in selecting an answer. They ask themselves, what evidence and reasoning will the judge require if he is to answer the question in the manner desired, either affirmatively or negatively depending upon the debater's perspective. It is important that the debater think of his problem in this way: what is necessary to help the *judge answer the question*—and not simply in terms of what evidence or reasoning is simply relevant to an affirmative or negative answer. The distinction may not seem important until one hears debaters who engage in a contest of testimony reading and wonder why the judge still is unsatisfied. They must understand that one quote balanced against another quote by the other side does not help the judge make up his mind. And two more quotes equally balanced will be no better. If a debater is truly interested in bringing a judge to his answer, he will be motivated to go beyond the pure testimony and seek to provide the judge with facts and reasons as well.

Let us return to the example issue: Did Mr. X break and enter? The affirmative or prosecution must ask itself what will be necessary to bring the judge to an affirmative answer. Obviously, if direct evidence is available, the job will be relatively simple. Thus, if three eyewitnesses observed Mr. X take an ax, chop down the door, and walk in, the contention would be developed this way:

I. Mr. X did break and enter, because
   A. Witness No. 1 saw him do it
   B. Witness No. 2 saw him do it
   C. Witness No. 3 saw him do it.

The negative would be in trouble.

However, debaters rarely are fortunate enough to have direct evidence. Usually a broader inference is involved between fact and conclusion. For instance, the prosecutor may have at his disposal only the testimony of a policeman that Mr. X was in the house and the door was broken, and there was no one else in the house who might have broken the door. In this case, the testimony is only circumstantial to the conclusion that Mr. X did break and enter. An inference is involved that any stranger found in a house with a broken door probably entered by breaking down the door. The contention would be developed in this way:

  I. Mr. X did break and enter, because
     A. Mr. X was found in the house, because
       1. Officer O'Brien saw him there, and
     B. The door was broken down, because
       1. Officer O'Brien saw the broken door, and
       2. The broken door itself can be shown to the judge, and
     C. No one else who could have broken the door was in the house, because
       1. Officer O'Brien found no one else there, and
       2. The owners of the house testify they were not at home, therefore

  I. It is reasonable to conclude Mr. X did break and enter the house.

With this development, a debater could feel strongly the judge might decide in the affirmative, but the debater would realize that only a probability had been established and that the negative might still produce argument and evidence to reject an affirmative conclusion. For example, the negative might build its contention this way:

  I. Mr. X did not break and enter, because
     A. The door was broken down with an ax, because
       1. Ax marks can be seen on the broken door, and
     B. Mr. X had no ax with which to break the door, because
       1. Officer O'Brien found no ax in or near the house, and
     C. Another person could have broken the door and left before the police arrived, because
       1. Nothing argued by the prosecution denies this possibility,
       2. No other explanation for the broken door seems warranted, therefore

  I. It is reasonable to conclude Mr. X did not break and enter.

Observations on the Examples

A number of observations can be made about the foregoing examples of argument. First, it must be noted that for both affirmative and negative it was not enough simply to present or read testimony. It was necessary to present a line of reasoning to make a logical bond between the testimony and the conclusion. In each case, the sentence following the capital letter states a reason which the debater hopes will combine with other reasons to lead the judge to agree with the contention. In each case, the sentence immediately following the arabic numeral describes the testimony of a witness or describes what can be observed by the judge himself which constitutes evidence of the validity of the reasoning designated by the capital letter.

A second observation about the examples is this: even after both sides have said all they can to bring the judge to agree with their position, it can be seen how reasonable men could disagree. That is, two judges sitting together could disagree as to whether Mr. X did or did not break and enter, and neither of them would be deserving of criticism.

Observation number three would call attention to the fact that each judge would be better able to describe the reason for his decision after hearing the arguments above than he would having heard only conflicting testimony or no debate at all. The debaters have helped increase the likelihood of a rational decision, and that is their purpose!

Meaning for the Teacher

A few comments to the teacher of debate analysis can now be made with greater meaning. First, quite obviously neither debater represented in these examples could have done an adequate job of analysis without considering how the other side might go about arguing the same issue. The affirmative can never feel satisfied with its development of a contention until it is satisfied the negative has no line of attack which is not accounted for. This does not mean the affirmative must be able to guarantee it will win every issue, but it does mean the affirmative cannot know whether it has done its best until it knows what negative arguments must be faced.

On the other side, the negative cannot begin its analysis until it has seriously considered how the affirmative will go about developing its side. In a very real sense, then, no debater can say he is ready to debate one side of an issue until he can say he is ready to debate either side of the issue! It is quite possible the student is ready to discuss *neither* side of a good many important issues, and it may well be that he has not prepared an overall strategy or case for both sides; but with regard to a single issue, thorough preparation for one side will result in preparation for both. This rejects the notion that debating both sides is too demanding for some debaters and they should be allowed to be either affirmative or negative. If they are truly prepared for one side, it requires relatively little additional effort to prepare the overall strategy to debate both sides. Probably more important, this reasoning suggests that permitting a debater to consider himself affirmative or negative is pedagogically undesirable because it leads students to rely on one-sided preparation. No matter how hard the teacher tries to motivate students, they probably never do the thorough job of analyzing both sides that should be done until they are obliged to defend both in actual debate. To those who reject two-sided debating on ethical grounds, it need only be said that such experience can come in practice debates or tournament debates exclusively, and for public appearances debaters can stick to defending their chosen side and will do a better job of it because of the two-sided practice.

Another comment to the teacher of analysis is this: the student must be exhorted to perform both basic steps in analysis—discovering all the essential elements or potential issues of the resolution, *and* developing available argument both affirmative and negative for each one.

A final note to the teacher is that it is often helpful to use simple legal cases for student practice in discovering essential elements and developing pro and con arguments. Any casebook for law students is filled with brief statements of fact which suggest one or two issues that can be discovered and discussed by non-law students even though they will not do so with the expertise of lawyers. (See Chapter 8, reference to footnote 3 on "You Be the Judge.") The value in this kind of exercise lies in keeping students' attention on one issue at a time until they have developed a clear concept of the relationship that exists between resolution, issue, argument, and evidence. A relationship which has been illustrated this way follows:

Resolved that Mr. X is guilty of burglary   (RESOLUTION)

Did Mr. X break and enter?   (ISSUE EXPOSING AN ESSENTIAL ELEMENT OF THE RESOLUTION.)

  I. Mr. X did break and enter.   (CONTENTION TO COMBINE WITH ALL CONTENTIONS TO LEAD TO THE AFFIRMATION OF THE RESOLUTION.)

    A. Mr. X was found in the house.   (ARGUMENT OR REASON TO COMBINE WITH ALL REASONING TO LEAD TO THE VALIDITY OF THE CONTENTION.)

      1. Officer O'Brien saw him there.   (EVIDENCE OR FACT TO COMBINE WITH ALL EVIDENCE TO LEAD TO THE VALIDATION OF THE CONTENTION OR SUPPORTING OF THE WARRANT.)

By focusing students' attention for a time on such a case, they will be prevented from considering the whole case as they plan to present it at the first tournament; this often leads to a confusion over the individual elements of an argument.

PREPARING STUDENTS FOR A RESOLUTION OF PUBLIC POLICY

When the teacher approaches the problem of preparing students to engage in analysis of a resolution of public policy—which is almost always used in national competition—he does not have the benefit of the regularity and precedent in law. Students cannot be told to search the statutes or common law for a statement of the essential elements of a policy resolution. How, then, can students be taught the process of analysis in such a complex problem? It has already been said that the typical practice is to use the concept of stock issues, but it might be useful to try an approach to such analysis from a somewhat different point of view. In the material that follows, an illustrative analysis will be made of a debate topic—first, trying to avoid the difficulties of the stock issue approach, and second, showing how stock issues can be used with good effect.

Suppose that a teacher had the task of starting a group of students off on an analysis of this resolution: "Resolved that the United States should limit its foreign policy to nonmilitary assistance." As none of the students had previously engaged in debate, nor did any know of stock issues, how should they proceed?

It would probably be useful to start by bringing the group together as a whole, or best, in groups of about six and by letting them talk about the subject in an unstructured way with only the motivation of a forthcoming debate deadline to keep them interested. What might they say to each other? Probably they would hit on one of various perspectives from which analysis could usefully begin. Conceivably, they might remember John Dewey and start with an effort to conceptualize the problem in terms of its scope and characteristics. They might ask, "What is our foreign policy?" "What is our present type of assistance?" "What is the difference between military and nonmilitary assistance?" This kind of discussion might lead in any one of a number of possible directions. For instance, the students might be motivated to end the discussion with the aim of seeking information to answer these questions. If they have already been doing some research, they may have information and be able to go on to ask, "What would it do to our foreign policy if we limited it to nonmilitary assistance?" It is not at all uncommon for students to want to jump quickly to questions about the proposed new policy and its possible beneficial or undesirable effects. They might begin to talk about how we would slow down world-wide arms races if the United States did not give military assistance; they might say the United States could save a lot of money if it did not give military assistance; or they might say that military and political unrest in various parts of the world might be lessened if the United States did not give arms and training to various factions in some dispute within a nation or among nations, and so forth.

A freewheeling discussion like this—with someone taking notes of the different comments made—could generate an important first step in analysis. When the students began to run out of suggestions such as those above, a teacher might ask: "Do you feel at this time that one important question in considering this resolution would be whether elimination of military assistance would reduce the tensions of arms races?" If the students agreed, the teacher could then say; "Let's make a note of that question, then, 'Would the elimination of U.S. military assistance reduce the tensions of arms races?' " The teacher could continue to do this with all the subject areas the students had mentioned in their discussion. Stating each in the form of a question which could be answered "yes" or "no" and phrasing them so as to put the burden of proof where it belonged—usually on the affirmative, but not always. Depending on the amount of general reading the students had done at the time of this discussion, they could generate between three and forty or more such questions which seem to have the potentiality of being essential elements in the debate.

At this point, it might be useful to distribute the questions among the debaters and send them out with the assignment to try to find either "yes" or "no" answers. It would probably be unwise to assign labels of affirmative or negative to the students at this time, for it would only tend to bias their reading in one direction or the other. It would be valuable to have more than one student seeking to answer each question, however, so that a variety of points of view could be brought to bear on the issue.

After a suitable period of research, the students should be brought together again to discuss what information they uncovered that might help answer the questions. The next discussion could be structured in the sense that the questions be considered individually. For instance, the teacher might say: "Last meeting five students were assigned to try to find some answers to this question: Would elimination of U.S. military assistance lessen military and political unrest in various parts of the world? What have you five students learned?"

A student might answer that India and Pakistan used U.S. military equipment to fight each other rather than the Chinese Communists, and that if the United States refused to give them any more equipment they might be less likely to get into another war. Another might add that the two countries might be less likely to resist Communist China as well if we gave no further military aid. A third student might have learned that India and Pakistan have been fighting or threatening to fight each other since the two nations were created by the withdrawal of Great Britain, and that U.S. military equipment played little or no part in the start of actual fighting.

At this point, the teacher might indicate that several questions seem to have emerged from this discussion. For example:

(1) Did U.S. military assistance play a significant role in the outbreak of war between India and Pakistan?

(2) Would the discontinuation of U.S. military assistance reduce the likelihood of a further outbreak of war?

(3) Would the discontinuation of U.S. military assistance reduce the capacity and willingness of India and Pakistan to resist the spread of Chinese Communism?

Probably other students would want to mention other illustrations of a relationship between U.S. military assistance and political and military unrest. Tension between Israel and the Arab nations might be discussed; or the internal unrest in Latin American nations receiving military assistance, and so forth. In each case, the teacher would be wise to let the students themselves develop the discussion, interrupting only to phrase each new topic that came up in terms of a question. Thus, the teacher might say, "Did U.S. military assistance play a significant role in the development of tension between Israel and the Arab nations, and would the discontinuation of U.S. military assistance reduce that tension?" In each case, the teacher should be sure that the newly-phrased question was recorded by each student.

When the students had once again exhausted their information and interest in the discussion, it would be appropriate for the teacher to distribute the recently generated questions among the students for the development of answers. Notice, that at this stage in the development, the teacher is not asking the students to build arguments but rather to try to *answer the questions*. One of the signal impediments to good analysis in debate is the tendency to leap into argument over questions for which empirically verifiable answers are available. Such debate is not only foolish, it delays the search for the real potential issues relevant to the resolution.

At this stage of analysis it would be useful for the teacher to instruct the students to develop their possible answers so as to parallel all the data suggesting an affirmative answer with all that suggesting a negative answer. Thus, a student paper might look like this:

QUESTION: Did U.S. military assistance play a significant role in the outbreak of war between India and Pakistan?

I. United States assistance did play a significant role in the India-Pakistan war, because
A. Pakistan has received substantial U.S. military aid,
  1. Reports of the U.S. government aid programs show this amount . . . over these years. . . .

B. India received U.S. arms when China invaded Bhutan,
  1. United States gov. reports say so. . . .

C. United States arms were used by India and Pakistan against each other,
  1. *New York Times* article says so. . . .

I. United States assistance did not play a significant role in the India-Pakistan war, because
A. India and Pakistan have deep and fundamental differences unrelated to U.S. aid,
  1. They have deep religious differences according to authorities.
  2. They have conflicting claims to the Kashmir territory, per *United Nations Report*.

B. Both Pakistan and India have received military assistance from communist countries,
  1. Pakistan has received help from China, according to *U.S. News & World Report*.
  2. India has received help from USSR according to *New York Times*.

C. Most of the equipment used in the war was not U.S. equipment,
  1. All the evidence displayed in photos by India and Pakistan reveals only a small amount of equipment and some empty boxes of ammunition, according to *United States News*.

It is quite possible that after reviewing such a paper in the group, the debaters might want to look for further information or add further reasons to the answers. They might, for example, after reading the negative answer, want to know how strong Pakistan would have been without any U.S. aid and whether it would have been able to become strong enough to challenge a nation as large as India, if it had had to rely on Communist China for all its assistance. On the other hand, the students might generate still another question arising out of this conflict. A student might observe, for instance, that in the case of India and Pakistan, the

United States cut off further military assistance as soon as the fighting broke out. While this involved a discontinuation of aid, it did not mean the elimination of military aid as a whole. The student might then ask the teacher whether the possibility existed to question if the present policy of military aid might have adequately adjusted itself to cope with the India-Pakistan problem without making a major change in the policy itself. The teacher would reply that the question seemed quite relevant and word it thus: (4) Is the present capacity of temporary discontinuance of specific-aid projects sufficient to cope with problems of military and political unrest? The students could go on to search for answers to that question.

By way of summary, what has this student group accomplished in the way of analysis so far? The students developed an interest in the relationship between U.S. military assistance and military and political unrest in the world. Through alternating discussion and research, they have generated such specific questions as these:

(1) Did U.S. military assistance play a significant role in the creation of military and political unrest in the world?
   (A) Did U.S. military assistance play a significant role in the outbreak of war between India and Pakistan?
   (B) Did U.S. military assistance play a significant role in the development of tension between Israel and the Arab nations?
   (C) Did U.S. military assistance play a significant role in the creation of internal political unrest in some Latin American nations?

(2) Would the discontinuation of U.S. military assistance significantly reduce the likelihood of military and political unrest in the world?
   (A) Would discontinuation of military assistance reduce the chance of war between India and Pakistan?
   (B) Would discontinuation of military assistance reduce tension between Israel and the Arab nations?
   (C) Would discontinuation of military assistance reduce the likelihood of internal political unrest in some Latin American nations?

(3) Would discontinuation of military assistance reduce the capacity and willingness of former recipients to resist the spread of communism?

(4) Is the present capacity of temporary discontinuance of specific aid projects sufficient to cope with problems of military and political unrest?

For each one of these questions, the students would have prepared a statement of all the available evidence and reasoning suggesting an affirmative or negative answer. In so doing, they would undoubtedly have discovered some questions to be rather clearly answered either "yes" or "no" and thus unlikely to constitute a significant focal point of difference in a debate. This in no way means the work was done in vain. On the contrary, that information is to be kept for that time when it will be used in arguing an answer to a broader question. Also, in seeking answers to these questions, numerous other questions certainly will have been discovered which stand independently in need of an answer. These should simply be stated clearly and added to the list for research.

An attitude conducive to the discovery and articulation of new questions is particularly important in allowing students to broaden their analysis. That is to say, while doing research on one question a student may become curious about an area quite unrelated to the one at hand. For instance, while looking for information on the India-Pakistan war, a student may run across an article dealing with the impact of military assistance on the U.S. balance of international payments. He may not know what a balance of payments is, but the article may lead him to suspect that it is a problem that may arise from the aid policy. He should be encouraged to record these questions:

(1) Is an imbalance of payments harmful to the United States?
(2) Does U.S. military assistance contribute to an imbalance of U.S. payments?
(3) Is it probable that U.S. payments will be brought into balance while continuing to send out military assistance?
(4) Would discontinuation of military assistance significantly increase the likelihood of balancing U.S. international payments?

In this way, a student has greatly expanded the scope of his thinking about the debate topic as a whole, thus freeing himself from the need to restrict his arguments to questions of military and political unrest. It may well be that he will never discuss both unrest and the balance of payments problem in the same debate, but this should in no way cause him to avoid such breadth in his analysis generally. At this stage of the game, the student ought not to be thinking of a specific case for a specific debate—he simply is not ready!

When to Begin Active Debating

The teacher may well ask how long students can be expected to go through rigorous research and analysis, then more research and then more analysis without a chance to get into a debate. The students need both a chance to begin to learn how to express themselves orally and the motivation of active participation to keep up their interest in the laborious study work. The answer to this question is that students should begin debating as soon as they have developed possible answers to the first set of questions posed, and depending upon the students this can be within one day or, at most, one week of their first meeting.

This does not mean the students engage in formal one-hour debates. Rather, they should begin with nothing more demanding than an oral statement of the specific question assigned to them along with the possible answers they had developed. Each student, in this case, would be simply making a 2- or 3-minute speech on a specific subject and covering both sides. They would not engage in refutation of each other's ideas at this time; rather they might discuss how each speech had been organized and presented in terms of logic, evidence, structure, delivery, etc., as well as what possible analysis and research might still be done on the topic. Emphasis would be on positive reinforcement of what the student had done well.

Discussion by Two Students

From this start, it is a small step to assigning two students to the same specific question—still not mentioning the overall debate resolution—with one assigned to prepare a short speech developing an affirmative answer and the other discussing a negative answer. Still the students do not engage in direct refutation of each other, but now the two presentations can be discussed with regard to the way in which the two possible answers clash, seeking to discover how a judge might go about selecting an answer. In this task, it is useful to have other debaters who are not speaking act as judges to select one of the proposed answers and be prepared to say why. Notice the judges do not pick a winning debater but rather the most probable answer! The emphasis in discussion after each set of speakers is directed again toward complimenting the students for their successes and suggestions of research and analysis that might be useful in seeking to answer the specific question. In a short time, the group should have generated enough different important questions so that the entire squad could divide into groups of two for the discussion of a different question.

Discussion by Groups of Two Students

The next phase in debater development of analytical skills is obviously the assignment of groups of two debaters to discuss possible affirmative and negative answers to a specific question—still not talking about the whole resolution—and to take into account what the other has said. In this case, each debater would be allowed to present his position and then speak again after hearing his opponent. All other debaters listening to this debate should continue to act as judges of the content and try to follow the flow of argument. This will prepare them to engage in analysis during their own debates, as well as providing valuable feedback to the speakers.

As these exercises continue, the debaters should be in the continual process of doing research on the questions already articulated as well as seeking out new questions to be potential issues. They still have not developed a case or planned the overall strategy for a full debate, nor do they as yet have reason to think of themselves as either affirmative or negative. They have merely been discussing individual topics, sometimes on one side, sometimes on the other.

Direct-Clash Debates

A next exercise can be a full direct-clash type of debate, which is essentially what the debaters have already been doing. For this exercise, the students can be divided into groups of from two to five each and given a side—affirmative or negative. For the first time, the full debate resolution is the focus of the debate. Each side is assigned the job of selecting two or three of the specific questions they have been discussing which they consider to be fundamental to the resolution itself and which constitute a coherent discussion of the resolution. The teacher will probably actively participate with each group in selecting questions to be used at first. During the debate, each team is allowed time—usually no more than five or so minutes—to state the resolution, define basic concepts, and advance their chosen questions as being worthy of debate. The teams should be given an opportunity to respond to the other's analysis or definition if it feels moved to do so. The object of this analysis period is to come up with three different questions—two to be advanced by the affirmative and one by the negative—which both teams agree are worthy of debate and are well worded. The teacher should feel free to participate in this effort, even making a final selection of the questions for debate if the two teams cannot decide for themselves or if they choose unwisely.

Once the three questions are selected, the teams should prepare assignments for speaking, seeing to it that the initial speakers on each issue are particularly well prepared to discuss the issue and that no speaker in any clash debate is assigned to speak twice before all others on the team have spoken once. From there, the clashes begin. The first speaker from each side on each issue should be given three or four minutes to establish a position, and the speakers who follow should have no more than two minutes, with the initiating team having a two-minute summary at the end. Each clash can involve as many different speakers as the teacher deems appropriate, but usually four or five speeches per clash is enough. At the end of each clash, either the teacher or the judging students, or both, should indicate their decision as to the side demonstrating the greater probability in favor of its answer. On the middle or second clash, the negative typically initiates the issue it has suggested, speaking both first and last. The side winning two or more of the three clashes has won the debate.

Even after moving to full direct-clash debates, the teacher would be wise to insist upon having a variety of issues discussed by the various groups of debaters, even to the point of assigning different issues than those which the debaters feel most significant at the moment. Students should not be allowed to settle on a specific group of three issues which they discuss over and over. The students also should be rotated from group to group and from side to side for as long as possible. Ultimately, of course, assignment of two-man teams so students can work together is necessary; but even then, in practice, the students can be moved around during direct-clash debates so as to forestall the advance of intellectual rigor mortis which frequently sets in as soon as two students have developed "our case."

THE VALUE OF THE STOCK ISSUES CONCEPT

The reader knowledgeable in debate theory has already recognized that the foregoing examples fit quite comfortably into the stock issue concept, and he may, by this time, be wondering why so much effort has been made to avoid mentioning them. The answer is that there is nothing inherently wrong with the concept of stock issues in a question of policy when thought of as a universal pattern which debaters may use to guide them to the discovery of real issues and to help them construct a coherent and logical case for one side or the other. The problem lies in the effect the stock issues concept has on the thinking of debaters and judges.

Specifically, the idea of stock issues is to provide a knowable and universal pattern with which to begin the analysis of any resolution of public policy, just as the legal or statutory concept of burglary provides lawyers with a useful pattern to start their analysis of any specific case of burglary. Obviously, the absence of universal acceptance by common law or statute or any similar standards prevents the stock issues of policy from ever being as valuable a tool as in the legal concept. Furthermore, the very nature of questions of policy—involving as they do such a widely varying complex of facts, values, and motives—means there can never be the similarity between one question of public policy and another as there can be between one case of burglary within a given jurisdiction and another. The two involve quite different forms of decision-making.

Nevertheless, when a student asks, "Where do I begin?" "How will I know if my case is prima facie*?" the teacher will find it meaningful to answer that almost any question of policy generates these general questions:

(1) Is there a need for a change from the present policy to a new one?

(2) Is the need inherent in the sense that the present policy is structurally unable to correct the need?

(3) Is there a workable plan or a new policy which can correct the need?

(4) Would it generally be desirable to adopt that plan? Would its payoff exceed its cost; its advantages outweigh its disadvantages?

The student should examine his research materials—or potential issues if he has developed them—to see if they provide for a discussion of each of these general areas. Thus, to return to the previous example (see p. 134), the question, "Did U.S. military assistance play a significant role in the creation of military and political unrest in the world?" would relate to stock issue No. 1 concerning need; the question, "Is the present capacity of temporary discontinuance of specific-aid projects sufficient to cope with problems of military and political unrest?" would relate to stock issue No. 2 concerning inherency; the question, "Would discontinuation of U.S. military assistance significantly reduce the likelihood of military and political unrest in the world?" would relate to stock issue No. 3 concerning plan; and the question, "Would discontinuation of military assistance reduce the capacity and willingness of former recipients to resist the spread of communism?" would relate to stock issue No. 4 concerning overall desirability.

Of course, the question, "Is an imbalance of payments harmful to the United States?" would relate to the stock issue of need as is true of the one mentioned above, and so would any number of other quite distinct questions relate as well! This is one of the

---

* See Chapter 7 for a more complete discussion of this concept.

weaknesses of the stock issues concept: once students have found a *need* they are inclined to adhere to it as if it were *the need* of the entire resolution, and thus blind themselves to all the other potential subject areas from which a need for a change might be found.

Moreover, the tendency to label issues as either need issues or plan issues leads students to think of them as different entities. Of course, the question of how to cope with political and military unrest remains the same whether it is being discussed from the perspective of the U.S. military assistance program and its possible discontinuance, the efficacy of temporary versus permanent discontinuance, or its relation to the power to resist the spread of international communism. By the same token, ways and means of balancing U.S. international payments remain the same subject whether discussed in terms of the effect of U.S. military assistance payments, their discontinuance, or—and this is significant—when discussed in terms of the effect of economic assistance, tourism, trade, etc. The subject is not distinct as a need for the discontinuation of military assistance, but is distinct as an economic problem to be dealt with in the most desirable manner whether that involves military assistance or not. The student must not be permitted to fractionalize these problems in his thinking to suit his concept of debating—rather he must adjust his concept of debating to provide the most meaningful pattern in which to discuss the problems! The Procrustean tendency to slice up problems in terms of needs and plans also leads to some awkward and repetitious discussions within debates as debaters try to talk about one problem as a need, then another problem as a need; the first problem as a plan, then the second problem as a plan; and the first problem in terms of desirability, then the second problem in terms of desirability, and so forth. A much more coherent discussion is usually to be found by talking about each problem individually—including its characteristics as need, plan, and desirability, and so forth, before moving on to a new topic.

Another outgrowth of the stock issues procedure is the constant difficulty with the comparative-advantages type of case structure as compared with the stock-issues structure. This distinction will be discussed in the section following, but let it be said here that some debaters and judges become so committed to the stock issues concept that unless a debater announces and demonstrates he has a *need* the judge will vote against him, and debaters sometimes use the comparative-advantages structure as if it were a miraculous way of advocating a new policy for which there is no particularly strong reason. Both attitudes are unbelievably myopic.

Finally, the stock-issue approach must be criticized to the extent it leads debaters—particularly inexperienced ones—to come to substitute the stock issue for the real issue. Thus, young debaters often announce that their contention is "There is a need for a change," after which they commence to read a series of quotations, all in some way relevant to describing the evils of the present system, which range over the full spectrum of subject areas and leave the audience and their opponents in such a state of confusion as is unlikely to be overcome in the ensuing fifty minutes. Debaters *must* keep in mind that their contention is not that there is a need, but that military assistance contributes to unrest, or imbalance of payments, etc., and these problems combine to constitute what might be called a need. They must also remember that in the final analysis the only way a given allegedly evil phenomenon can be measured to see if it does truly constitute a need for a new policy is (1) when it is considered in terms of its inherent effect, (2) the capacity of present policies to cope with those effects, (3) the capacity of a new policy to cope with those effects, (4) the capacity of X number of other potential new policies to cope with those effects, and (5) the overall cost of implementing any one of the new policies as compared with the cost of retaining the present policies including undesirable effects. In other words, debaters cannot meaningfully talk about *needs and plans* but only problems and solutions, taken as they are found in the extensional world.

Therefore, the concept of stock issues seems to have a real value for the teacher of debate analysis, but that value is quite restricted and the use of stock issues should be similarly restricted. Stock issues become positively evil when they are allowed to pervade the entire thinking of debaters and thus warp the process of debate itself.

Summarizing, analysis in debate has been described as a two-step process of discovering what questions are essential to the decision on the resolution itself, and the discovering of the available reasons and evidence to help answer the questions. Analysis has been spoken of as a process of inquiry as distinct from advocacy. In that sense, it has been recommended that to the extent debaters are permitted to begin to think of themselves as affirmative or negative advocates of a given set of arguments they will tend to short-circuit the process of analysis.

A pattern of analysis has been advanced, which begins by permitting the debaters to select their own point of demarcation as they must and will ultimately cover the entire problem if their analysis is complete. From the starting point, debaters have been encouraged to ask questions, then try to answer them, and to re-ask questions and discover new questions, and search for more answers. This search is to be made in terms of various subject areas relevant to the resolution and not in terms of a case for a specific side.

The final product of this kind of analysis is a file box, or notebook, or full brief consisting of forty or more distinct questions, all of which interrelate in terms of the overall topic of debate and some of which fall into small groups of questions centering around a large subject area. For each of these questions the debater has written (in as logical and coherent a manner possible) all the available reasons and evidence suggesting both an affirmative and a negative answer. In some cases, the answers are one-sided; in others, there is a well-balanced clash. The debater never considers himself finished—he only pauses from time to time to engage in a debate before he returns to look for better answers or more questions, or both.

Finally, the debater has practiced the dynamic analysis which must take place in a debate by participating in direct clash debates. In so doing, he has learned to think of a debate in terms of one issue at a time, to keep his arguments relevant to the issue at hand, and to recognize when the debate has left one issue and moved to another.

With this preparation, the debater is now prepared to build a case.

SUGGESTED READINGS

Capp, Glenn R., Robert Huber, and Wayne C. Eubank. "Duties of Affirmative Speakers—A Symposium," *Speech Teacher*, VIII (March 1959), 139–49.

Hellman, Hugo E. "Building Your Constructive Case," *Debaters Magazine*, II (December 1946), 235–38.

Kruger, Arthur N. "Teaching Analysis to a Debate Squad," *Gavel*, XXXIX (November 1956), 9–11.

Marsh, Patrick O. "Prima Facie Case: The Perennial Debate Topic," *Gavel*, XLV (November 1962), 13–15.

Moore, Wilbur E. "Assumptions Underlying Analysis in Debate," *Forensic of Pi Kappa Delta*, XXXIII (March 1948), 45–46, 51.

Nadeau, Ray. "Hermogenes on 'Stock Issues' in Deliberative Speaking," *Speech Monographs*, XXV (March 1958), 59–66.

Newman, Robert P. "Analysis and Issues: A Study of Doctrine," *Central States Speech Journal*, XIII (1961), 43–54.

Sattler, William M. "Some Values of Discussion in the Investigation and Analysis Phases of Debate," *Gavel*, XXIV–XXV (March-May 1943), 54–55.

Scott, Robert L. "On The Meaning of the Term Prima Facie in Argumentation," *Central States Speech Journal*, XII (Autumn 1960), 33–37.

Shaw, Warren C. "Systematic Analysis of Debating Problems," *Quarterly Journal of Speech*, II (October 1916), 344–51.

CHAPTER 6

Research in Debate
Don F. Faules

Students of debate are concerned with reasoned discourse and the reasoning which occurs is a result of previous observation or supposition. In a debate an appropriate cliche is: "Come let us reason together"; however, an even more important statement might be: "Come let us reason *from something.*" One must possess the raw materials of argumentation before productive advocacy can take place.

THE NATURE OF DEBATE RESEARCH

Good research involves systematic inquiry into the total problem area. The antithesis of this concept is illustrated by the debater who conceives of research as "quotes on cards" or research as a means to verify preconceived ideas. Perhaps all coaches have had the experience of hearing a debater say "I have my case; now all I have to do is find the evidence to support it." The coach should be careful to make the distinction between case and analysis. The preceding chapter on analysis explains the difference in considerable detail.

Ideally the debater should have a grasp of all the subject matter in a resolution. However, it soon becomes apparent that it is rare for a debater to comprehend a technical discussion of a specialized area. When a debater poses a question to an expert, it is not uncommon for the specialist to point out that the student would need several years of study before he could understand the answer. Although such a comment may be legitimate, it does not solve the problem for a debater who must be prepared to advocate a position.

The debater is forced to utilize materials that he understands. The problem and its solution is best illustrated by a continuum. At one end there is journalistic material that is digested for the public and at the other end there is scholarly material that is available for scholars and other specialists. The difficulties of material at one end of the continuum have been discussed. The scientist did not write for the debater. That was not his purpose; and the debater is not a scientist. But what of the other end of the continuum? The debater is not the public and it is doubtful that the journalist had him in mind when he wrote the article.

Although a journalist may base his writings on scholarly work, his purpose is different than that of the scholar. It is not unusual for such material to contain the few sensational items that may be found in a study. Part of a journalist's purpose is entertainment and his writing is geared to interest readers. The very process of selection may insure readers, but at the same time distort the total meaning of scholarly inquiry. The embellishments added by a journalist may make an article very interesting, but these same embellishments may distort and emphasize the unimportant.

At the same end of the continuum with the journalist is the special-interest group or advocate. The extreme statements of such groups can be frightening as well as entertaining. Such statements are rarely established in a debate where all the evidence is carefully examined. The purpose of the special-interest group is to advocate a particular position and persuade the reader. Because of a one-sided presentation, one can conclude that this material is propaganda. It must be granted, however, that not all special-interest groups are radicals. In addition, debaters will be examining evidence and devising some propaganda of their own. The important point is that the debater must view all the evidence and devise the rhetorical argument. It is not enough to seek out extreme statements on both sides of an issue.

It is apparent that the debater must make a compromise if he is to engage in intellectual discourse. In other words, he must search for mediate answers. Somewhere along the described continuum there will exist data and scholarly discussions that can be understood. The coach should keep in mind that this part of the continuum makes more demands on the students because they must look at the data and formulate arguments of their own. However, this is the purpose of debate training.

Developing Research Attitudes

The coach will do himself and his students a service by discouraging the search for ready-made arguments. The debater must realize that different sources have different purposes. The journalist cannot be expected to provide primary materials for the debater because part of his task is entertainment. Special-interest groups tend to design arguments that are extreme and these groups seldom explain the basis for their argument. A case in point can be seen in the arguments advanced by special-interest factions during the right-to-work controversy. Highly emotionalized materials were distributed by both sides. The student should know that extreme examples can be found on both sides of an issue and the quality of a debate depends on what materials are used.

The competent coach will train his students to search for explication of the issues by competent authorities who also provide intelligible data. The teacher must understand that one of the primary goals of forensic training is to help the student acquire research skill. When the student is willing to settle for mediocre research and analysis, he will never experience the satisfaction and knowledge that comes from intensive investigation.

THE ROLE OF THE COACH

The coach of debate has the responsibility of developing critical tendencies in his students. This means that he must develop some standards of his own and adhere to them. The following suggestions are helpful for the coach who endeavors to implant a valuable and permanent skill.

(1) Teacher aids are just that and should not replace instruction. Once the research process is short-circuited by handbook cases or preconceived notions, productive research is replaced by gamesmanship. In other words, there is a tendency to look for evidence that will support a case that was not derived through analysis. The case may be a poor one and no amount of evidence can make it respectable. If the student learns that analysis and research precede case construction, he will be prepared to engage in realistic research for future efforts.

(2) Students should examine the evidence and construct their *own* rhetorical arguments. It was pointed out earlier that special-interest groups tend to overgeneralize and emotionalize their arguments. It is unlikely that a competent debater will draw the same conclusions after examining the evidence that he did before examining the evidence. It is the responsibility of the coach to see that his debaters do not settle for the conclusions of others without a careful examination of the evidence.

(3) It is the coach's responsibility to distinguish between rhetoric and sophistry. Perhaps one way to make this distinction is to describe the different ways that a logician, rhetorician, and sophist would examine an argument. The logician would ask, "Is it logical?" The rhetorician would ask, "Is it logical and how will the audience react to it?" The sophist would only ask, "How will the audience react to it?" Coaches can instill sophistic habits within their students without realizing it. Whenever students ignore analysis and engage in a search for persuasive arguments, they are following a blueprint for sophistry. Whenever a student is willing to settle for quoting any argument that might support his position, he runs the risk of sophistry. It is important for the coach to teach a student to examine the evidence and formulate rhetorical arguments of his own. The coach must then decide if the arguments are indeed rhetorical rather than sophistic.

(4) The student should be given the opportunity to determine for himself what evidence is important and what that evidence means. However, the coach is responsible for evaluation and instruction. When the coach receives the usual free literature from special-interest groups, he should be more than a disseminator. Some of these materials can serve as useful instructional aids. If

the students have done a careful job of analysis, inadequacies can be determined by comparison of facts and inferences. It is not enough to destroy such materials or to tell a student not to use them. The student must understand why the materials may be inadequate.

(5) The attitude that the student holds toward evidence is developed by the coach. It is not uncommon for students to try to please the coach, rather than meeting the requirements that are imposed on evidence. For example, the coach may criticize the debaters in practice for using weak evidence. In the next practice he may find that the debaters are using different evidence with the same weakness, a different arrangement of the same evidence, or only slight modification of the same evidence. A coach must insist that the evidence meet the requirements. He should observe carefully to see how a debater responds when his evidence is exposed as faulty. If the debater attempts to distort, the behavior of the coach becomes extremely important because his reaction will determine his student's attitude toward evidence. The coach must insist on precision and point out clearly the fruits of sophistry. Sometimes the charge of inability is more effective than that of unethical behavior. The competent debater does not need to distort! If a coach can obtain an expert in the particular area of concern, this will do much to examine the value of evidence presented. When a team has constructed what it considers to be a good case, the expert can listen and evaluate from a different perspective.

RESOURCES

Although the coach should not do research for his students, he is obligated to direct them toward all available resources. These resources will be discussed and in addition a list of titles and addresses will be included at the end of this chapter. It is apparent that the coach will not have a budget that will permit him to order all the materials that are available. He must be selective and have a clear understanding of what he is purchasing.

Library Facilities

It is both necessary and desirable to have an area where debate materials can be collected and made available to students. The ideal situation is a debate library that contains the major sources of materials. However when this is not possible, a special section of the school library should be used for relevant materials.

The coach should know the limitations of his particular library and compensate for them. For example, if the debate resolution involves a legal question, a law library is not always readily available. In this case, the coach should prepare his team for a day's visit to a law library at a nearby school. Before this visit is made, the coach should go to the library first to locate relevant materials. This pre-planning can make the day's work productive. Some libraries serve as repositories for government documents. The coach and students should understand the workings and contents of all libraries that are accessible.

Sometimes debate materials are relevant to a number of areas of study. In this case the coach can justify the use of a library budget to supplement that of his own. There are some materials that may exist in the library but which must be duplicated by the coach because of their constant use or the nature of that use. For example, the *Congressional Record* is quite lengthy and sometimes cumbersome. It saves time to cut material out of this publication and arrange it for maximum efficiency.

Debate Sources

Handbooks

It has been pointed out that teaching aids sometimes replace teaching. One of the fundamental goals of debate training is to train the student to analyze. This goal cannot be met if coaches and students are willing to settle for ready-made cases and arguments. Some of the debate handbooks that have been published are even questionable when placed in the category of teachers' aids. The bibliography in such handbooks is no more extensive and certainly not as selective as a bibliography compiled by a competent debate squad.

Some common reasons that coaches give for the use of such handbooks are: (1) a handbook gives a hint of what others might be using, (2) it helps to get the student started, (3) it saves time, and (4) the bibliography is useful. However, the soundness of these reasons is questionable. A team rarely dares to use a handbook case or analysis. When it does, it offers mediocre competition and such cases lend little to a learning experience. The coach must remember that helping a student start in the right direction is more important than just getting a student started. If the coach wishes to train the debaters, himself, the handbook can actually waste time. The process of analysis cannot be circumvented and retraining is often more frustrating and time consuming. Part of a debater's training is gathering a bibliography and composing an analysis of his own.

Special Analyses

Students always hope that they can find an intelligible and scholarly discussion of the debate resolution early in the debate season. One such analysis is made by the American Enterprise Institute. Although this analysis may have some limitations, it is distinctly superior to handbooks in terms of material and also with regard to intent.

The Congressional Digest usually devotes an issue of their publication to an analysis of the current debate topic. This issue also features "Pros & Cons" which contains statements by various dignitaries. The major value of this publication is its historical approach and reference to other materials. Much of the pro and con material is of little value for debate.

High-school coaches can obtain useful analyses by writing to the National Committee on Discussion and Debate. Special issues of *Current History* focus on the questions that are helpful for an analysis of the high-school debate topic.

An analysis and bibliography of high-school and college debate topics can be obtained free of charge through the Legislative Reference Service.

Government Documents

In order to find the available materials in a topic area (example: Labor-Management Relations) the coach should examine the

Monthly Catalogue of U.S. Government Publications. In addition, he can obtain price lists on topic areas from the Superintendent of Documents. The U.S. Government Printing Office also supplies a biweekly listing of selected government publications. This list can be obtained free of charge by simply asking to be placed on the mailing list.

Government agencies can provide newsletters, reports, and news about reports that are going to be released. The coach and students should compile a list of the agencies that are relevant to the topic area.

Newspapers and Periodicals

Students will find the most complete reporting in national newspapers, such as the *New York Times* and the *Christian Science Monitor*. A major value of newspapers and news magazines is their reference to primary evidence. Thus, the student should find out where the reporter obtained his story. Newspapers often report the preliminary findings of studies and they also alert the reader about the expected date of study completion. The student who is willing to go to the original source of the news will benefit from newspapers and periodicals.

International Agencies

The data compiled by international agencies usually has direct or indirect relevance to the debate topic. Such data may even expose an issue that might have gone unnoticed. For example, during a debate on compulsory health insurance, figures from world health organizations indicated that the United States might not have the best health program in the world. The description and addresses of such agencies can be found in the library.

Special-Interest Groups

The coach will not have to search for free materials from special-interest groups. Some addresses are included at the end of this chapter with the thought that the student will want to determine what data are used for the arguments advanced. The student should realize the shortcomings of such material. Recently a union retained two college debaters to write an analysis of compulsory arbitration which was then made available to high-school debaters. It is obvious that college debaters are not experts in the subject matter of compulsory arbitration. Nevertheless, the style of such a book might be most appealing to a student who wishes to avoid analysis.

Guest Speakers

A discussion with an expert can be helpful if debaters are prepared for such a discussion and if the results are used properly. The students should prepare questions for an expert and the emphasis should be on analysis. Debaters should not expect the speaker to build a case for them or verify a case that they have constructed. Such interviews should not be used as evidence for a case. It is too easy to distort what the speaker has said. In addition, all debaters should have access to the materials used in a debate. When a debater quotes material that has been given in an interview, he is violating the rules of the game. An opponent has no way of checking the accuracy of such materials.

Summer Institutes

Summer institutes and workshops for high-school students can be both a blessing and a curse. If the research and analysis done at a workshop is kept in proper perspective, it is of great assistance to the coach. Both the coach and the student should recognize that the workshop is designed to get a student started. The student must still continue to examine the problem area and the coach must continue to instruct.

High-School Speech Leagues

The high-school coach can usually obtain materials or listings of materials from his state speech league. Some state speech leagues provide bibliographies that have been compiled at summer workshops.

RESEARCH PROCEDURE

The start of a debate season presents the coach with a challenge. Students want to know how and where to start. It is helpful to think of a research problem as having centrality and circumference. The centrality of a resolution is represented by the essential questions that must be answered by analysis. This procedure is explained in Chapter 5. The development of potential issues also indicates the broad scope of a resolution. The circumference of a resolution is developed by discovering all of the potential issues. This in turn indicates the kinds of materials that will need investigation. In most cases this means that a variety of sources must be examined. It is unlikely that any one debater can examine all of the relevant publications for pertinent information.

Division of Labor

An organized research effort by all members of a debate squad can result in efficiency and comprehensive investigation. The coach can assign individual members of the debate squad to ex-

(Example of Primary Evidence)

10228 CONGRESSIONAL RECORD — SENATE *May 17, 1966*

search for world peace, this proposed trade act has a part to play which serves the interests of the United States. I am persuaded, moreover, that the sooner this act is permitted to play that part, the better it will be for this nation and the world.

Mr. MAGNUSON. Mr. President, I ask unanimous consent that some documents and statements in connection with this subject to be printed in the RECORD at this point.

There being no objection, the material was ordered to be printed in the RECORD, as follows:

Imports from Sino-Soviet bloc, January to December

[In millions of U.S. dollars]

	S. Union		China		Poland		Czechoslovakia		Rumania		Bulgaria		Hungary		E. Germany		Total	
	1965	1964	1965	1964	1965	1964	1965	1964	1965	1964	1965	1964	1965	1964	1965	1964	1965	1964
G. Britain	331.7	252.8	82.9	68.9	135.3	134.7	48.6	47.3	31.3	24.9	15.1	12.0	19.0	20.4	33.5	28.8	697.4	589.8
W. Germany	275.3	234.3	72.7	51.8	108.9	90.7	84.1	72.0	72.4	61.3	41.3	30.3	71.9	61.8	314.4	259.3	1,041.0	861.5
Japan	240.2	226.7	224.7	157.7	1.9	2.1	7.0	6.0	19.0	11.9	6.1	5.8	0.4	0.6	1.2	3.3	500.5	414.1
France	146.8	142.5	43.8	31.1	31.2	31.1	26.8	23.0	29.0	29.4	7.3	8.1	15.9	11.8	15.9	14.3	316.7	291.3
Italy	181.1	147.8	38.2	23.8	61.1	53.2	35.9	36.4	61.1	55.4	30.7	19.9	51.3	42.8	14.2	14.8	473.6	394.1
Belgium	46.3	50.1	14.2	13.7	13.7	13.4	20.9	15.1	3.6	7.0	2.5	2.5	7.8	7.6	26.3	23.0	135.3	132.4
Netherlands	52.7	35.8	25.4	20.2	15.1	13.7	27.9	26.6	5.6	4.5	3.6	2.5	12.6	12.3	32.6	30.5	175.5	146.1
Finland	229.3	245.5	5.9	6.4	31.3	30.0	10.9	10.1	3.9	2.8	1.7	1.4	5.0	7.8	15.1	15.1	303.1	319.1
Norway	28.2	25.8	4.7	3.4	10.6	11.5	11.4	12.9	1.1	1.4	1.4	0.8	3.6	5.0	11.7	9.8	72.7	70.6
Sweden	72.5	70.0	15.1	12.3	38.5	33.3	22.0	20.4	7.3	3.6	2.8	1.7	12.6	10.9	25.1	29.7	195.9	172.9
Denmark	33.5	26.0	6.4	7.5	31.5	31.6	14.2	12.3	0.8	0.6	0.8	0.6	6.7	6.7	25.1	21.0	119.0	106.3
Austria	53.0	52.6	5.0	3.4	45.8	40.3	38.2	27.4	20.7	19.6	11.7	8.1	31.5	27.4	26.5	22.1	232.4	200.9
Switzerland	12.0	8.1	12.6	7.6	13.1	10.4	19.5	13.7	5.6	9.0	2.2	0.8	20.0	19.9	7.5	6.2	92.5	75.7
	1,702.6	1,518.0	551.6	407.8	538.0	496.0	367.4	323.2	261.4	231.4	127.2	94.5	258.3	235.0	549.1	468.9	4,351.1	3,774.8

Exports to Sino-Soviet bloc, January to December

[In millions of U.S. dollars]

	S. Union		China		Poland		Czechoslovakia		Rumania		Bulgaria		Hungary		E. Germany		Total	
	1965	1964	1965	1964	1965	1964	1965	1964	1965	1964	1965	1964	1965	1964	1965	1964	1965	1964
G. Britain	126.9	106.4	69.5	49.6	68.1	66.9	35.7	35.3	26.8	23.0	10.6	7.8	21.2	24.1	22.6	14.0	381.4	327.1
W. Germany	146.3	193.6	79.0	25.4	91.5	78.4	100.6	82.9	115.6	82.7	55.2	39.0	76.8	74.0	296.6	289.8	961.6	865.8
Japan	168.6	181.8	245.0	152.7	5.4	2.4	8.7	2.8	15.2	19.2	10.9	7.5	2.3	4.0	1.1	0.1	457.2	370.5
France	72.5	64.7	60.5	50.1	35.7	40.0	35.7	16.2	44.1	43.4	23.7	21.3	20.9	24.6	69.5	26.6	362.6	286.9
Italy	89.6	91.3	56.4	14.8	49.4	31.4	41.6	36.4	46.6	41.4	32.6	27.7	37.1	31.9	16.2	11.8	369.5	288.7
Belgium	22.9	14.8	17.0	7.6	14.0	14.3	22.9	17.0	6.1	6.4	4.7	3.9	10.9	12.3	12.0	8.7	110.5	85.1
Netherlands	29.3	13.1	19.0	5.9	12.8	10.4	15.4	10.6	4.2	5.0	11.7	3.9	10.9	13.7	19.8	15.7	113.1	80.3
Finland	224.9	115.7	80.9	64.0	33.2	25.5	8.1	8.9	3.3	2.8	1.9	7.8	7.5	8.4	12.0	12.6	371.8	225.0
Norway	18.4	17.1	5.3	5.9	12.6	10.4	10.0	9.5	1.7	0.8	4.7	1.1	5.6	3.9	10.0	16.0	68.3	64.7
Sweden	50.5	87.6	13.7	14.0	30.9	22.4	18.9	14.0	7.3	7.0	5.9	2.0	9.5	10.6	32.4	26.3	169.1	183.9
Denmark	30.7	35.0	1.9	1.1	17.0	11.2	10.9	7.0	2.0	2.0	2.8	1.7	6.7	4.2	22.6	18.5	94.6	80.7
Austria	57.5	48.2	1.7	0.6	32.1	23.8	37.4	29.1	22.0	23.8	25.4	18.2	42.7	43.7	28.5	19.6	247.3	217.0
Switzerland	15.1	10.1	18.1	10.4	14.5	9.5	18.7	16.0	8.1	9.8	6.9	3.4	11.2	10.4	8.4	6.3	101.0	71.9
	1,053.2	1,031.4	668.0	346.5	417.2	346.6	364.6	282.8	303.0	267.3	197.0	145.3	263.3	265.8	541.7	465.7	3,808.0	3,150.7

(Example of Secondary Evidence)

e tariff on Rumanian cheese is 7 cents
pound—for its competitors, 5 cents a
und. On Rumanian glassware—both
ateglass for industrial use, and table-
are—the tariff is 60 percent while other
untries bear only a 15- to 50-percent
riff.

"We are between the anvil and the
ammer," says the Rumanians. "If we
wer our prices sufficiently to overcome
e tariff barrier, then we are accused of
mping."

Undoubtedly, the inability of the
resident to grant the most-favored-
ation treatment to Rumania has greatly
paired the effectiveness of our ef-
rts to assist Rumania in steering the
dependent course which she seeks for
erself.

The Senate Commerce Committee has
ng maintained a deep interest in the
evelopment of mutually advantageous
ast-West trade relationships. Last fall
e committee was represented by staff
unsel who served as a consultant to
e U.S. trade mission to Poland and
mania—the first such mission spon-
red by the U.S. Government—and at
e invitation of the Department of
mmerce, the committee will again be
presented in October as the United
tates sends its first trade mission to
ungary and Bulgaria.

Mr. President, in his letter of trans-
ittal, Secretary Rusk predicted that
panded East-West trade would pro-
uce a "growing understanding of the
lls, opportunities, and earnings of free
bor in the United States." The U.S.
ade mission to Poland and Rumania
st fall reported several instances which
ramatize the growth of such under-
anding.

Mr. James O. Ellison, of San Fran-
sco, for example, was the trade mis-
on's machine tool expert.

I am told that no one who witnessed
s electrifying tours through Rumanian
nd Polish factories could doubt the wis-
om of promoting commercial contacts
tween American businessmen and
eir Communist counterparts. From
he moment he crossed the threshold of
plant, it became evident that this man
mbodied that quality—American know-
ow—which the Europeans most covet.
he Rumanian expression for know-how
know-how. Quietly, politely, not un-
ke a patient teacher, Jim Ellison would
read his way through each factory,
ausing to acknowledge and praise that
hich was sound, but seeing with a com-
rehending eye and identifying those
aps which were the product of tech-
ological isolation.

At the Red Star truck plant in
rashov, Rumania, the technical direc-
r sought his advice on the possibility
f licensing American technology to solve
persistent production problem. The
ant had begun producing a high-speed
ngine which wore out its camshaft in
to 5 months. Ellison paused for a mo-
ent and then replied that they did
ot really need a license—the problem
ould be simply solved by redesigning the
amshaft with double, rather than single
bes, so that it need revolve only half
s fast.

In the Nova Huta Works, near Kra-
kow, Poland, the mission watched an
American rolling mill smoothly and ef-
fortlessly turning out galvanized steel,
while nearby a new piece of Russian
equipment had broken down. I could
give many other examples such as these.

In neither country could one tell where
admiration for the American and his
machines ended and where admiration
for the economic and political system
which produced them began.

I think it is high time that we take a
step forward on this road toward better
world understanding. As I have stated
on so many occasions, legitimate trade,
nonstrategic trade, is a tool for peace.

Mr. President, the Senate should know
that the Senator from Montana [Mr.
MANSFIELD] would be here this afternoon
were he not confined to the Bethesda
Naval Hospital with a slight touch of the
flu. He has prepared a statement on
the bill which he has asked me to make
for him.

STATEMENT BY SENATOR MANSFIELD READ BY
SENATOR MAGNUSON

Mr. MANSFIELD. Mr. President, I
am about to introduce a bill which is reported to have been already consigned
to the legislative junkheap. And, indeed,
that may prove to be the case. At this
point, certainly, there is far more reason than not to concur in the bleak
journalistic forecasts of the future of the
so-called East-West trade relations bill.
That is a most unfortunate situation
especially since the measure has been requested by the President and asked for
by the Secretary of State in letters to
the Vice President and the Speaker of
the House.

I do not suppose that in the great
equations of peace and war a few million
dollars of trade with Bulgaria or Rumania looks like a very urgent or major
matter. In the rising flames of the Vietnamese conflict, it appears almost incon-
gruous to put forth a legislative effort
which has as its purpose the enlargement
of commerce with some countries in
Eastern Europe.

Nevertheless, the leadership is going
to introduce this East-West trade relations bill. It will be introduced now because the President and the Secretary
of State have asked for it. It will be
introduced now because the majority
leader welcomes an initiative along lines
which he has believed desirable for many
years. The measure will be introduced
now because even the act of doing so or
failing to do so does have some relevance
to the great equations of peace and war.
It will be introduced now, not in spite of
the Vietnamese war, but, if anything, because of it.

Finally, Mr. President, the leadership
will introduce this measure because it
is an entirely proper vehicle for a hard
legislative look at the incongruities and
anachronisms which have long characterized the policies of the United States
toward Eastern Europe. These bar-
nacles on American commerce not only
plague businessmen, they also hamper
the diplomacy of the President and the
Secretary of State in seeking to develop

useful and peaceful relations with various nations in that region.

Whatever their original justification,
certain of the conditions which we ourselves imposed on our commerce years
ago and with which this act, in effect, is
designed to deal have become self-de-
feating, often meaningless, and very cost-
ly to individual Americans and to the
Nation as a whole. The measures were
largely an expression of the fear, hos-
tility, disgust, or whatever with which
the United States greeted the appearance of certain systems of government
and economics in Eastern Europe. They
were in the nature, too, of reprisals for
hostile acts against us. And they were,
finally, vaguely designed to defend the
West against communism from the East.

I think, by this time, it is clear that
while many factors may be involved in
determining the future of communism
in Eastern Europe, the trade policies of
the United States are at or near the bottom of the list in terms of significance.

I would point out in this connection
that, for many years, we have had no
trade to speak of with certain of the
Eastern European countries but, at last
report, they still had Communist governments. And the truth is that over
the years we have had trade with Yugo-
slavia and Poland and even aid but, at
last report, they, too, still had Communist governments.

Let us, therefore, if we are going into
a consideration of this bill, go in with
our eyes open. Let us not tilt with wind-
mills. If past trade policies have had
little significance for the future of communism in Eastern Europe one way or
the other, it may be said that this bill
does not have much significance either,
one way or the other. I doubt that it
will strike very much terror or very much
joy in the hearts of the Communist pur-
ists of Eastern Europe.

The basic question in this bill, in short,
is not what it will do to communism in
Eastern Europe. The basic question is
what this bill will do for the United
States.

The bill has no automatic and direct
effect on trade between Eastern Europe
and the United States. Rather, the bill
deals with the relationship of the President and the Congress in delineating the
patterns of that trade. It gives the
President substantially the same kind of
control over U.S. commerce with the entire region of Eastern Europe that he
now has by law over trade with Yugo-
slavia and Poland.

The bill says to the President, in effect,
if opportunities present themselves to
enlarge the trading relationship in
peaceful goods with various Eastern
European countries, go ahead and explore them. If the occasion arrives to
promote better and more stable relations
by adjustments in peaceful trade with
these nations do not hesitate to take advantage of the occasion. In short, this
act would authorize the President to use
his judgment in setting certain rules and
approaches for the conduct of trade with
Eastern Europe. The passage of this act
would make clear that the President is
trusted by the Congress to act in this

amine specific publications. For example, one student might be assigned to examine the *New York Times* each day and report any relevant materials. If different students are assigned to the various indexes in the library, a comprehensive annotated bibliography can be compiled within a few weeks.

Selecting Evidence

The careful development of potential issues will help set limits on what kind of evidence should be recorded. However, the student will still be faced with the question of what to keep. This decision should be made on the basis of what evidence is the most potent and relevant to the issues. The student should not expect to use all the evidence that he gathers. A student who has done a careful job, will probably utilize only ten per cent of the evidence. This does not mean that ninety per cent of his time was wasted. Considerable research must take place before a student can select the strongest evidence. A debater who has done extensive research will feel confident that he is ready for any opponent.

Research should not be equated with the amassing of evidence cards. The number of such cards is far less important than a thorough analysis of issues. An indiscriminate collection of data may give the debater a sense of accomplishment, but this is short-lived when he is required to manage and apply the data.

Evidence is selected on the basis of its probative value and its psychological value. Both types of evidence are needed to construct a rhetorical argument. For example, statistics may be necessary to convince an audience of the extent of poverty; however these statistics cannot describe or convey the conditions of poverty. This must be done by examples that create an awareness of the problem. Students must be cautioned about the exclusive use of either type of evidence. The error is most commonly made in the direction of evidence that has psychological value.

Recording Evidence

Differences in views on recording evidence can be witnessed at any debate tournament. There are those who carry their evidence in an envelope while others struggle with suitcases and trunks.

There are some instances that make the use of a book or document advantageous. If the evidence found in a book deviates considerably from current thought, the book itself might add credibility. Copies of documents, treaties, or other such primary evidence may add to the precision of evidence. However, if a book simply refers to a document this is secondary evidence and an evidence card is more manageable and sensible. The difference between primary and secondary evidence can be illustrated by examples from the *Congressional Record*. (See pages 154 and 155.)

Evidence that is placed in a file box must be organized so that it is manageable. The broad categories of affirmative and negative evidence are rather obvious. One way to organize the subcategories is by the potential issues that have been produced by analysis. The advantage of using evidence cards lies in the fact that they are uniform in size and can be arranged quickly. In addition, a large amount of information can be stored in a file box. When clippings and photographs of material are used, they should be mounted on uniform size paper, placed in a notebook, and indexed. The debater who takes five minutes to arrange his materials before he speaks will incur the wrath of a judge. If cards are cumbersome to the debater, he can arrange issues and evidence on sheets of paper, place them in a notebook, and index them for rapid reference.

MAXIMIZING RESEARCH

Although debaters are expected to compete against one another, they are also expected to cooperate for the benefit of the entire organization. The sharing of information can be handled in several ways. Some debate squads have a central file which holds copies of all the evidence. Each time a debater researches a piece of evidence, he adds it to the central file. Sometimes a student secretary is responsible for typing and filing the evidence. Another method of sharing information is simply arranging for an evidence exchange periodically.

In a research organization there will always be some who do more research than others and there will be those who have the ability to apply the research. The coach must be aware of the student that is doing neither. The student who does not have the ability or the interest to engage in a cooperative effort, will gain little from participating in such an activity. A debate team will only be as strong as the debate squad and the words "my evidence" and "my case" should be discouraged. The task of the coach is to maximize research without destroying individual initiative and creativity.

Cooperative research does present some problems. Aside from the fact that some students are not mature enough to take part, there is danger that poor evidence and inaccurate evidence will be placed in the files. Some students will feel compelled to produce usable evidence and a change of a word here and there can make someone a temporary hero. The coach must devise safeguards against faulty or irrelevant evidence. The files must be examined for such materials and debaters must be made aware of the risk of using the material of others. When the evidence just seems too good, it should be verified.

Research and analysis is a continuing process and the debaters must search for new questions and develop them in depth. The mediocre debater is satisfied with stale evidence while the superior student continues to search and refine for greater effectiveness. After the debate season is under way, the student should be encouraged to reread earlier references. Many times the references mean more and point the way to fresh analysis and different cases. Research cannot be divorced from analysis because the student must know what to search for and why he is searching for it.

LIST OF SOURCES GENERALLY USEFUL IN RESEARCHING DEBATE TOPICS

1. Legislative Reference Service, Library of Congress analysis of high-school and college debate topics pursuant to Public Law 88–246, published each year in separate volumes for high school and college and may be obtained by writing:

Superintendent of Documents
U.S. Government Printing Office
Washington, D.C. 20402

or by writing a Senator or Congressman.

2. Write to your representative in Washington asking him for copies of hearings which have been held relevant to your subject. Write as follows to a member of the House of Representatives:

The Honorable (give your Congressman's name)
United States Congressman from (name your state)
House Office Building
Washington, D.C. 20402

Write to your Senator as follows:

The Honorable (give your Senator's name)
United States Senator from (name your state)
Senate Office Building
Washington, D.C. 20402

3. Write for a list of titles of all relevant federal government publications from all agencies of the government at this address:

Superintendent of Documents
U.S. Government Printing Office
Washington, D.C. 20402

To find titles to be named specifically in writing to this office, refer to the Catalogue of U.S. Government Publications which should be in your library. Also use this address when ordering subscriptions to the *Congressional Record.*

4. Write to the department in the Executive Branch of government most likely to have information relevant to your topic. For example, the Department of Health, Education, and Welfare, The Department of Defense, the Agency for International Development, etc. Simply give the name of the cabinet officer, the name of his department, and Washington, D.C. To learn which departments might be useful in this respect,

refer again to the Catalogue to see which departments are publishing relevant material.

5. Write to the chairman of the Congressional committee responsible for the area of study in the resolution. Learn his name by reading a newspaper, the *Congressional Record,* or the directories published by the government.

6. For an analysis of the debate topic that has few of the liabilities typical of handbooks, write:

>American Enterprise Institute
>1200 17th Street N.W.
>Washington, D.C. 20036

7. For relatively scholarly studies of current problems, write:

>Brookings Institute
>722 Jackson Place
>Washington, D.C. 20406

8. For well-developed statements of possible economic policies, foreign and domestic (with documentation), write:

>Committee for Economic Development
>711 5th Avenue
>New York, N.Y. 10022

>Bureau of Business Economic Research
>Michigan State University
>Box 592
>East Lansing, Michigan 48823

>Council on Foreign Relations
>58 East 68th Street
>New York, N.Y. 10021

>Export-Import Bank
>811 Vermont Avenue, N.W.
>Washington, D.C. 20005

>Bureau of International Programs
>Department of Commerce
>Washington, D.C. 20230

Commodity Credit Corporation
Department of Agriculture
Washington, D.C. 20250

Editorial Research Reports
1156 19th Street
Washington, D.C. 20036

Department of State Bulletin
Department of State
Washington, D.C. 20520

Bureau of Economic Affairs
Department of State
Washington, D.C. 20520

9. For statements of special-interest pleaders which will be in
   the form of persuasive statements rather than research documents, write:

AFL-CIO
815 16th Street, N.W.
Washington, D.C. 20406

Chamber of Commerce of the United States
1615 H Street, N.W.
Washington, D.C. 20006

American Legion
720 5th Avenue
New York, N.Y. 10007

American Farm Bureau Federation
2300 Merchandise Mart
Chicago 54, Illinois 60654

10. For special analyses on the high-school topic, write:

The Committee on Discussion and Debate
National University Extension Association
Box 5152, University Station
Eugene, Oregon 97403

Current History
1822 Ludlow Street
Philadelphia, Pa. 19103

11. For analysis and "pros and cons" on intercollegiate topic, write:

The Congressional Digest
3231 P Street, N.W.
Washington, D.C. 20407

12. For a one-volume collection of the latest facts and figures on the economic, political, and social structure of the U.S., order:

Statistical Abstract of the United States
Superintendent of Documents
Government Printing Office
Washington, D.C. 20402

13. For an index to indexes in the library, examine:

Reference Books by Mary Neill Barton
assisted by Marion V. Bell
Basic Reference Sources by Louis Shores
Guide to Reference Books by Constance M. Winchell

14. For a guide to books of recent publication, check the reference room of your library for:

Subject Guide to Books In Print, edited by Sarah L. Trakkn

15. For a directory of information sources concerning the physical and social sciences, write to:

National Referral Center for Science and Technology
Library of Congress
Washington, D.C. 20540

16. For access to sources of information concerning education, write to:

ERIC
Division of Research Training and Dissemination
Bureau of Research

Office of Education
Washington, D.C. 20202

ERIC engages in acquiring, abstracting, indexing, storing, retrieving, and disseminating nationally the most significant educational research and research-related documents.

SUGGESTED READINGS

Abernathy, Elton. "Canned Debate Material," *Southern Speech Journal*, VIII (September 1942), 26–27.

Buehler, E. C. "The Role of Opinion as Related to Persuasion and Contest Debate," *Southern Speech Journal*, XXV (Fall 1959), 21–26.

Crocker, Lionel. "The Debater and His Handling of Facts," *American Forensic Association Register*, XI (Spring 1963), 18–22.

Dresser, William R. "Studies of the Effects of Evidence: Implications for Forensics," *American Forensic Association Register*, X (Fall 1962), 14–19.

Fotheringham, Wallace C. "The Law of Evidence and the Debater," *American Forensic Association Register*, VI (Spring 1958), 18–36.

Hellman, Hugo E. "The Varsity Debate Researchers," *Gavel*, XXVIII (May 1946), 52, 54.

Kaplan, Abraham. *The Conduct of Inquiry*. San Francisco: Chandler Publishing Co., 1964.

Montrose, J. L. "Basic Concepts of the Law of Evidence, *Law Quarterly Review*, LXX (October 1954), 527–55.

Olson, Donald O., Phillip Tompkins, and Gloria Temple. "The Cooperative Squad File," *Gavel*, XL (November 1957), 15.

Scott, Robert L. "Discourage Handbooks?" *American Forensic Association Register*, IX (Convention issue, 1961), 14.

CHAPTER 7

Case Construction in Debate
Richard D. Rieke

Of all the questions discovered in analysis for which a debater has developed affirmative and negative arguments, some are quite distinctly more critical to the resolution than others; some are clearly more inclined toward one side rather than the other; some are more susceptible to oral explanation than others; in any event, there are too many to talk about in one debate of an hour's length. Therefore, a debater must make a selection of those few specific questions he expects to raise in each debate. His final selection, when revised to smooth out relationships and organized for oral presentation, constitutes a case.

The teacher of forensics must remember that tournament debating is a very specialized, stylized context, and that cases appropriate for successful tournament debating may require characteristics not suitable for other situations. This is not to say that tournament debating is not a useful student experience in anticipation of real-life situations. It merely means that the teacher must be aware of the differences and see that students do not become so engrossed with contest debates that they are unable to make the transfer into other contexts.

The focus of this discussion will be on the development of cases for tournament debates, with an effort made to point out the key places in which they vary from the everyday arguments the students will encounter upon graduation.

It must first be noted that the approach to debate in high school and college is the reverse of what might be considered

natural. That is, in school debates, the students are given a proposed new policy for which they must go out and find a reason.
Typically, we expect that after graduation students will encounter
reasons for which they must devise proposed new policies. What
is the effect of this reversal? For one thing, it leads to substantial
discussions of what kinds of reasons are to be considered within
the resolution. For example, one year college students debated
whether Congress should be given the power to reverse decisions
of the Supreme Court. For most of the year, it was common to
talk about the substantive decisions of the court with regard to
the questions of law involved in a specific appeal. One team, however, came up with a case which concerned, among other points,
those decisions of the Supreme Court to review or not to review a
case on appeal—the decision to grant or deny certiorari. The team
also discussed nonunanimous decisions. The team did not choose
to argue about unanimous, substantive decisions of the Supreme
Court. Great discussion among debate judges arose over whether
or not this team was living up to its obligations as described in
the resolution which mentioned simply "decisions." Some judges
declared they would not vote for such a case on the grounds that
the team did not accept its proper burden.

In another case, teams were debating whether or not non-
Communist nations should form an economic community. A great
many teams conceptualized an economic community as a structure
similar to the European Economic Community which involves,
among other things, the formation of a relatively free trade area
among a group of sovereign nations. Some teams, however,
thought of an economic community as common monetary policy
providing for easy and secure international exchange among a
group of sovereign nations. Again judges were concerned that a
case talking about international monetary policy was outside the
resolution and therefore illegitimate. Many declared they simply
could not vote for a team using such a case.

At least two ideas are involved in this kind of judge behavior.
In the first place it involves a feeling by some judges that they
know what is contemplated in the resolution. They know, for
instance, that "decisions" was meant to indicate all substantive
decisions, and not those granting or denying certiorari and they
know that an economic community must involve more than a

common monetary policy. This knowledge comes from two possible sources: (1) the judge may be well informed in the subject area and have valid reason to believe that a team's conceptualization of a term is simply not acceptable in any knowledgeable context; (2) a judge may have a strong belief that he knows what was in the minds of the writers of the debate resolution. In the former case, a judge has an opportunity to inform students and get their analysis on a more useful track. In the latter case, a judge is letting his intuition interfere with his judgment and penalizing students on the basis of prejudice. The problem is trying to know which source of knowledge is operating. The recommendation to the judge is to listen carefully to the whole debate before drawing any such conclusion. The recommendation to the case-building debater, however, must be that some judges are so certain of themselves as to make a judgment about a team's position at once, make a mental (if not actual) commitment to vote against a team, and close their minds to the rest of the debate.

Therefore, case-building in contest debate involves the decision both by debaters and judges as to whether a specific case is within the concept of the debate resolution and whether it fulfills the full burden of that concept. While in practical argument outside the school, it is expected that decision-makers will listen to the reasons and the proposed policy and make their decision on the merits of the issues, in the contest debate the reasons and policy, no matter how meritorious per se, will ultimately be judged in terms of the pre-set national or specific resolution.

Why must this be so? In establishing area-wide or even nationwide debate tournaments it is necessary that students from many different schools be able to come together on the same day well prepared to debate with each other. This makes it necessary to have a relatively common concept of what is to be debated. Otherwise, the students would be faced with the necessity of debating, in six debates, six different resolutions. The door is thus opened to extensive gamesmanship: teams plan to win by virtue of presenting a case so tenuously relevant to the resolution as to catch the opponent unprepared to talk about it; or they prepare so bizarre an analysis that the debate is over before the opponent has adjusted his thinking to the unexpected context.

What is the danger in requiring commonality of meaning in the resolution? A first danger has already been suggested: judges with erroneous ideas of correct concept make their decision at the first of a debate and refuse to listen to arguments. Related to the first danger is the tendency among contest debaters to hit upon a perspective regarding the resolution and stay with it all year failing to discover other quite legitimate and creative perspectives. Furthermore, some remarkable maneuvering of ideas is used to make worthwhile problems conform to the current concept of the debate resolution. For example, when college students were given the resolution that the U.S. government should establish a program of public work for the unemployed, many ended up with talking about the whole question of economic growth and the full utilization of natural and human resources, and then almost frantically relating such resources to public works projects. An economist, unfamiliar with school debates, might have listened to these debates with interest until they reached the point of trying to relate this substantial economic discussion to the single concept of public works projects. He might have observed that it seemed as if the students had started with the full panorama of economic problems and then tried—in the Procrustean manner—to fit them in with a public works program, rather than starting with the full capabilities of public works to make a positive economic contribution and limit the debate accordingly.

The second idea is tied in with the determination of a judge that a given case does or does not live up to the expectations of the resolution: the decision in contest debate is made in terms of the team doing the better job of debating, and not in terms of the preponderance of argument and evidence generated around the specific issues of the debate. It is not impossible for a team to win all the issues of the debate and lose the judge's decision. This may simply signal a judge's feeling that the team's case represented a poor job of analysis of the debate resolution. Therefore, the case constructed by a contest debate team must be designed not only to provide sound arguments in favor of a certain policy, it must also see that the policy is logical in terms of the stated resolution and the individual judge's idea of good analysis. A teacher will be wise to see that students keep these requirements in mind as they prepare their case.

SELECTING A BASIC POSITION

If debaters have prepared their analysis in the manner described in Chapter 5, they will have at their disposal the equivalent of a full brief on the resolution, outlining numerous potential issues arising from a variety of quite different topics or points of view. In preparing a case, the debaters can draw from this selection and experiment with various points of view and different combinations of arguments until they find what seems best.

In setting out to make such selections, debaters will benefit if they have been taught that a variety of strategic approaches and organizational structures is available to them.

Strategic Approaches that Are Available

Both affirmative and negative cases may be developed to set out and defend either a very broad or very narrow argumentative position depending on which approach seems strategically most advantageous. Of course, this is not an either/or choice; the positions may range anywhere between broad and narrow. For example, an affirmative team may choose to level an indictment based on a broad range of alleged evils of the present system under the strategy that their opponents will have much difficulty countering such a universal attack. On the other hand, a team may choose to focus on one specific evil which is expected to allow them to develop the argument in such depth and with such strength that their opponents will never be able to prove otherwise. The former strategic approach has the value of presenting a variety of attacks, some of which may survive even though the opposition weakens or destroys part of the case or even though the judge disapproves of one line of thought. This strategy also has the value of allowing a team to combine one line of thought that is quite typical and understandable with another which is unique and perhaps hard to explain. Sometimes this is necessary since to rely on the unique argument alone may lead the judge to discount the position before he fully understands it, come to a mental commitment and stop listening before the team has successfully explained its argument. The latter strategy—the narrow approach—has the value of discarding weaker arguments which draw immediately successful opponent attack and thus lead to an impression that the case as a whole is weak.

However, the *broad case*, when carried to the extreme, has a high chance of spreading a team so thin in terms of time in which to explain and defend arguments that in the end the team may have carried none of its many lines of reasoning. This is a common failing of inexperienced debaters and early-season debaters who have not become well enough informed on the topic to judge between good and bad arguments and have not developed sufficient evidence to defend any single line of reasoning with sufficient depth. Frequently this effort to compensate for inexperience or ignorance results in a case containing seven or ten separate attacks on the present policy and virtually no evidence. Unless the opponents are equally inexperienced or ignorant, such a case will die a sudden death as the first negative speaker demands the fulfillment of the burden of proof in each contention.

The *narrow case* has the obvious weakness of putting a team's argumentative eggs in one basket. It is simply not possible to defend, successfully, a narrow case if a team does not in fact have a clearly defensible point and more than enough information to support it. In other words, the team using an extremely narrow case exposes itself to considerable scrutiny by the opponents. If there are weaknesses to be found in the case, it can be expected that the opponents will find them. The team must be satisfied that it can sustain the argument even though every weakness has been found and argued by the opposition! In tournament debating, it is sometimes said by debaters that there is a hole in their case, but it is unlikely that the opposition will have the proper information and time for thought in the course of a given debate to find the hole. The team feels secure in this gamesmanship of time, and it is unfortunately true that this can be a successful strategy. However, particularly in narrow cases, the strategy frequently breaks down. It might also be noted in passing that such a strategy presumes ignorance or stupidity, or both, on the part of opponents. While such a presumption is often warranted—not all debaters are brilliant storehouses of knowledge—in almost every series of debates a team can reasonably expect to face one or more teams which are competent. When this happens, cases with hidden holes tend to fall precipitously. The poetry of this lies in the fact that the team probably would have defeated the ignorant debaters under any circumstances, and the defeat at the hands of competent teams frequently comes in crucial rounds such as eliminations. Little is accomplished by beating four or five bad teams in the preliminary rounds only to lose, in eliminations, to the first good team that comes along.

It is not the intent of this discussion, though, to suggest that all narrow cases are weak. On the contrary, some of the most successful cases—both affirmative and negative—are ones which hit on a specific point and stick to it successfully. This kind of conversation has been known to occur between two tournament debate judges:

> Say, that affirmative team I just judged has an awfully narrow case.
>
> Did you vote against them?
>
> No! The negative threw everything it had at them including their file cases, and they never touched the affirmative point. That point may be narrow, but it's broad enough to carry the proposition and it seems to be true.

Another strategic decision open to debaters has already been suggested: a case can either exploit the common and fairly obvious lines of reasoning, or it can seek to build arguments which, though clearly within the boundaries of the resolution, are quite original and creative. Again the distinction should be thought of as a continuum and not as either/or.

There are several advantages to a case which is quite typical. Most obviously, the commonly used arguments represent what most debaters and their coaches perceive to be the best arguments in favor of one side or another. To this extent, the common arguments will probably be favorably received by the judge who is also a coach. The debater will be able to achieve a clear understanding of his position with a minimum of communicative effort. The judge has probably spent considerable time working with his own debaters in building just such a case. Using typical arguments leads to frequent use of communicative short cuts in the sense that everyone understands this line of reasoning and does not require the elaborate explanations necessary in talking about a new line of argument. Debaters using such a case can concentrate on its presentation and defense because of the time saved that would have been used in special analysis.

The strategy of the *typical case* is simply this: the team does not choose to rely on surprise or complex analysis, but rather will depend on its ability to organize, express, and defend a common case better than other teams. To this end, the team will try to structure its case in a more logical and communicative way than others do; it will seek to be more fluent in talking about the case than other teams; it will be more clear and sophisticated in answering opposition attacks than others. By virtue of frequent defense of the same analysis the team will become more knowledgeable about the points of attack to be expected and they will be better prepared to deal with a variety of attack than they would be with less experience. Such a team will seek to inspire this kind of remark by the judge:

> That is certainly a run-of-the-mill case, but this team did a better job with it than I have heard before.

There are also advantages to the *unique case*. Debaters who refuse to go along with arguments that most others are using (and this still refers both to affirmative and negative) and instead continually look for a new way of thinking about the topic are likely to turn up some creative and refreshingly original arguments. Judges—either coaches or otherwise—quickly become hypnotized by the typical case. In the course of one tournament, and then a series of tournaments, they hear the common analysis time after time. Cases tend to blur together. In a debate a judge may forget what these teams have said as distinguished from the last two teams he heard. To hear eight such debates in two consecutive days—which is not as unlikely today as it once was—may cause a judge to become bored from hearing the same arguments and same evidence to the extent he does not welcome the opportunity to hear them again. In this case, the teams that present a new and unusual approach will be received with gratitude for relieving boredom if nothing else. The judge will be more likely to listen to their ideas carefully simply from the excitement of having to analyze a new set of issues.

There is another and perhaps more significant advantage in

searching for an *original case*. For the most part, coaches and debaters approach each year's resolution as laymen, not experts in the subject matter. While they are usually intelligent and learn quickly from their reading of the experts, they nevertheless lack the sophistication usually necessary to deal with complex problems in their full complexity, at least at the start of the year if not later. Consequently, the typical case for much of the year features much superficiality as students grasp for simple answers to complicated problems. It usually falls to the debaters searching for original cases to do the research and expert consultation required to prepare themselves to argue the topic in greater depth. Such debaters frequently turn up significantly better cases which others copy so that ultimately the "typical" case improves. These same debaters, by virtue of their willingness to work, often stay ahead of the group for the entire year, coming up with better and better analysis while leaving others to continue to argue the points they left behind.

The disadvantages of the typical case have already been suggested. That which is common is often mediocre, and the debaters who choose to go along with the typical case run the risk of failing to develop their analysis to the extent they are capable of doing. While they may become quite expert in presenting and defending a certain case, they may fail to learn how to engage in creative analysis and case building, and how to learn to defend a new case quickly. Students who use the common case tend to find themselves in a class with the majority and less frequently ahead of the group. They tend to be the students who attend the elimination rounds to hear what new ideas are being used by winning teams. It is very hard to continue to do the best job with a common case, when so many other good students are trying to do the same thing. Finally, the very fact of judge boredom is an important disadvantage to the common case.

There are disadvantages in using very original cases as well. There is a very fine line dividing the truly successful creative development of a case and random analysis. Most students find it very difficult to distinguish between cases that open up a sophisticated avenue of argument on the topic and those which are simply exotic. The very fact that the students and their coaches are not experts in the field under study makes it difficult to evaluate an original case idea. It often takes the use of such a case in a number of good rounds of debate—both in practice and in tournaments—to discover whether it is good or simply "different." Debaters must have the courage to resist the immediate scorn of fellow-debaters and coaches, since it is not uncommon for people to scorn that which they do not understand. But often after debaters have done research on an unusual case, they find it is valid; hence the case scorned this week may become the best two weeks later. In the meantime, the creative debaters have lost a good many debates. Yet many original cases turn out, after general study, not to be valid, and debaters will never win in this situation. It can be quite discouraging to a student to develop faith in a creative analysis, only to learn a month later (and many losses later) that the case has little or no merit after all.

The role of the coach in selecting cases is very important although difficult. When a student comes up with an extraordinary case which the coach believes to be of little merit, what should be done? Clearly, for the coach to point out that it is a bad case and forbid its use in competition will probably not only stifle a student's creativity but will also likely lead to rebellion. On the other hand, for the coach to approve the use of the case, knowing or feeling strongly that it will fail to win a single decision, may lead both to discouraged debaters and a very poor tournament record. Debaters may also lose confidence in the coach's analytical powers because he failed to warn them of the case's weaknesses. Probably, the best the coach can do in such a case is first to discuss what he feels to be the logical inadequacies of the case with the debaters, hoping they will either correct them or point out how they are not inadequacies. It is important not to try to force these criticisms on the debaters, but rather to present ideas and ask the debaters to discuss them in such a way that they themselves come to see the weaknesses of the case. A second approach of the coach, in trying to reveal to debaters that they have a bad case, is simply to give them good competition in practice debates. This will probably force them to face up to the weaknesses in the case and try to correct them. In the final analysis, however, it often happens that debaters remain unconvinced. Then, after logical discussion of what the coach feels to be fatal weaknesses, and the development of problems in practice rounds, if the debaters still believe in the case idea they should be allowed to try it out in competition. There seems to be little doubt that it is better to lose some important debates than to develop intellectually resentful students.

Should the debaters come home with a bad record but remain convinced in the value of their case, the coach has work to do. First, he must discuss with his debaters what happened in the debates, considering judge evaluations as well. If a pattern of rejection of the case is clear, the coach must stress the probable need to try a new case idea. If the debaters will not listen to this, the coach must then try to help the debaters make the case as effective as possible on the chance that the idea is good but the presentation is not adequate to communicate the idea. Still another opportunity to try the case in competition is warranted. Finally, it is the coach who must decide if the debaters are simply being quixotic, for the coach cannot wash his hands of responsibility for his student's persistent failure. A time may finally come when the coach decides his students lack the maturity to recognize their error and forbids them to continue using the case. But this is a grave decision, and must be only a last resort.

There are various other minor strategies relevant to case construction which might be mentioned. At this point, it is useful to distinguish between affirmative and negative considerations.

Affirmative Strategies

The general affirmative obligation in a debate is to present and successfully maintain a prima facie case. A coach, of course, must have a thorough understanding of the concept "prima facie," which is explained in any good text on the theory of argumentation. Briefly, a prima facie case is one which presents as much argument and evidence to affirm as many of the essential elements of the resolution as the judge or other decision-maker feels necessary to sustain the resolution itself, and does so on its face or in and of itself. That is, the affirmative must initially set out a case which would warrant the adoption of the resolution if there were no negative attack. Without at least that much, there would obviously be no need for debate since the negative could lose every argument and the judge would still be unwilling to adopt the new policy. To refer to the discussion of analysis, in the legal situation the affirmative would be obliged to present evidence and argument to affirm each of the essential elements of the concept "burglary" before the judge would require the defense to answer. It has already been noted that in policy debate the essential elements are not so clearly outlined, and therefore the above definition of prima facie states that as much as the judge deems necessary must be presented without saying how much that must be. Judges vary, some demanding more of the affirmative than others. All affirmative strategies, then, must aim toward bringing the judge to believe that the sum total of the affirmative case— that which is presented in the constructive speeches—is adequate to affirm the resolution so long as the negative does not destroy an essential element of that case. In every judge's mind, how much is required, and what constitutes an essential element of the case is a variable the debaters can only infer. Sometimes even after the decision is made, the debaters remain unsure of the judge's thinking. Therefore, in planning the case, the affirmative debaters must make an inference as to the probable demands of the typical judge, and realize they will inevitably fail to satisfy some judges no matter how great a burden of proof they accept.

This much the affirmative knows: before the end of their two constructive speeches they must present a prima facie case. But how they proceed—what sequence of ideas is used, what forms of emphasis, and so forth—is a matter of strategy over which each team has discretion. Some of the frequently manipulated variables are these: (1) how should the labor of case construction be divided between first and second constructive; (2) should the specifics of the affirmative plan be withheld until the second speech; (3) how should evidence be utilized in terms of use in supporting original constructive points and reserved for use in rebuttal; (4) how can the sequence and relative emphasis of ideas be prepared both for maximum communication and defense against negative attack? These four variables are discussed as follows:

(1) For many years it was typical to divide the affirmative case between first and second speakers this way: the first speaker developed the full need or indictment of the present system, and the second speaker advanced the plan or proposed new policy and

discussed how it would relieve the evils desirably. In the first place, this is a logical sequence of ideas in an affirmative case since the team should give its reasons for a new policy before advancing it. Second, the reasons for the plan (whether in the form of need or advantages) usually constitute at least half or more of the affirmative argumentative time in construction, and the first speaker could use a full ten minutes on that alone.

Recently, college debaters in particular have been constructing their cases so that the entire affirmative constructive position can be presented in the first ten minutes. Strategically, this tends to draw the first negative into discussion about most, if not all, of the case. This establishes the negative position earlier than is true when only half the affirmative case has been presented. This form also leaves the second affirmative speaker free to develop a speech in rebuttal which conforms more completely to the character of the negative attack. He can devote his time to the discussion of those points which seem most likely to receive negative comment.

However, a ten-minute speech which covers an entire affirmative case necessarily must be cut to a bare minimum of evidence and reasoning. The debaters typically present the basic outline of the case, and read some evidence very, very quickly and close with a rapid summary and almost no elaboration of their ideas. The first negative, then, must respond to a case which neither he nor the judge is likely to understand fully. He may waste some of his time clashing with positions which, as the affirmative explains later, were not intended to be in their case. Unscrupulous debaters may even plan their strategy to achieve this. They may try to draw negative attack to false issues and thus divert attention from the actual intent of the case. Or, the affirmative may intentionally sandbag with their evidence, using weak testimony in the first speech to arouse negative attack. Then, in the second affirmative speech, a devastating barrage of hard fact is given with even greater effect than if it had been used initially. While this may have strategic and psychological value, it is morally and rationally unacceptable. The teacher should discourage this and judges should punish such practices. If affirmative teams are to continue to develop a full case in the first speech, they must take special care to avoid confusion and misunderstanding.

(2) The placing of the affirmative plan in the constructive speeches is related to the form of the case as just discussed. That is, in the standard format, the logical sequence of need, plan, and advantages leaves the plan to the second speaker. Some debaters prefer this method as it denies the negative time to think about the plan and prepare attacks. Of course, when the entire affirmative constructive position is given in the first speech, the plan is revealed early.

There are some reasons to suggest that presenting the plan in the first speech is wise regardless of other considerations. The belief that withholding the plan from negative thinking for a time will decrease the severity of attack on it is not a good one. The difference of ten minutes will usually mean only that the negative will develop their attack in full fury in the rebuttals rather than in constructives. In this instance, the affirmative will only have reduced their opportunity to answer the negative attack, for they will have two and sometimes only one rebuttal in which to answer a strong attack on their plan. If the plan appears in the first affirmative, it is possible that some idea of negative attack will come at once, and that it should have reached its maximum by the end of the constructive speeches. Finally, to use a plan which relies on delay for its success is another case of hoping for incompetence in the opposition which is a poor basis for a case.

Finally, all affirmative debaters must define critical concepts at the start of their presentation. It is often impossible to characterize what the affirmative will mean by the policy stated in the resolution without actually describing the plan they intend to propose. It is therefore efficient to say, simply, ". . . by economic community we will mean a plan in which nations eliminate all barriers to trade among themselves"; or, ". . . by compulsory arbitration we mean the following plan . . ."

(3) The use of evidence for construction and rebuttal has already been discussed in part. It has been said that affirmatives must not sandbag with evidence. On the other hand, it is not expected that a team will exhaust its supply of evidence in the original presentation of the case. If there is so little evidence available that all of it is required to make an original point, debaters

should consider the possibility that there is not enough strength
in the point to warrant its presence in the case.

The key question here is what evidence to use in the first presentation of the case and what should be kept for rebuttal. In the
first place, the teachers must educate the debaters in the theory of
evidence. Too often debaters (and many coaches) have a vague
idea that evidence is anything that appears in print which might
lead a judge to believe an argument. In a persuasive sense, this is
not far from wrong. However, debate is designed to educate
students in a rational system of decision-making, and for this
reason it is expected, if not always true, that judges will strive to
reward debaters more for the rational quality of their evidence
and not its psychological quality. To this end, the teacher will be
wise to refer to a good book on the theory of argumentation and
use it to educate the debaters. At the very least, the students must
come to distinguish between pure testimony and more factually
oriented evidence. For example, some evidence will relate empirically verifiable data—"The U.S. Department of Labor Annual
Report, 1967, indicates that the rate of unemployment for white
workers averaged 3.5% last year while unemployment for non-
white workers was 7%." Other evidence will present an opinion
by a person in whom the judge is expected to have faith: "Secretary of Labor Wirtz said in an October, 1967, speech that the
United States, '. . . has a problem of severe unemployment among
non-white workers.'" The difference can be characterized in this
way: the first kind of evidence presents information from which
a conclusion could be drawn, while the second kind gives a conclusion presumably based on reliable information. An argument
benefits from both kinds of evidence, for the judge likes to be
trusted with the data from which an argument was drawn and to
know that experts agree with the conclusion. However, when
debaters must limit themselves to one kind of evidence or the
other for initial presentation, it is both strategically and rationally
wise to rely on the former—factually oriented—kind of evidence.
Such a practice would be rational in the sense that the facts supply the raw material for a rational decision by the judge, rather
than requiring him to proceed on his faith in an observer. The
practice is strategic in the sense that most judges are more im-
pressed by factually oriented evidence than by testimony; to use

such at the outset will establish a tone of good scholarship on the part of the affirmative and distinguish them from the large number of debaters who rely exclusively on the reading of one allegedly expert opinion after another. Opinion is often cheap while empirical data are hard to get but meaningful when available.

(4) Debaters often feel some conflict over clarity and strategy in the development of their points. At the extreme, naïve young debaters sometimes say they want to keep their case vague so as to keep the negative debaters in the dark and prevent them from developing a good attack. Other debaters, more deviously inclined, like to construct their case so as to hide the real crux of their argument in a subpoint so as to misdirect the negative attack until, in the rebuttals, the affirmative suddenly begins to indicate that this was the focus of their case all along, but the negative confused the issue. The judge will look at his notes and find the affirmative actually did make that point in the first speech. Some judges are gullible enough to let the affirmative convince them that they simply misunderstood the point as did the negative. Most judges, fortunately, will recognize this as a so-called "affirmative shift" and cannot be fooled.

A coach will be wise to teach his debaters that there is no conflict between strategy and clarity. He should convince them that the case which most clearly communicates specifically what the affirmative wants to defend is the most defensible case. When the negative is confused, the judge often is too; then judges are inclined either to punish unclear debaters by assuming they are doing poor debating or by misunderstanding their case by believing it to be weaker than it is. A team should be able to articulate clearly the crux of their argument, and place it in the prominent place in the case it deserves. Subpoints should be just that. If the affirmative relies on a broad-value assumption as the basis of its argument, it would be wise to say so and state the assumption.

Students may resist such a policy on the belief that clarity involves unnecessary risk. Why, they might ask, must they make everything so explicit? The answer is that it is better for *them* to do it than the negative from both a communications and strategy point of view. Once more, it is foolhardy to rely on the hope that the negative will not think to attack fundamental points of the affirmative case if they are hidden. It is a waste to prepare to defeat only incompetent opponents, and if the case is so vulnerable that it will fall as soon as the negative understands its major points, then it would be best to look for a new case.

By way of summary, it has been suggested that principles of logic and communications constitute the best guide to affirmative strategy.

Negative Strategies

Many questions of negative strategy revolve around the theory of negative debating generally. As the teacher learns from the study of debate theory, debate propositions in school competition do not involve, necessarily, one side saying "yes" and the other "no." The negative has options as to its position in the sense that its only assignment in the debate is to prove the answer to the question is "not yes." That is, if the resolution were "Resolved that the United States should adopt a policy of compulsory arbitration in basic industries," the overall question is: "Should the United States adopt compulsory arbitration . . . ?" The affirmative, by virtue of the burden of proof, must prove the answer is probably "yes" if they are to win the debate. The negative, on the other hand, need not prove that the United States should not adopt compulsory arbitration, only that the affirmative has not proved we should.

From this point, it can be seen that the negative can proceed in various ways. The negative can argue (1) the affirmative has not proved its case; (2) the negative can prove the United States should not adopt the policy because the present system is superior; (3) the negative can prove the United States should not adopt the policy because it would do more harm than good; (4) the negative can prove the United States should not adopt the policy because there is another, distinctly different, policy which is superior to the present policy as well as the proposed policy.

From a strategic point of view, how does the negative decide which of these positions to take? The answer must be in at least two parts: first, these positions are not altogether mutually exclusive, and second, the negative must be prepared to take any of these positions to the extent they might be appropriate to different affirmative positions. The negative simply cannot prepare a single case. It probably cannot even select a single philosophical position to be defended in all debates. It is possible that some affirmative cases will rely upon alleged evils which the negative can destroy, and thus allow the negative to take the strict refutation position. Other affirmative cases—on the same resolution—may set out evils which simply cannot be rejected. Then, the negative will be obliged to turn to the present policy to show its superiority either as presently constructed, or as it might be improved through minor repair. Some affirmative plans may be set up so as to be vulnerable to many charges of disadvantages which almost certainly will accompany them; other affirmative plans may be much less susceptible to such attack. In very rare cases, the negative will be obliged to turn to the advancement of a counterproposal because the present policy simply cannot be successfully defended. It is possible that within a single proposition, each of these negative cases might be needed to respond best to different affirmative analyses.

Furthermore, negative teams may choose to take several positions in the same debate without inconsistency. For example, a negative first speaker might begin by saying this:

> The negative case will involve three basic positions. First, the affirmative cannot prove its own contentions through inadequacies in logic and evidence; second, the negative will constructively prove that the present policy ought to be retained; and third, the negative will constructively prove that should the affirmative plan be adopted it will create more disadvantages than can be offset by any good it could do.

So long as the negative is clear as to what it is doing, it is not inconsistent to say that there is no need for a change, but even if it were as the affirmative charges, their plan would not correct it. The three positions stated above could easily be translated into contentions which the negative would advance vis-a-vis specific affirmative ideas.

Commonly, the negative will seek to advance all three of these lines of argument in each debate, but plan to do so specifically in reference to each affirmative case. Therefore, the negative will probably try to develop as comprehensive a full brief as possible as described in Chapter 5, on analysis. As it hears the specific affirmative case, the negative will select from its files the arguments that apply to the affirmative case, and then they will structure them to do both the job of refuting the affirmative arguments and to construct a negative position. The negative should not let itself be distracted from discussing the inherent strengths of the present policy simply because it does not fit into the affirmative case. The negative would be wise to be prepared to advance a contention that adoption of the affirmative position would necessitate the loss of inherent values of the present policy, even though these values have not been discussed by the affirmative.

The trend toward increased use of comparative advantages cases by affirmative teams (discussed below) suggests that it is unusual that the present policies are so inherently weak as to be indefensible. Similarly, negative debaters should rarely find it necessary to resort to a counterplan. The teacher should discourage debaters from dreaming up creative alternatives simply because they are appealing. The students must be reminded that when the negative abandons the status quo it assumes a burden of proof equal to that of the affirmative and loses the strength in defending the presumed position. Moreover, a negative counterproposal must be directed toward the correction of any evils the affirmative proves either by argument or negative admission, but it must be incompatible with the affirmative policy. If it is not, the affirmative may simply absorb the negative's ideas, incorporate them into the affirmative case, and leave the negative without a position to defend. Sometimes the affirmative attack on the present policies is so limited that the negative can extend the analysis of inadequacy to suggest that evils of greater magnitude exist for which the affirmative policy is an insufficient remedy while the negative counterplan would do the job. But most of the time, the negative would be wiser to stake their rejection of the proposition on a defense of present policies than on their capacity to generate an altogether different alternative.

Probably the teacher's chief obligation in working with negative debaters is to be sure that they have a case at all. It is very easy for students to prepare "blocks" which outline an attack to selected potential affirmative arguments and then use those that come up in each debate. They may add to this a list of ten or more "disadvantages" which are presented sequentially and independently of each other or a fundamental negative philosophy. In this way, the negative more or less commits itself to talk about only those issues the affirmative brings up, with the exception of the list of disadvantages. In doing this, the negative sacrifices the strength that comes from issues heavily weighted in favor of the negative and which the affirmative, therefore, seeks to avoid. It also loses the strength that comes of a unified and coherent position toward which each individual argument is directed. The negative should set out an overall position at the start of the debate, and follow it through both in refutation of the affirmative and construction of their own arguments.

Comparative-Advantages Cases

Recently, much discussion among coaches has taken place over the differences between a comparative-advantages case and a stock-issues case. Unfortunately, these discussions often take place from the point of view of affirmatives with and without needs rather than the logic of policy decision-making. Coaches would benefit from some study of modern decision theory to help them understand how to teach this aspect of case building.

In actual practice, there is little difference between debates that begin from the "stock issues" point of view and those oriented to comparative advantages, for in most cases the affirmative is obliged to resort to a discussion of the values obtained in the new policy compared with those in the present policy because it is usually impossible to expose a fundamental and inherent weakness in the status quo that outweighs all of its advantages per se. This statement deserves some explanation.

The concept of the stock-issues affirmative case is essentially a deductive one. The affirmative sets out to discover a fundamental principle or principles on which the present policy can be indicted, thus revealing inherent evils in this policy which demand change. The affirmative then offers a new policy which it argues can diminish or eliminate the evils. In a strict deductive sense, an affirmative might argue this way:

(1) Any U.S. foreign policy that increases rather than diminishes the chances of war ought to be eliminated.

(2) Military assistance, by providing the equipment and knowl-
    edge for war, actually increases rather than diminishes the
    chances of war.

(3) The United States ought to eliminate military assistance,
    and restrict its foreign aid to that which does not supply
    equipment or knowledge for war.

In this affirmative case, the team has isolated a principle—
opposition to war—and identified it with the status quo—military
assistance—and proposed a plan to correct the evil—limit aid to
economic assistance.

How would the negative likely respond to this case? Can they
be expected to come out in favor of war? Not likely! The chances
are good they will deny that military aid increases the chances of
war; they will argue that it in fact decreases the likelihood of war
by providing a deterrent to aggression. They will also probably
argue that to limit aid to economic assistance will be undesirable
to the extent it will allow weak allies to fall under the domination
of communism. The negative might, however, by the end of the
debate challenge the affirmative to select between policies which
increase the chances of war and those which increase the chances
of world communist domination. While they have not come out
foursquare for war, they have suggested it has certain values
which must be compared with other values in setting public
policy.

The concept of the comparative-advantages case, on the other
hand, is less concerned initially with striking causal relations between the status quo and existing evils. But such a case also sets
values that public policy is expected to gain, and then charges
that the present policy is unlikely or less likely to achieve these
values than is the proposed new policy. Such an affirmative might
use these arguments:

(1) The United States must adopt that foreign policy which is
    most likely to contain communism without war.

(2) Military assistance, by putting military equipment and
    knowledge in the hands of foreign countries, is less likely to
    contain communism without war than is economic assis-
    tance alone.

(3) Economic assistance alone, by denying foreign nations access to military equipment and knowledge, while strengthening their economies and improving the welfare of their citizens, will be better able to contain communism and less likely to cause war.

How would the negative likely respond to this case? Again they would probably not choose to defend war per se, but they probably would argue that whatever value the affirmative might achieve by lessening the chance of war—and they would still deny that military assistance increases the chances of war—would be more than offset by the loss of nations' capacity to resist militant communism. Just as in the first debate, the decision would turn on the comparison of the advantages of lessening the chance of war against the increasing weakness to resist communism.

In both cases, the cost of the new plan must be measured against its value. Cost, in this case, includes all the satisfactions denied by selecting the policy—such as this: without military assistance, the United States could no longer use the aid simply to reward foreign leaders for support in other international ventures, as well as the external costs that might be involved in the actual change from one policy to another.

If it helps one think about comparative advantages cases, it can be said that such a case does indeed involve a need in this sense: the present policy is inherently incapable of achieving a value as well as the proposed policy. The evil is the absence of value that might be achieved. As one study of decision-making stated:

> . . . examination of policies proceeds through comparative analysis of no more than the marginal or incremental differences in the consequent social states rather than through an attempt at more comprehensive analysis of the social states.[1]

"It can best be expressed," these authors continue, "by stating how much of one value is worth sacrificing, at the margin reached in a given situation, to achieve an increment [slight increase] of another."[2]

Is the comparative-advantages case an easier position for the

---

[1] David Braybrooke and Charles E. Lindblom, *A Strategy of Decision* (New York: The Free Press of Glencoe, 1963) 86.
[2] *Ibid.*, 88.

affirmative? Does it permit them to get away with a very slim position only a little bit better than the present policy? The comparative advantages position is easier than the stock issues perspective only in the sense that it permits the affirmative to state clearly its position vis-a-vis the status quo when it does not choose to accept the burden of a basic and fundamental indictment of the status quo. To the extent the affirmative does not feel able to argue a fundamental weakness in the present policy, the comparative-advantages case provides a framework for a case. It certainly does not let the affirmative get away with anything more than any other case form, except to the extent the negative team fails to adapt to the comparative advantages perspective. The negative must proceed to discuss the total cost (as described above) of the affirmative policy; they must show that affirmative strengths and weaknesses in comparison with negative strengths and weaknesses do not leave a positive value on the affirmative side. However, if after all costs have been subtracted from values, on both sides, the affirmative is still a little bit better, then the affirmative has fulfilled its burden of proof. On the other hand, the comparative-advantages case is a weaker position than one which exposes an inherent evil in present policy. If the affirmative can level an inherent indictment at the status quo, they would be foolish not to take advantage of that strength.

Why have so many teams been using a comparative advantages approach recently? The answer probably lies both in the character of the topics being debated and a changing attitude of debaters and coaches. Resolutions which call for an extension of greater freedom for police, or substantial reduction in foreign policy commitment, or a limitation of foreign aid to economic assistance only, and so forth, tend to invite comparison of values between the two policies rather than a discussion of philosophical differences. Debaters find it difficult to strike at the very essence of the present policy when much of that essence must necessarily appear in the affirmative plan as well. Furthermore, modern thinking is much less likely to think about things as being altogether good or evil than was the case in the past. Rather than seeking to expose direct causal relationships between policies and evils, debaters are inclined to think in terms of correlations or groups of contributing factors, and to perceive policies as being on a continuum somewhere between good and evil. Furthermore, recognizing the complex of values that may be operative in any policy discussion, the debaters may feel the need to think of policies on several value continua, thus rejecting forever any notion that a policy can be characterized as either good or evil. Both of these tendencies increase the relevancy of the comparative advantages approach to affirmative case building.

ORGANIZATIONAL STRUCTURES THAT ARE AVAILABLE

Books on the theory of argumentation and debate generally discuss a variety of types of cases available to affirmative and negative teams. The fundamental differences among affirmative and negative cases have been discussed already in terms of the broad-narrow, stock issues-comparative advantages, strict refutation, repair, status quo, counterplan, and other choices open to students. But within any of these argumentative positions, it is possible for students to structure their cases in various ways. (See Chapter 10.) The coach will want to discuss these options with the students.

In the first place, the students must be brought to understand there is a difference between the logical and persuasive requirements of a debate speech. For instance, no matter how a debate speech is presented, logically it should be prima facie. On the other hand, it is quite conceivable that what one judge perceives to be prima facie another will not, quite regardless of the logical content of the speech. This difference may depend upon the communicative structure of speeches. The teacher of debate must understand and teach both logical and persuasive structure and presentation.

In tournament debate, however, there are certain strongly rooted role expectations which debaters are wise to fulfill. Specifically, the tournament debate speech must follow certain patterns of structure which might be less appropriate for argumentative speeches outside the academic environment.

As commonly practiced, debate speeches are expected to follow an Aristotelian structure in the sense that the speaker is to state first each major point in his argument (contentions), and then take them one by one and state each contention once again and supply proof for it. For example, after brief social amenities, a hint of the significance of the topic and its verbatim statement, and definitions (all of which typically requires no more than a minute or so) a debater might say this:

The affirmative will advance these contentions:

    I. Strikes are harmful to the U.S. economy
   II. Present labor legislation is unable to achieve satisfactory labor-management agreements without the harm of strikes
 III. Compulsory arbitration could achieve satisfactory labor-management agreements without the harm of strikes

The debater would then restate his first contention, and present proof:

    I. Strikes are harmful to the U.S. economy because
      A. Strikes reduce the gross national product
         1. Evidence
      B. Strikes reduce per capita income
         1. Evidence

and proceed to develop his speech in very much the same structure as that used in the process of analysis. Of course, debaters may phrase their position in various ways such as the stock-issues method used above, or by topic, or as a chain of reasoning, and so forth. But, regardless of the wording, tournament debaters are under strong pressure to present their speeches with emphasis on the clear statement of contentions, arguments, and evidence, and frequent summaries. It is not typical for a debater to present a persuasive speech in which the structure is hidden in smooth wording and the speaker's specific intent is not made explicit until the end. In fact, many judges do not seriously listen or take notes until the debater signals, by stating his specific contentions, that he has begun the body of his arguments. Debaters who interweave their organization too subtly into the text of their comments may discover they have failed to communicate.

On the other hand, too much devotion to argumentative structure often leaves the debate case devoid of style to the point of being dull and mechanical. One of the great challenges to the debate coach is to bring debaters to the point where their cases satisfy the requirements for logical structure without sacrificing persuasive style.

To summarize, it has been strongly urged that the development of cases for contest debates presents a number of options to the student. While case building for tournament debate has many characteristics peculiar to that medium, the experience is viewed as relevant to argument in general. In preparing a case, the teacher's task involves making debaters aware of the variations open to them. If they have prepared their analysis in the form of a full brief, they will be ready to see the variety of cases which might be used in defense of the same resolution. The teacher must encourage and permit experimentation even though it means the loss of some important debates. At many turns, strategies open to debaters allow sophistry or gamesmanship which may lead to some success at the expense of rationality and self-respect. A teacher must guard against such practices. Finally, case building presents a threefold challenge to fulfill the demands of logic, persuasion, and the role expectations of the tournament debater. The teacher of debate must teach students to balance these demands so that concern in one area does not damage the case in another.

SUGGESTED READINGS

Giffin, Kim. "A Study of Case Construction in Tournament Debates," *Gavel*, XLIV (November 1961), 11–14.

——, and Kenneth Megill. "Stock Issues in Tournament Debates," *Central States Speech Journal*, XII (Autumn 1960), 27–32.

Kruger, Arthur N. *Modern Debate: Its Logic and Strategy*. New York: McGraw-Hill, Inc., 1960.

——. *Modern Debate: Its Logic and Strategy*. New York: McGraw-Hill, Inc., 1960.

Nebergall, Roger E. "The Negative Counterplan," *Speech Teacher*, VI (September 1957), 217–20.

Patterson, J. W. "Obligations of the Negative in a Policy Debate," *Speech Teacher*, XI (September 1962), 208–13.

Thompson, Wayne N. "The Effect of a Counterplan upon the Burden of Proof," *Central States Speech Journal*, XIII (1962), 247–52.

CHAPTER 8

Refutation in Debate

Don F. Faules

If any single measure could be applied to determine the potency
of a debater, that measure would examine refutation skill. Refutation takes place throughout the entire debate. Even when the
student constructs a case, he should be thinking in terms of refutation. In other words, the builder of the case should know the
weakness of that case. Beginning students sometimes attempt to
convince themselves, as well as others, that they have built the
perfect case. Experienced debaters realize that natural logic is a
myth and that if both sides in a debate are competent, sound
constructive arguments will be presented by both sides. The
winner will be determined on the basis of who is able to refute his
opposition, and at the same time, defend his own case. A study by
Keeling revealed that the greatest difference in the scores of winning and losing debaters occurred in the area of refutation. In
addition, winning debaters were scored superior more frequently
for refutation than any other item.[1] The reader might ask at this
point, and rightly so, just how does one teach refutation skills?
First, students must understand just what refutation is.

---

[1] Russell M. Keeling, "An Analysis of Refutation and Rebuttal in Interscholastic Debate" (unpublished M.A. Thesis, Department of Speech, Baylor
University, 1959), 86–91.

THE NATURE OF REFUTATION

Refutation can be defined as the process of weakening or destroying an opponent's arguments. This process is dependent upon a student's ability to examine evidence, reasoning, and the relationship of evidence and inference. Everyone attempts to refute the arguments of others in everyday living and the verbal procedure of attack and defense is practiced on the street as well as in the United Nations. It is important that the student and the coach have some notion of how the student perceives the process of refutation. In order to determine this, it is helpful to provide exercises that will serve as testing and instruction devices. Such devices allow the coach to teach refutation rather than just teach about it. One such exercise is the hypothetical case. This is constructed by (1) selecting a topic that is familiar to the student, but one that he does not have extensive knowledge about and (2) writing the case so that it has a liberal amount of fallacies. It is easier to explain refutation in terms of a familiar topic because students do not get caught up in the mystique of subject matter that is associated with a political or economic question. It is common for beginning debaters to rely on evidence alone and ignore analysis. Sometimes this occurs because the students have not been given the opportunity to discover how they think. Instead of analyzing a particular position, they memorize certain arguments and the corresponding evidence. This practice results in a type of recitation rather than argumentation and students are baffled when they face different arguments or stock arguments that have been modified.

The following hypothetical case is designed to examine the student's approach to refutation. Once the students discover what principles are involved in attacking a familiar topic, the application of the same principles to the unfamiliar becomes easier. The following hypothetical case is an example of the type that the coach can construct for purposes of illustration. This type of exercise is especially helpful for the beginning debater because it is necessary that he master the fundamentals. In addition, the exercise can be used to illustrate what argumentation means. This is most appropriate for students who would like to debate but hesitate because they are not sure that they can.

> TOPIC: Resolved that the large state university should limit its undergraduate population.
> I. Large universities are unable to provide individual attention to students.
>   A. Classes are very large because of mass enrollment.
>   1. Ohio State University—40,000 students
>   2. University of Minnesota—40,000 students
>   3. NYCU—50,000 students
>   B. Students become numbers rather than individuals.
>   1. Work must be done by IBM.
>   2. Students become represented by test scores.
>   C. The number of students necessitates the use of graduate assistants for teachers.

PATTERNS OF REFUTATION

The foregoing hypothetical case is usually submitted to a student who is given a time limit of five minutes. Students are asked to write their arguments and number them in the order of presentation. In this way, the instructor can determine the pattern of refutation. The student should be made aware of the different patterns of refutation and their application.

Direct Refutation. Because the initial burden of rebuttal belongs to the negative, it is useful to force the student to attack the arguments and evidence of the affirmative first. Again, this is one of the values of the hypothetical case. Novice debaters tend to avoid direct clash by presenting a countercase that contains evidence which favors the status quo. Direct refutation consists of examining the structure and evidence of an opponent's arguments.

Indirect Refutation. If a debater attacked the hypothetical case by presenting arguments that favored the large state university, his refutation would be largely indirect. Although the affirmative is responsible for answering indirect refutation, the negative is obligated to refute the case presented by the affirmative. Also it is important to remember that the affirmative has *the* burden of proof. If the negative does not engage in direct refutation, they lose the advantage of presumption.

Direct and Indirect Refutation. A negative debater who presents direct refutation and also presents strong constructive arguments for the status quo, puts considerable pressure on the affirmative because the affirmative must answer the challenges to its own case and also deal with the negative constructive arguments. This approach can be presented in several ways. The negative may attack the entire affirmative case and then present counter-contentions that favor the status quo. Another alternative is to state the negative position at the outset, engage in direct refutation of the affirmative case, and then develop the negative position.

Running Refutation. The most skilled negative debaters not only refute the arguments of the affirmative but present counter-evidence and arguments immediately after each challenge. In other words, the negative constructive arguments are interwoven with the direct refutation of the affirmative arguments. This procedure is recommended for only the most experienced debaters. The difficulties of organization and clarity are apparent.

Affirmative Refutation. The affirmative has the burden of establishing its case and this should be the primary concern. The affirmative should present its refutation by stating the original arguments and referring the negative attack to those arguments. After the affirmative case has been established, the negative constructive case can be attacked. Although most of the affirmative refutation is of a defensive nature, the best defense is a good offense. In other words, the affirmative should be alert to negative assertions and should make the negative take a position. The negative has *a* burden of proof.

THE ESSENTIALS OF REFUTATION

Organization

Before a debater can master the skill of refutation he must know precisely what his opponent has said. This means careful listening and careful note-taking. Students must be capable of outlining the major arguments of an opponent and the evidence used to support each argument. This process can be taught by using a tape recorder to present various cases. The student is asked to outline the case and indicate major arguments and their support. Once a student can follow a well-organized case it is time to present scrambled cases to him or cases that are badly organized and delivered poorly. One such case might be constructed with a number of arguments that are not mutually exclusive. If a library of such tapes is in existence with answer sheets that outline the case, the student can practice on his own.

After a student is capable of outlining a case he must know how to approach the task of refutation. The student should learn to examine the general reasoning of his opponent before he attempts to analyze specific evidence and causal relationships. He will ask himself the following questions. What is the general approach to the resolution? What is my opponent basically trying to prove? What unproved assumptions does he rely upon? If we return to the hypothetical case it can be seen that the advocates believe that size and quality are related. The major assumption is that students need individual attention to meet the goals of education. Until this assumption is proved, no amount of specific evidence will strengthen the case. It is also assumed that (1) limitations do not exist, (2) large enrollment means large classes, (3) depersonalization is undesirable, and (4) graduate assistants are not capable teachers. Not all cases contain this many unproven assumptions, but all cases rely on certain presuppositions and premises. It is necessary to teach debaters to examine the philosophy and general reasoning of any case. People sometimes come to believe ideas without knowing why they believe them. The 1959–60 intercollegiate debate topic is a good example. (Resolved: That Congress should be given the power to reverse decisions of the Supreme Court.) A frequent contention of affirmative teams was that the Supreme Court was not democratic. Negative teams went to great lengths to deny this by proving that the Supreme Court was democratic. However, some negative teams recognized the basic assumption and challenged the affirmative to prove that the Supreme Court should be democratic. In a more recent debate a young lady advanced the idea that unless a resolution was adopted a communist government would take control of a developing country. When her opponent challenged the assumption that communism was evil, she was completely baffled. She could not explain why communism was evil, but simply asserted that everyone knew that it was.

It should be noted that many times it is not enough to question the basis of an assumption. The debater must generate doubt about the assumption so that the challenge is more than a strategy to consume time.

Presentation

The presentation of refutation will decide its potency. The effective debater can state the essence of an opponent's case in an orderly fashion and in an order that suits his purpose. His first task is to place the burden of proof. In other words, he is able to state precisely what the opponent must prove in order to establish a case. The first contention of the hypothetical case provides a good example. (Large universities are unable to provide individual attention to students.) It is tempting to deny this at the outset. However, the first line of attack is to place the burden. In other words, (1) make the affirmative prove that individual attention is necessary, and (2) present evidence to the contrary. One should not try to disprove his opponents' assertions, but make them take *the burden of proof*. It is well to remember that assertions come in a variety of subtle forms.

There are three essential steps of refutation. (1) State precisely what is to be refuted. (2) Refute by the use of evidence and reasoning; rather than merely questioning an opponent, make him accept his burden of proof. And (3) point out just what effect the refutation has had. In other words, was an argument destroyed? Was it demonstrated that no relationship existed between premises and conclusions? If the refutation had no effect, it was not refutation. Debaters may discover minor points that they can disprove. However, if this will have no effect on their opponents' case or it will not rebuild theirs, it is *not* refutation. In essence there has been a waste of time. The skilled debater is above all a pragmatist. He asks himself, what difference would it make if my statements were valid?

The language of refutation must be precise and potent. A lack of clarity results from such phrases as "in regard to this point," "they said," "we say," and "it has been quoted." The experienced debater speaks in terms of issues, arguments (contentions), and evidence. He identifies precisely and relates the process of refutation to the overall scope of the debate. In addition to clarity, the language of refutation determines persuasiveness. Consider the difference between "we question the workability of the affirmative plan" and "compulsory arbitration could never yield satisfactory labor contracts." It is the responsibility of the coach to help the student make the best use of language. This is achieved by asking students to write out arguments and examine them. The growth of vocabulary will help the student employ more effective language in the extemporaneous situation.

Debaters must be able to follow the trend of a debate and a good debate usually has movement and change. Just what happens to the refutation during the debate? If one team advances strong challenges at the outset of a debate, but then fails to capitalize on them by not following them through each speech, the effort has been wasted. Teamwork is especially important in refutation. The debaters should be trained to give a running account of what has happened during the debate. They can then maximize or minimize what has taken place by additional arguments and evidence. This skill can be developed by holding a practice debate that deals with just one issue. A shortened series of speeches that are recorded allows for examination of this skill. (See direct-clash exercises recommended in Chapter 5.)

Fruitful teamwork also involves division of labor. By careful planning, negative team members can divide their refutation duties and thereby mount a more extensive attack. The second negative speaker might spend the major portion of his time attacking the affirmative plan in the second negative constructive speech. The first negative rebuttal speaker will then devote his time to an attack on the need issues. In this way the negative speakers can avoid overlap of arguments and develop their arguments more fully.

Rebuttal periods are designated for an analysis of arguments that were presented during the constructive periods. If the refutation has been effective, crucial areas of agreement and disagreement will be revealed. Novice debaters sometimes only summarize and repeat earlier arguments. When this happens, little is accomplished in the rebuttal period. Experienced debaters realize which arguments must be destroyed or defended. The most important concept in rebuttal is *selection.* Arguments are selected on the basis of how well the opponents have defended those arguments and which arguments must be established before the opponents can establish a case. The coach should keep in mind that not all debaters can make maximum use of the rebuttal period. A helpful exercise consists of stopping a debate after the constructive speeches and asking the debaters to explain what the most crucial arguments are, why the arguments are crucial, and just what they intend to do. In essence, this is what they will be expected to know if they are going to employ effective refutation. The coach may also play the role of judge at this point and tell the debaters exactly what he perceives at this particular time of the debate.

Knowledge of Special Techniques

Certain methods of refutation are probably called "special" because they are strategems. Debaters should be reminded that such methods are designed to examine reasoning and are not used to exhibit cleverness. The debater who attempts to be clever may know the score, but he may also lose the game. These special techniques should emphasize rationality; however, when misused they can result in trickery. For example, an opponent's argument might be extended beyond its natural limits for the purpose of raising more objections. The more exaggerated and general a statement becomes, the more open it is to attack. The coach can train the debater to use these devices if the debater is prepared to ask the right questions. The following questions illustrate the use of special devices.

(1) How far can I extend my opponent's reasoning? (Reducing the argument to an absurdity.) If we turn to the hypothetical case concerning large universities it can be seen that the individual attention theme is a likely target. Just how much individual attention is necessary and what type of student needs individual

attention? One might extend this reasoning to demonstrate that it would be impossible to staff a university.

(2) Can I use my opponent's argument or evidence to my advantage? (Turning the tables.) For example, one might say that the second line of reasoning in the hypothetical case actually favors the large university. Perhaps the enrollment assures adequate testing and counseling services.

(3) Do the opponents remain consistent with arguments and evidence? (Exposing inconsistencies.) The consistency of the hypothetical case can be questioned in view of the last argument. First there is concern about individual attention and then it is assumed that graduate assistants do not count. When an opponent is inconsistent the issue should be forced because he will not only lose credibility, but he must give up part of his case.

(4) Are the arguments related to the major premise or issue? (Exposing irrelevant arguments.) In terms of the hypothetical case, the second argument is irrelevant. The argument has little to do with teaching and the limitation of undergraduate population will not remove IBM and test scores.

(5) Can I limit my opponents to alternatives that are equally damaging to their position? (The dilemma.) In refuting the hypothetical case, one might contend (a) that limitation according to a set number would violate the principle of education for all or (b) that limitations of size would create a large number of universities without proper facilities or trained teachers.

Special techniques are useful if the student understands the reasoning that is required to apply them. The name of the technique is useful for analysis but is not necessary for application. The use of familiar subjects helps to get the student started. Once he understands the principle, he can apply it to more complicated material.

Examining Evidence

How does a coach train his students to examine evidence? Perhaps the first step is to remove some obstacles to analysis. One such obstacle is created by the debater himself when he employs certain crutches. One such crutch consists of asking an opponent for more evidence. It is granted that there are occasions when this is justified. However, in most cases this is a weak attack. Even if an opponent cannot give a large number of examples, the examples he uses may be enough to convince a judge. Another crutch that is employed is the strict use of counterevidence. When in doubt the debater simply reads evidence that seems to show the opposite. This approach may have its place but eventually a decision must be made as to which evidence is most accurate or which evidence best supports the validity of the reasoning used. One way to avoid these pitfalls is to train debaters to employ direct analysis of the evidence advanced by an opponent. The purpose of this discussion is to explore some of the central questions that will help the debater analyze evidence.

(1) What is the ultimate source of the evidence? Testimony by an authority is usually nothing more than an assertion. The fact that an authority has made a statement may add to its credibility, but the ultimate test is a determination of how he arrived at his conclusion. The debater must trace the origin of that opinion. If the authority has reasoned from certain evidence, both the reasoning and evidence should be scrutinized. It is helpful to realize that all authorities have their prejudices, although some are more objective than others.

Numerical proof should also be reduced to its formulation. The meaning of data is dependent upon the means used to gather that data. The method of study will determine what can be said of the data, and the data are simply a reflection of the thinking that went into the study in the first place. For example, a study of unemployment will need to have a definition of what unemployment is and the resulting figures will depend on that definition.

(2) How specific is the evidence? It is not unusual for debaters to use general statements or general figures to support a specific point of view. One must be aware of the specific category that needs support. Then it is a matter of dissecting the statement or figure. For example, in the hypothetical case cited earlier the figures are general and do not support the resolution. These figures represent more than the undergraduate population. The figures include graduate students, special students, students

in night school, and so forth. A recent debate topic required that the affirmative demonstrate that qualified students should be guaranteed a higher education. It was common for the affirmative to cite the figures of those who were not getting a higher education. However, these figures did not specify that the same individuals had tried to obtain assistance. Another case in point concerned the question of compulsory health insurance. General figures of those who did not have health insurance or of those who did not obtain adequate medical treatment did not tell why this was the case. In essence it is a question of just what the evidence means.

(3) Does the evidence support the argument? One way to examine this question is to determine if other equally sound conclusions can be drawn from the evidence. The specificity of the evidence is also important. The first argument of the hypothetical case asserts that classes are very large because of mass enrollment. However, no evidence indicates how large the classes are or what kind of classes might be large. In fact we do not know what constitutes a large class.

(4) What was the method of study and what do the figures mean? Today's debater must have a knowledge of quantitative methods because qualitative problems are expressed with statistical concepts that are designed to give precise description. The results of any study will depend on how the study is conducted and what particular statistic is used to describe the outcome. Although this discussion will not detail the many considerations of quantitative study, it seems important to review some of the general items that are necessary for a minimal understanding of quantitative studies. First students should be trained to recognize the difference between descriptive statistics and inferential statistics. (See Chapter 12.)

Descriptive statistics are used when a total population is examined. For example if one were to study the income of unskilled workers it would be necessary to define income, unskilled workers, and then obtain the income figures of all the unskilled workers. The income figures might be based by the hour, year, or month. The resulting income figures could be described in at least three ways: the mean (average), the median (the midpoint of the incomes), and the mode (the most frequent income or income range). Although all three figures would be different, they would also be accurate. The discerning debater must decide what figure best answers the point at issue. He must also determine if the basis of the study is sound. Percentage figures can be particularly misleading. The size of a percentage may mean very little. For example, if the base figure is one we can add one more and end up with a 100 per cent increase. On the other hand, an increase of thousands will mean little in terms of percentage increase if the base figure is in the millions. The significance of percentage figures may depend on other existing factors. A case in point is a controversy over inflation and food prices. The situation is depressing if past food prices are compared with those of today on a percentage basis. However, some relief is to be found if one compares the percentage of total income spent on food in the past with the percentage of total income spent for food today.

Inferential statistics are a reflection of sampling methods. A sample is taken of a population and then inferences are made about the total population. Television rating systems and other such polling devices are illustrative of this method. Students should be made aware of the requirements for such studies. Is the sample adequate? Is the sample representative? Was the sample taken randomly? When was the sample taken? How was the sample taken? If survey methods are used in such studies, it is important that students realize some of the shortcomings of the survey method. For example, one of the basic problems in the survey method is obtaining a response that accurately reflects the feelings of the respondent. The construction of a questionnaire or interview can decide the results of a survey.

The coach will do well to train students to do more than question the results of a study. The student should be prepared to trace the very beginnings of the study. If the procedure of a study can be indicted, it is not necessary to deal with the figures presented.

Examining Reasoning

In order to refute the reasoning of an opponent a debater must be able to perceive what reasoning is being used. This means that the student must be trained to see unstated relationships as well as those that are stated. It is helpful if the instructor starts with broad concepts and commonplace examples. Two concepts that are basic to an approach to an argument are *form* and *content*.

The form of an argument can best be described by examining deduction and induction. Deductive reasoning employs a generalization to arrive at a specific conclusion. Even more important, the generalization dictates the conclusion and the conclusion comes as no great surprise. An examination of the hypothetical case provides an example.

Effective education requires individual attention (unstated).

Large universities do not provide individual attention.

Large universities do not provide effective education.

The debater should remember that once he grants the truth of the major premise it is no great problem for an opponent to illustrate that truth. When deductive reasoning is used, the debater should be aware of the specific generalization advanced. Is the generalization an "allness" statement or is it qualified? If the generalization is qualified, the conclusion must be qualified. The inductive form of argument moves from the particular and arrives at a generalization that is based on probability. The debater can attack the particulars in the chain of argument or he can show that other probable conclusions follow from those particulars. The structure of argument can also be used to illustrate false reasoning. In a debate concerning direct foreign aid a debater asserted that countries did not want direct aid because certain conditions were stipulated. This assertion was supported by a quotation from the prime minister of country X who stated that country X would not accept U.S. aid if strings were attached. A negative debater destroyed this line of reasoning quite effectively by utilizing structure and evidence. He pointed out that the major premise was that country X would not accept aid if strings were attached. He then produced evidence that country X was receiving U.S. aid. The conclusion was obvious and the effectiveness of such refutation is also obvious. The coach should be able to elicit two questions from his debaters during practice in regard to *form* of argument. What is the structure of the argument? What must you do to weaken the argument?

The content of argument is examined by determining the truth value of the statements that appear in the structure of argument. It was pointed out earlier in this discussion that the debater should analyze the general reasoning of his opponent before he proceeds to examine specifics. The coach trains his debaters to ask the right questions—both general and specific.

Examining the General

Affirmative Case Analysis. Are the evils cited by the affirmative caused by or related to the present policy? Faulty case analysis is not uncommon. There is a tendency for some teams to find a problem and attach it to the resolution. Some teams that debated the "right-to-work law" spent considerable time demonstrating that corruption existed in labor unions. This approach contained the assumption that the lack of a right-to-work law had something to do with corruption. In addition it was assumed that a right-to-work law would correct the problem. Negative teams not only questioned a causal relationship, but cited cases of corruption in states that had right-to-work laws.

It was pointed out earlier that one of the fundamental questions that a debater asks when approaching a case is "Basically what is my opponent trying to prove?" Attack on specifics can sometimes obscure the pivotal point of a controversy. For example, some debaters used the following series of arguments when attempting to establish the policy of creating a national system of Public Work: (A) there is unemployment, (B) unemployment wastes human resources, and (C) Public Work will create employment. The first line of attack is to discover the pivotal point of these arguments. This cannot be done by examining each argument in turn because they seem too reasonable. However, an examination of the general reasoning indicates that it is assumed that Public Work will actually make full use of human resources. The issue is: "Do make-work programs utilize human resources?" This example indicates that it is not necessary to deny any of the arguments although this was the first impulse of many students.

The Nature of the Contentions or Arguments. A contention is an argument that is designed to support an issue. The debater should decide first of all if the contentions are truly indictments of the present system. Sometimes contentions are only descriptive of the status quo and point to an argument that may not be stated at all. For example, during a debate on the matter of applying antitrust legislation to labor unions a team contended that labor unions were very large. One could hardly dispute this. A negative speaker in this case was quick to point out that this was quite descriptive but was no indictment. The negative then moved to contentions that were truly arguments. The debater must view all the contentions and decide if they are independent of each other or if they represent a chain of reasoning. Sometimes contentions are meant to be independent, but in reality they are not. In this case the debater can save much time by demonstrating that the arguments are not mutually exclusive and that they depend on one central idea. The debater then refutes that central idea. If the arguments represent a chain of reasoning, the debater should select the weakest link and destroy it. The coach can train his debaters to examine contentions by structuring cases that are designed to mislead. Students are then tested on their approach to each case.

Examining the Specific

Causal Relationships. Perhaps the most common method of reasoning is causal. We observe an event and then assign a reason to the cause (effect to cause—present to past). If we observe an event and predict a result of that event we are reasoning from cause to effect (present to future). Sometimes it is easier for students to think of the time factor when examining relationships. It is normally difficult to establish single causes that produce single effects. This is especially true of complex problems and it is better to train debaters to think in terms of major causes and major effects. A common fallacy of effect to cause reasoning occurs when two events occur in sequence and the second event is assumed to be the result of the first event. In this case debaters should be prepared to destroy the idea of a direct or major relationship. This is accomplished by demonstrating that other significant causes have produced the result. Reasoning from the present to the future by an opponent presents at least three opportunities for refutation. Does a contemporary problem exist? Will other effects occur that will overshadow the effect asserted by the opponent? Will other causes prevent the predicted effect from occurring?

Sign Relationships. When two or more events are related in such a way that the presence or absence of one may be taken as an indication of the presence or absence of the other, a sign relationship exists. For example, when college football begins we can conclude that the school year is under way. Although some football coaches may not agree, we can also observe that the football season did not cause school to begin. Sign relationships always rest on a generalization. In order to test the validity of sign reasoning it is necessary to test the validity of the generalization. If this test is applied to the above generalization (implied) that college football begins when school begins, the results indicate that the sign relationship is faulty. If one saw the college all-stars who play during the summer, he could not conclude that the new school year was under way. Another test of such reasoning is that of examining the other signs that may corroborate the relationship or deny it. For example, one would not conclude that the economy was falling apart on the basis of one undesirable stock market report. Another avenue of attacking sign relationships lies in the debater's ability to point up events that are related to the sign that contradicts those asserted by the opponent.

Reasoning by Example. The number of examples that support a line of reasoning may or may not be important. The psychological impact of an example is more important than the number of such examples. If an employee committed an act that destroyed the company, it is unlikely that he could preserve his job by telling the boss that it had only happened once. It is better to train debaters to examine the specificity of the example and its relationship to the generalization. The debater should also be prepared to demonstrate that the example is not representative and that important exceptions are not accounted for.

Reasoning by Analogy. The analogy is essentially a comparison between items. The literal analogy compares items that are in the same class and the figurative analogy compares items that are in different classes. Coaches would do well to train their debaters to avoid extensive use of analogies. The beginning debater frequently uses an analogy because he is not disciplined to reason precisely. Figurative analogies are sometimes used to illustrate a particular line of reasoning. However, in most cases the debater who uses a figurative analogy has no line of reasoning to illustrate. When he can state his reasoning there is usually no need for the analogy. The following questions are essential when the debater examines an analogy. Is the analogy literal or figurative and how is it applied? Are the similarities of the items compared essential similarities? Are the major differences between items of any consequence? For example, if we compare the unemployment figures between the United States and Europe, the results are quite startling. However, much of this difference is due to the difference in the definition of the term unemployment. Analogies are normally time-consuming, misleading, and they often offer an easy target for refutation. If the analogy cannot be refuted, it can usually be muddled to the extent that everyone will be confused.

AFFIRMATIVE AND NEGATIVE STRATEGY

It has been pointed out that the debater may not need to deny a particular argument if it assumes a more general truth that needs to be demonstrated. When arguments are strong the technique of minimizing is more productive than attempting to destroy. Constant attack on an argument gives it importance by the very nature of selection. Rather than deny the validity of the argument, the debater must be prepared to minimize the importance of the argument and its necessity for the acceptance or rejection of the resolution.

Negative debaters must be made aware of the *shifting case*. One affirmative strategy is to advance a number of arguments to determine the strength of the negative attack in the constructive speeches. Then in the rebuttals, the affirmative selects the arguments that have received the least attack and claims that these arguments represent the real issues. The shifting case has a number of variations and can be employed in subtle ways. For example, a stock-issues case can shift to an advantages case in the rebuttal. The coach can prepare his teams for such cases by preparing some for practice. The negative debater should be trained to make an affirmative team commit themselves in the constructive speeches. One method is to declare the affirmative's position for them and thereby force a decision early in the debate. Cross-examination debate is especially suitable for this technique. When, and if, a shift of emphasis is detected it should be pointed out to the judge.

Refutation by the affirmative consists of (1) rebuilding the affirmative case by answering challenges of the negative and (2) attacking the negative position. The first obligation of the affirmative is to establish its case. Each affirmative speaker should restate the major affirmative arguments, state the negative arguments that are related to the affirmative arguments, refute the negative arguments, and then point up the effect of the refutation. If the negative has failed to attack a key argument, this should be made abundantly clear. When the affirmative debaters are trained to continue with the case that they have presented and keep it in the foreground, there is less likelihood that they will become disorganized. In addition, this type of organization prevents the affirmative team from leaving their case to wander on negative ground. Once an affirmative team has left their case, they are completely on the defensive and the probability of establishing the case is very slight. This method of presentation also helps the affirmative point up negative arguments that may have been discarded or altered. It is always tempting to jump on the argument that can be crushed at the outset of a speech. However, debaters should be trained to follow a pattern that allows for efficiency and clarity. When the affirmative team has rebuilt their case, they are then free to attack the negative position or related arguments that may have an influence on the outcome of the debate.

The affirmative team should be aware of negative opponents that probe for weaknesses but never develop a position of their own. In this situation the affirmative should try to get a commitment from the negative. Otherwise the negative has considerable latitude and does not have to worry about consistency of argument. In addition the negative is relieved of the responsibility of developing a position.

There is no formula that guarantees effective refutation. Nevertheless it is important to establish an organizational pattern of refutation and also delegate the duties of the speakers on a negative or affirmative team. The outcome of a prescribed approach may be mechanical at first, but the basics are necessary before refinement can take place. The coach should insist on the basics during practice debates and if necessary he should ask each speaker to describe his organizational plan before each speech. One special problem of refutation that the affirmative must learn to cope with is called the "shotgun attack" by the negative. This usually occurs in the traditional debate format which allows the negative team a fifteen-minute block of time during the second negative constructive speech and the first negative rebuttal speech. This gives the negative team the opportunity to amass a large number of arguments against the affirmative position. The first rebuttal speaker for the affirmative will be expected to answer these arguments. Although it may not be justified, there is normally suspicion about an affirmative team which waits until the last speech to answer arguments that may be crucial. Therefore affirmative speakers must be prepared to deal with large numbers of arguments. Several key questions point toward a method of handling this problem. (1) Are the arguments advanced by the negative indeed seperate arguments? If the arguments are all variations of the same theme or the same assumption, they can be grouped and answered without answering each one separately. (2) Are the arguments relevant and did the negative establish this relevance? The affirmative team can do much to decrease the number of negative arguments by forcing the negative to establish the relevance of each argument. (3) Has the negative team employed the process of selection? If the negative has not placed a priority on some arguments, the affirmative should do so and then convince the judge that they have answered the most important arguments. It may be an advantage for the affirmative team to declare that all the negative arguments are about equal in importance and the majority of them have been answered. However, this is a dangerous practice because one of the unanswered arguments may appear important to the judge and there are some judges who insist that all arguments must be answered. The coach can prepare his team for "shotgun" approaches by preparing such cases and utilizing them in practice. It is especially effective to contrive lists of arguments that are not mutually exclusive. This prepares the debaters and also gives the coach information about which students can best handle the first affirmative rebuttal.

COMMON ERRORS OF REFUTATION

There are some weaknesses in refutation that are common to the novice debater. It is well to identify these weaknesses early and explain why such procedures are not productive.

The Witch Doctor Approach. Sometimes students become so enmeshed in evidence that they assume that everyone sees the same argument they do and therefore they do not make a separation between argument and evidence. As a result they are inclined to read to refute an opponent's argument with the hope that it will go away. The process of drawing an argument from the evidence is left to the judge. Sometimes both teams engage in a vehement reading contest and little debating actually takes place. In some cases the debaters do not actually have an argument, but silence is intolerable and they wish to create the illusion that they are accomplishing something.

The Curiosity Syndrome. Challenges to an argument are sometimes made in the form of a question. It should be remembered that the question is usually a form of assertion. It is risky for a debater to ask a question unless he knows the answer. This is particularly true in cross-examination debate. In most cases it is better for a debater to be positive about the challenge and point out what the opponent must do to establish his argument. If we return to the hypothetical case given at the outset of this discussion, an example is apparent. The first contention of the case was that large universities are unable to provide individual attention to students. Contrast the following approaches: (1) "Is individual attention necessary?" (2) "Until the affirmative can demonstrate that individual attention is necessary, they cannot establish their case. Besides, evidence exists to the contrary."

The Magic of Terminology. It is important that students learn terms that categorize reasoning. This makes for efficiency and also helps the student realize what is required for validity. However, the student must be able to explain precisely what he means when he uses the terms. A debater may be justified in concluding that his opponent has not established an inherent need, a prima facie case, or a causal relationship. However, he is obligated to explain just what he means when the terms are used. He should not expect the judge to fill in the gap.

Pat Arguments and Persuasion. As the debate season progresses, debaters tend to respond to arguments with stock answers that have been found to be effective. Eventually this approach becomes a type of shorthand and consequently the persuasive force of an argument is lost. The debater must remember that all judges may not have heard the argument and even valid arguments must be persuasive.

Identification of Arguments. It is the obligation of the debater to identify clearly what he is refuting and why. The debater should not assume that a judge will see what he sees. The relationship between evidence, argument, and issue should be explained clearly.

The Missing Step of Refutation. The most frequent omission in refutation procedure is the last and most important step. Debaters fail to point out what their refutation has accomplished or what it means in terms of the total debate. This probably occurs because the debater feels that the conclusion is obvious. However, the judge cannot be expected to draw the conclusion for the debater.

Lack of Movement. When debaters are following the trend of a debate they are expected to do more than summarize. A good debate has movement, and crucial arguments evolve that must be reinforced or destroyed. The areas of agreement and disagreement ought to be made clear in the rebuttal period. Arguments are not established by merely repeating them.

The Problem of Selection. It was pointed out earlier that the beginning debater is always tempted to refute the easiest argument or piece of evidence at the outset of his speech. However, it is necessary to refute crucial arguments and drive into the heart of an opponent's case. It is important then to follow the organization of an opponent and at the same time select those arguments that will make a difference as to the acceptance or rejection of the resolution. The debater should devote the most time to those arguments that will make the difference and he should remember that when he selects an argument to refute he has indicated a preference. If the argument is unimportant, he has given it importance by virtue of selection.

It is unlikely that a debater can deal effectively with all the arguments and evidence of an opponent. However, it is usually not necessary to do so. There is danger in attempting to answer too much because an attack can be spread too thin. The same principle applies to the negative attack that is a barrage of "one liners." It is better to develop a number of arguments in depth that will actually influence the outcome of a debate. If this has been done, then other arguments might be added as a means of strategy. Speaking in ideal terms, a negative debater should win if he can destroy an issue of the affirmative's case or if he can destroy the underlying premise of the affirmative's case. If this were true, the debate might be over after the first negative speech. Indeed, this speech might take only thirty seconds. However, such thinking does not take into account the human factor of judgment. Judges differ on what they expect of a negative team. Some are satisfied if the foundation of a case has been removed while others want the case razed. Therefore the debater should be trained to deal with "first things first" and then proceed to utilize the remaining time for additional destruction and weakening.

Disproving Assertions. The debater is frequently armed with so much information that he is anxious to disprove any argument advanced by his opponent. There is a tendency to forget that "he who asserts must prove." The debater gives his opponent an edge when he is willing to disprove the opponent's assertions. It is wiser to make an opponent take the burden of proof because if the assertion cannot be supported, it is a waste of valuable time to attack it. In addition, credibility is given to an assertion if the debater is willing to try to disprove it. A stronger approach is to make the opponent support his assertions and then examine the support.

Defending the Indefensible. The superior debater knows when to keep quiet and when to shift the emphasis of his case. If an argument has been destroyed, it is better to establish the issues with other arguments. Defending an indefensible argument only draws attention to an inadequacy.

Need-Plan Issues. The shifting case was described earlier and the following problem is only one variation. However, it occurs frequently enough to warrant special attention. This situation arises when the affirmative cites far-reaching problems in the development of the need issue. However when the plan is presented to meet this need, the need area is reduced so that the plan can take care of it. This shift can be made in a subtle way and the negative must be alert and prepared.

Negative debaters sometimes grant too much to the development of the need issue. Several questions concerning analysis are in order before the negative engages in specific refutation. The negative debater should ask himself: (1) What is the relationship between the need cited by the affirmative and the resolution? and (2) If the affirmative need is based on common goals, are these goals being met at the present time? There is a tendency for some affirmative teams to assume a relationship between the problem area that they have found and the resolution.

Poor Argument—Poor Refutation. There are times when debaters wonder how they could have been beaten by a weak and seemingly ridiculous case. Rather than looking at the judge as a reason, the debaters would do well to examine their refutation. Abraham Kaplan gives us an example which expresses the problem. "Some fool has put the head of this nail on the wrong end." "You idiot, it's for the opposite wall!"[2] One is hard put to choose between the worth of these two statements. It is not enough for a debater to label an argument as foolish. He must explain its inadequacy.

COMPONENTS OF EFFECTIVE REFUTATION

The following principles of refutation summarize the preceding discussion. They are not intended to represent a formula; never-

---

[2] Abraham Kaplan, *The Conduct of Inquiry* (San Francisco: Chandler Publishing Co., 1964), 35.

theless they are essential and should be acquired by the debater even if the acquisition is mechanical at the outset.

Procedure

It is obvious from the hypothetical case advanced at the outset that the debater cannot give all the arguments that he can think of in a five-minute period. He must be selective and drive into the heart of a case. The concept of *priority* must be made clear to the student. The student's first obligation is to examine the general reasoning of the case and place the burden of proof if the case contains assumptions that are questionable. After the nature of the contentions have been examined, the relationship between contentions and evidence should be analyzed. The evidence itself must then be investigated.

The *potency* of an argument or its quality will be determined by its effect on the relationship that exists between resolution and issue, issue and argument, and argument and evidence. The debater must always ask himself why he is refuting a particular argument or piece of evidence.

The *quantity* of arguments that one can advance in refutation is important. The superior debater not only uses quality arguments, but he also uses a quantity of arguments. This puts additional burden on an opponent and insures extensive coverage for the benefit of the judge.

Presentation

The language of refutation is precise and persuasive. An organized attack should reveal significant areas of agreement and disagreement in terms of issues, arguments, and evidence. The superior debater never lets the judge forget what his opponent must do to establish a case and what has happened to the refutation. In the rebuttal period, the debater makes a decision as to what arguments are significant enough to decide the outcome of the debate and acts accordingly. Teamwork in refutation requires division of labor and close attention to what has happened to the arguments of a colleague. Knowledge of special methods of refutation helps the debater to analyze arguments and employ challenges that have a psychological impact on a judge.

Preparation

The best refutation is a result of a thorough understanding of issues, evidence, and refutation techniques. The coach can prepare his debaters for the task of refutation by examining their ability to recognize the essential questions that must be asked of controversial topics. One such exercise was illustrated earlier. Another exercise that helps the debater to realize what an essential question or issue is, can be found in the series "You Be the Judge" located in the *Saturday Evening Post* (July 10, 1948– August 26, 1961).[3] These law excerpts provide a number of facts of a law case and the reader is asked to decide what decision was given by the judge. It is not important that the debater decide what the decision was. He should be asked to formulate the question that was the basis for the judge's decision. If he can do this, he has selected the essential point or issue of the controversy. Once the debater has indicated that he understands what he should be looking for, it is time for him to analyze a more complex topic.

Although the debater is obligated to deal with the arguments presented, he can prepare some of his refutation in advance of a debate. Analysis generally produces certain stock arguments. The debater can prepare for such arguments by preparing "blocks" of refutation. It is important to refine such blocks continually so that they do not become stale and ineffective. This means a continuing search for better arguments and better ways to present those arguments. (Review Chapter 5 for construction of "blocks.")

It is important for the debater to remember that reasoning does not occur by itself. When one reasons, he reasons from something. The debater who believes that he can become a superior debater without having a command of the evidence and issues is only deluding himself. Eventually he will be called upon to defend his presuppositions.

---

[3] This series, under the same title and edited by Ashley Halsey, Jr., has been published in book form by Fawcett Publications, Inc., 67 West 44th Street, New York City.

CROSS-EXAMINATION

Although it is often thought of as a distinct form of debate, cross-examination is nothing more than a means of extending the process of refutation that occurs in debate generally. If the coach keeps this in mind, teaching students to cross-examine their opponents will be easier.

When thinking of it in the abstract, most scholars of debate become excited over the contribution of cross-examination to effective refutation. When observing it in operation, they are frequently dismayed at the way the questioning caused the debate to deteriorate into a "dog-fight." This is attributable not to an inherent weakness in the cross-question method, but probably to one or more of the following factors: (1) almost all debates in college and a proportion of those in high school do not use questioning, and many coaches never bother to teach the debaters how to cross-question; (2) because it brings competitors into close interpersonal discourse, cross-examination requires great maturity and self-discipline of the debaters if they are to avoid invective; (3) cross-examination in academic debate differs in purpose and scope from the highly popularized legal process with which most people are familiar and which students are inclined to use as a model; (4) debaters tend to expect more from a cross-examination than they reasonably should; and (5) questioner-control and severe time limits increase the likelihood of sophistry through questioning. This discussion of the teaching of cross-examination debate will be organized around these five points.

Cross-Examination Requires Time and Attention

One of the ideas stressed in Chapter 2 suggests that often the exigencies of the forensic schedule dictate the educational goals of the program. The facts, first, that many of the debate tournaments attended in high school and college do not use a cross-examination method, and second, that debate coaches typically find themselves totally occupied with preparing students for those events immediately forthcoming help explain much of the neglect to teach cross-examination. It simply does little good for the student to be given a few words of advice and a couple of practice debates just before going to a cross-exam tournament. The students, nervous about the unusual situation, tend to become more concerned with finding a series of questions that *can* be used that will fill the time allowed than they are with integrating the examination with their refutation as a whole and exploiting the unique values of the questioning technique.

Students thus left very much to rely on their ingenuity of the moment, often hit on questions that are clever or tricky per se; questions that the judge may enjoy in a consummatory way, but which do not become instrumental to his decision on a particular issue or the debate itself. Similarly, respondents with little training look for answers that will display cleverness and wit, with cleverness usually being defined as evasiveness and refusal to cooperate with the questioner in even the most fundamental way.

Perhaps the most useful thing a teacher can do for students of cross-examination is to decide to integrate practice in it throughout the year and not wait until the week before a cross-exam tournament. This could be justified first because the cross-examination experience would probably sharpen the students' capacity for refutation and analysis generally, and second because it is the only way they will really learn the process. If they are given systematic practice in questioning, the students will be able to overcome their tendencies toward display. They will, through trial and error, begin to see where questions will actually enhance their overall refutation as opposed to serving only a consummatory function.

Cross-Examination Requires Self-Discipline

As long as a debate remains impersonal (debaters talking to the judge and ignoring each other) it is relatively easy to stick to issues and avoid personal attacks. Even then, of course, some debaters lose control under the stress of a tough debate. Imagine how much more likely one is to lose control when he is engaged in face-to-face interaction with an opponent who is scoring point after point. Cross-examination is as close as academic debate comes to common invective argument. Such arguments are characterized by charge and countercharge, "you're one and you're another" kinds of exchanges which tend to become more and more incoherent as opponents search for a way—any way—to hurt each other. Irrelevant and ad hominem attacks become the order of the day as the participants run out of legitimate lines of argument without having satisfied their need to argue.

In fact, it has been this author's observation that a norm exists in academic debate in both high school and college toward antagonistic interpersonal behavior that would not be tolerated in most other social situations. Debaters who are most civilized in their normal social relations and even in orthodox debates suddenly become sneering, sarcastic animals when the cross-examination begins. Students who are Bill and Bob to each other outside debate become *Mr.* Smith and *Mr.* Jones (with the "Mr." being pronounced in the most condescending manner possible). Students coached to stand in such a way as to be easily seen and understood by the judge take this as license to turn their back on the person to whom they are speaking. Students begin to operate under the generalization that any courtesy or affirmative response toward their opponent is to be avoided. "Would you agree that the sun is hot?" asks a questioner searching for an obviously feeble figurative analogy which could not possibly hurt the respondent. "Only if you present conclusive evidence to that effect in your next speech," is the confident reply by the student smug in the knowledge that once again he has avoided a simple "yes" answer.

To be sure, some coaches behave toward each other in much the same way, and in fact counsel their students to avoid those from competing schools for fear that they might give something away. With this model to follow, it is no surprise that debaters respond to each other in an uncivilized and immature way when they come face-to-face under pressure.

Effective reasoned discourse cannot take place in such an atmosphere. It is the job of the teacher to refuse to reward such behavior, to counsel against it and reward with praise and decisions those students who prove able to discipline themselves. Above all, it is the job of the teacher to set an example of self-discipline—courtesy, dignity, maturity—in competitive situations.

Academic Debate Differs from Legal Cross-Examination

Perhaps one cause of the interpersonal antagonism among debaters is their use of legal cross-examination as a point of reference. This probably also accounts for some of the ineffective use of questioning in academic debate.

With cross-examination debate an infrequent occurrence, and with an inadequacy of formal instruction, it is quite reasonable that students should turn to their notions of legal practice for norms to apply in the academic situation. This is unfortunate from at least two lines of reasoning: (1) students' notions of legal practice are often based on stereotypes and fictions only slightly resembling legal reality; (2) actual legal practice involves some significant differences in the purpose for cross-examination. The first idea requires little elaboration, but the second should be developed.

Even though academic debate may take the idea of cross-examination from the law, there are some necessary differences, most important of which is that in law an attorney cross-examines a witness who has been called to testify by the opposing side; in academic debate, one advocate cross-examines another. In the former case, even though the witness was called by the opposition, he may have information to present which is quite favorable to the questioner. In any event, he is questioned as one having access to facts or expertise relevant to the arguments. To approximate such a situation in academic debate, it would be necessary to arrange for debaters to question the authorities quoted by their opposition. What actually happens in school debates is more like one attorney putting the other on the witness stand. The attorney could not be questioned as a *source* of facts or expertise, but only as a user of them in argument. Therefore, it would be relevant only to question him concerning the *use* of fact and authority, and his inferences from them.

In legal cross-examination, much time is spent trying to weaken or destroy the credibility of the witness as a fact-giver. Much time is spent comparing the witness's statements on direct examination and in pretrial examinations with current statements in search of contradictions, improbabilities, or absurdities. The question raised for judge or jury is whether they should believe this witness's version of the facts over that presented by witnesses for the other side. This effort may sometimes lead to attorneys behaving aggressively toward the witness in an effort to break down his story or humiliate him before the jury.

It should be kept in mind that the attorney does not always question with the purpose of achieving an immediately favorable impression by the decision-maker. On the contrary, an attorney has often the goal of building a total record of the trial that will read well much later when examined by the trial judge or an appellate judge. And he has plenty of time to ask all the questions he has in mind.

The academic debater, on the other hand, is questioning a fellow-debater who makes no pretense of being an expert on the subject or an eyewitness to a relevant event. The academic debater is not building a written record which can be examined in detail before the decision is made, but rather he is communicating to the judge—through the medium of questions of his opponent—who will make a decision at once without any possibility of review of the examination. Finally, the questioning is restricted to a few minutes.

What, then, can the academic debater hope to accomplish from his questioning? Will it be very useful to cross-examine the other debater as a fact-giver? Should such questions as, "Are you aware of the Treaty of 1801?" be asked? Probably not. If the purpose of the question is to enter facts into the consideration of the judge, it can probably better be done during an ordinary speech. Is it likely to be useful to probe the perceptions of the other debater with such questions as, "Do you really believe your plan will work?" Not likely. The debater is not an expert on the subject even if he were to say he did not believe in his plan, which he will not say. Will it be useful to ask an opponent to respond to hypothetical situations as an attorney might put to an expert witness such as, "If the Soviet Union were to stop feuding with China and rejoin forces with them, then your plan would probably fail, wouldn't it?" The witness will reasonably expect proof of a probable Soviet-Chinese reconciliation before responding to the question; the witness's affirmation that in such a situation his plan would surely fail is of very little help to the questioner as the witness is not an expert, and the issue will really turn on the question of probable Soviet-Chinese relations on which the witness has not responded; the witness can answer with a simple "yes" and do more to build his credibility than the admission would do to destroy it. Would it help to ask the other debater if he believes the Soviets are likely to get together with China in the near future? Obviously not, both because the debater is not likely to think so if it would hurt his position, and again, the debater is no expert on the subject of Soviet-Chinese relations and his opinion is of little consequence.

The academic cross-examination must concentrate on those aspects of the debate for which the respondent has responsibility and control: the case or arguments and evidence used to defend his position.

Without cross-examination, much time is wasted because debaters refute a position only to learn that the opponent either did not make such a statement or mean to; much time is given to following a "slippery" opponent using the shifting case discussed earlier in this chapter; much time is wasted waiting for the opponent to qualify his authorities more specifically so that they may be challenged; much time is wasted trying to be sure what the opponent actually means to include in a definition or a plan so that it may be refuted. In other words, cross-examination is a fine tool for quickly cutting through to the essence of the opponent's position and fixing it in place so that it can be refuted thoroughly and finally. One of the most common weaknesses in academic debate is the failure to generate specific issues; cross-examination can be effectively used to do this. One of the most common weaknesses in academic debate is the tendency to hear only a hasty reading of some testimony or fact without ever examining in detail the context in which it was made, the basis for the computations, or the competency of the expert testifying; cross-examination can be used to do this better than could ever be done in a series of alternating speeches. One of the common weaknesses in academic debate is the failure to expose unstated assumptions and premises utilized by a team and then force them to defend the idea; cross-examination can be effectively used to do this.

To learn where cross-examination debate can be useful, the teacher need only turn back in this chapter and ask at each point of refutation discussed how the process might be enhanced through the use of direct questions. The idea emphasized here, though, is that one goal of the teacher of cross-examination must be to bring the students to understand the unique functions of questioning in academic debate as opposed to legal practice or any other similar situation.

Debaters Tend to Expect Too Much from Cross-Examination

Just as failure to exercise selection and teamwork is a cause of difficulty in refutation generally, so does it cause problems in cross-examination. One product of inadequate practice in questioning is the inability to judge how much time can be consumed in following just one line of inquiry. It often happens a debater begins questioning the first part of an opponent's comments not because they constitute the place which deserves most attention but because they came first and the debater fully intends to get to the important arguments before he is done. To his dismay, he finds himself out of time before he even completes his questions on the first argument. Even if the debater had managed to hurry his questions so as to cover more of his opponent's case, the chances are good that his haste would have so diminished the effect of his questions that no productive refutation was accomplished. The principle to follow in cross-examination (as in refutation generally) is this: it is better to refute a single important argument *effectively*, than it is to attack the entire case so hurriedly that none of the questions have the desired effect on the judge. Sometimes debaters forget their communicative function and come to believe that having *stated* an argument or asked a question guarantees that the judge will comprehend what was said and appreciate its refutative effect. This is naïve.

Cross-examination is an effective tool for gaining information about an opponent's position that might be used to refute that position, but it is rare that the full potency of an attack—its full implication upon the total opposing position—can be made clear to a judge through questions. This should be done during a speech, when the debater is free to explain his attack without interruption by an opponent. The student needs the teacher's help in learning this; it is not likely to come simply from practice in questioning. The teacher, playing the role of the judge, can explain to a debater where he has failed to clinch an argument that was only suggested through cross-examination.

Finally, debaters tend to expect too much from questioning in the sense that they anticipate the opponent will become aware of the inadequacies of his case and confess his sins publicly. Suppose, for instance, an opponent is arguing in favor of some aspect of U.S. foreign policy and quotes the unsupported testimony of the Secretary of State. It would be quite realistic to expect an affirmative answer to such questions as, "Is the Secretary of State responsible for creating our foreign policy?" "Is the Secretary of State personally involved with the success or failure of our foreign policy?" "Is it typical for the Secretary of State to avoid criticizing our foreign policy while he is still in office?" But it would be quite unrealistic to expect the opponent to admit, even after an affirmative answer to these questions, that the Secretary of State is not a reliable, objective witness to the success of U.S. foreign policy. This is a conclusion that depends upon the viewpoint of the thinker, and it is simply expecting too much to ask the debater to confess openly that he has used poor evidence.

Again, such conclusions are best left to a speech where they can be fully advanced from one side's perspective. To ask an opponent to draw a conclusion favorable to his enemy is to risk not only failure, but also to chance that the answer given will weaken the effect of the information already brought out. The teacher must help students learn to ask those questions sufficiently free of the feelings of the opponent as to be dictated by criteria external to the opponent. It is one thing to ask, "Did you cite any evidence for this point?" It is another to ask, "Can you support that point with evidence?" The former answer will very much be dictated by the public record in the minds and notes of listeners and the opponent; the latter answer is largely a function of the opponent's faith in his evidence file and his aspirations to defend himself. Even though the questioner may feel strongly that no real support exists for the point, it is likely the answer will be affirmative and that the opponent will come up with something resembling support in time for the next speech.

Questioner-Control and Time Limits Increase Sophistry

The teacher faces a dilemma in teaching cross-examination: the strategy of successful questioning tends toward sophistry. It is the teacher's job to help students to be effective; it is the teacher's job to counsel against sophistry.

The strategy of successful cross-examination must be reviewed. First, the questioner must learn to retain full control of the examination. This is accomplished first by asking leading questions. The questioner must treat the respondent as a computer, offering a series of propositions to which a binary response (accept/reject; affirm/deny) is appropriate and necessary. For example, if the inquiry concerns the full meaning of a definition, one does not ask, "Would you please explain your definition more fully?" This would at once put the respondent in control of the situation. It would permit him to determine the information to be revealed, its sequence, and its duration. Rather, the questions follow this pattern: "Did you mean to include municipal courts in your concept of the federal judiciary?" "Did you mean to include the National Labor Relations Board in your concept of the federal judiciary?" And so on, until the questioner had satisfied himself on each potential ambiguity of the definition. This takes more effort and knowledge on the part of the interrogator, but it assures that the examination will go where he wants it to, will include specifically the information in which he is interested, and that the length of the response will be commensurate with the importance of the subject relative to the time limits and the other subjects to be covered.

Second, control is maintained by hiding the object of the line of questions from the respondent as long as possible. By starting with relatively harmless questions which cause the respondent to lower his guard, and moving climactically toward the object (sometimes even stopping the movement to go back to harmless questions for a while to confuse the witness), the examiner can prevent the respondent from structuring answers so as to frustrate the accomplishment of the goal.

Finally, control is maintained by cutting off answers as soon as the questioner is satisfied. Norms of debate, if not society at large, permit the interrogator to stop an answer at any time. If the witness is foolish enough to answer first and try to qualify the answer last, he is likely to be interrupted. The questioner must do this or the respondent may filibuster his way right out of the examination.

However, just as these strategems make for successful cross-examination from the point of view of the questioner, they make for the suppression of full information and explanation by the respondent. Even lawyers are divided over the end of cross-examination. Some say it is the greatest engine for truth ever created by man; others state it is an insidious mechanism for the generation of half-truths and misunderstanding. While the opponent will, of course, have some opportunity in later argument to explain his answers, the damage often has already been done, and irreparable confusion exists. On the other hand, as long as the extraordinarily short periods are provided for cross-examination, it would be foolish for an examiner to turn his respondent loose for a full explanation of each answer. This would amount to nothing other than turning a cross-examination into an additional rebuttal for the opponent.

Therefore, as in many of the other strategies connected with academic debate, it becomes the task of the teacher to explain effective techniques to students while at the same time cementing ideas of responsibility and restraint in their use. It is also the task of the teacher, when acting as a judge, to refuse to reward sophistic use of strategy. If debaters are given serious instruction in cross-examination, if they have a chance to use their skills in competition, and if they are constantly rewarded for responsible behavior, the results in practice will be impressive.

To conclude, the teacher must remember that cross-examination is an extension of refutation in general. The teaching of refutation will likely be enhanced through the use of cross-examination, just as cross-examination cannot be taught apart from refutation as a whole.

SUGGESTED READINGS

Copi, Irving M. *Introduction to Logic*. New York: The Macmillan Company, 1953.

Ehninger, Douglas, and Wayne Brockriede. *Decision By Debate*. New York: Dodd, Mead & Co., 1963.

Faules, Don F. "Measuring Refutation Skill: An Exploratory Study," *Journal of The American Forensic Association*, IV (Spring, 1967) 47–52.

Freeley, Austin J. *Argumentation and Debate*, second edition. Belmont: Wadsworth Publishing Co., Inc., 1966.

Huff, Darrell. *How To Lie With Statistics*. New York: W. W. Norton & Co., Inc., 1954.

Kerr, Harry P. *Opinion and Evidence: Cases for Argument and Discussion*. New York: Harcourt, Brace & World, Inc., 1962.

Kruger, Arthur N. *Modern Debate*. New York: McGraw-Hill Book Co., Inc., 1960.

Miller, Gerald R., and Thomas R. Nilsen (editors). *Perspectives on Argumentation*. Chicago: Scott, Foresman & Co., 1966.

Mills, Glen E. *Reason In Controversy*. Boston: Allyn & Bacon, Inc., 1964.

McBurney, James H., James M. O'Neill and Glen E. Mills. *Argumentation and Debate*. New York: The Macmillan Company, 1951.

Murphy, James J., and Jon M. Ericson. *The Debater's Guide*. New York: Bobbs-Merrill Co., Inc., 1961.

Organ, Troy W. *The Art of Critical Thinking*. Boston: Houghton Mifflin Company, 1965.

Peirce, Charles S. "The Fixation of Belief," *Chance, Love, and Logic*. New York: Harcourt, Brace and Co., 1923.

Saunders, T. Bailey. *The Essays of Arthur Schopenhauer*. New York: The Wiley Book Co., 1896.

CHAPTER 9

Coaching Individual Events

Robert E. Dunham

It should not be assumed that there is a best way of coaching individual speaking events in a forensics program, nor that the individual events will be the same in all parts of the country. It is the purpose of this chapter to discuss the elements of a good individual events program, the description and rationale for some of the standard individual speaking and reading events, and a few tips for the coach.

COMPONENTS OF A GOOD SPEAKING PROGRAM

There are three basic components in any good individual events program: (1) instruction on the principles of speaking, (2) practice in realistic situations, and (3) constructive criticism. The absence of any one or more of these parts will weaken the educational values of a forensics program.

Instruction

Occasionally, and perhaps more times than this writer would like to believe, one can observe a student in a speaking contest who does not have the slightest idea of the principles of speaking. He has never studied the concepts of oral communication. He has gone through the routine procedures of delivering a speech, very much interested in winning the contest, but without the slightest notion of what made the speech effective or ineffective. The practice means very little to him unless he wins. The criticism is meaningless because there is no foundation upon which to build. This student is somewhat to blame for participating in the contest without first of all knowing what he is doing, but more often the coach is to blame because he will send a student to a contest to participate in some individual speaking event without giving him adequate instruction in the principles of oral communication and without informing him of the specific rules and procedures for that particular event. The student entering a contest ought to consider the following questions:

What is my purpose for speaking to this particular audience?

What do I know about my listeners, their background, their interests, their attitudes, and so forth?

What is the residual message (often called central idea) I want to leave with my listeners?

Do I have the proper material selected which will help me accomplish my purpose, and are these materials arranged in a pattern which is meaningful to my listeners?

Having achieved a basic understanding of communicative speaking, he should then begin to "learn the rules of the game," for contest speaking, in a sense, is a game.

To send a student to a contest or to permit him to speak in public without a proper instructional base is educationally unsound and about as demoralizing and misleading as sending a football player into a game without teaching him the rules or how to block and tackle. Instruction prior to the speaking situation is extremely important.

Practice

Someone once said that practice makes perfect. Looking at it realistically we probably should conclude that practice does not necessarily make perfect but practice tends to make permanent. One could swing a golf club at the golf course without prior understanding of what is involved in the swing. It may be a good swing and yet on the other hand it may be a poor swing. What one does by practicing without instruction is to tend to make permanent the thing which he is practicing. In speech contests practice is important, but may be misguided. Once a student has acquired the basic principles of speech he needs to practice in order to improve the delivery, but primarily to determine how this message affects his listeners. Therefore, it is extremely important that the practice situations be as realistic as possible. If he learns that speech in a speech contest should be communicative speaking involving listeners and he does not practice with listeners, the learning effect from practice is diminished or eliminated. Perhaps one of the largest criticisms which we could aim at contests today is the fact that most contest speaking situations provide either a very small audience of other contestants or no audience whatsoever. In most cases the audience cannot be determined beforehand and therefore the speaker has difficulty analyzing his specific audience.

While delivery skills could conceivably be improved by practicing without an audience, the ongoing, dynamic process of communication cannot realistically take place without an audience.

Criticism

If I am to improve my golf swing, I should have a golf coach who will watch me as I practice, and will then make comments about how my swing can be improved. Merely to tell me that I rate a 75 or that I am an "average" golf swinger or that I am the third-best golf swinger in his class does not help me improve my swing. Although this is evaluation, it is not constructive information that will help improve my practicing. Likewise a student who has learned something about preparing himself to speak and who has practiced in a realistic situation will not really improve unless he has someone listen to his speaking and make some constructive statements about how to improve. Unfortunately, today in many forensic contests criticism is often discouraged and, indeed, in some contests, *prohibited*. It would seem that if our forensic contests are educational opportunities, and if the student has spent a great deal of effort preparing for this particular event then the least we can offer is sound, constructive criticism on how he might improve his speaking.

On various occasions a coach has been known to remark that he is somewhat hesitant about constructively criticizing a student speaker in the early round of a tournament because that student might improve and eventually beat his student in one of the following rounds. Undoubtedly the pressure of winning is great, and perhaps the coach has much at stake, but a truly educational contest will involve incidents such as occurred recently at a district tournament in one of our state leagues. A participant said that she had received criticism following the first round in her particular individual event and thought that in the second round she should try to adapt and incorporate some of these criticisms. She eventually won the contest! She was exceptionally grateful for the fact that what she had been told in the first round had worked in the second, and she felt much better about her communicative speaking. Such comments are indeed gratifying, but cannot be expressed unless the judges who are called upon to criticize first understand enough about the event so that they can *teach* a student in the criticism period, and second, are willing to help a student from some other school do a better job of speaking in the following round or following tournament.

In summary then we have seen that there are three constituents in any good individual event program: instruction, practice in a realistic situation, and constructive criticism. The elimination of any one of these would be detrimental to a forensic program.

SPEAKING AND READING EVENTS

Extemporaneous-Impromptu Speaking

Description

The meaning of the word *extemporaneous* is often confused, and for a good reason, because in the field of speech extemporaneous is used to mean at least two different things. If the term "extemporaneous" were discussed in a speech classroom setting it would probably be understood that extemporaneous means well-prepared, and perhaps delivered from notes but certainly not read from a manuscript nor spoken from memory. Most of the speeches given in a beginning speech class are called extemporaneous speeches. In the same classroom setting the word *impromptu* typically is used to mean without *specific* preparation or "on the spur of the moment." Although most good impromptu speakers are prepared in a general way, they are often not sure of their specific topic until a very short time before they are called upon to speak.

In the forensic contest arena the word extemporaneous is used to mean "on short notice" and without much specific preparation, and would come close to the classroom definition of impromptu. In an extemporaneous contest normally a student selects a topic and is then given from fifteen minutes to one hour (depending on the particular contest) to prepare himself on that specific topic. The topics which are chosen are normally current events topics and are usually gleaned from one of the news magazines such as *Time, Newsweek,* and *U.S. News and World Report.*

Nationally, the extemporaneous contest is extremely popular, and is usually the first individual event to be instituted in a state league. The format for the extemporaneous speaking contest calls for the speakers to meet and draw lots for speaking order, and then one at a time, usually five to ten minutes apart, they draw three topics at random from a large number of prepared topics. They may choose one of these three as the topic they will prepare on for the speech contest. Then they retire to a library or to a study room where they may search through scores of magazines they have accumulated and hastily prepare themselves to speak. Oftentimes students are found walking the halls talking to themselves in the practice "dry run" for this extemporaneous speech.

In the impromptu speech contest, which is included in very few tournaments, the normal procedure is to have a student walk into a room, pull a subject out of a hat, go up to the front of the room and begin speaking. In a "less traumatic" impromptu tournament the student has as much as two minutes of preparation time before he is called upon to speak. Normally, the time limit for the extemporaneous speech is five to seven minutes, while for the impromptu speaking contest the time is much shorter.

Following are some sample extemporaneous topics:

Discuss the Causes of the Geneva Conference Failure.

What are the Disadvantages of the Right to Work Law?

What New Safety Features Are Going to be Initiated in the Automobiles Which Will Be Built This Coming Year?

What is the President's New Educational Proposal All About?

Topics for the impromptu speech contest vary slightly and can be either topics such as "What is Your Favorite Book," "Elaborate on Your Favorite Current Event Topic" or very intriguing one-word topics such as "Building," "Communication," "Sin," and "Athletics" which are general enough for a person to take off on a number of different angles and still keep within the overall limitations of the topic area.

Rationale

Extemporaneous speaking can be a very valuable learning experience for students if they approach this event realistically. The student should be able to: (1) speak in an integrated manner on a central idea on very short notice, (2) organize his ideas effectively in a pattern which is meaningful to his listeners, (3) practice in a speaking event which is somewhat void of overly-polished delivery skill, and (4) learn a great deal about current events.

Of course, a student can negate the values involved in extemporaneous speaking if he becomes enamored with the contest atmosphere and decides to guess what topics he may get, and memorizes speeches on each of the probable topics. He may win a number of contests by this behavior but he certainly will not receive the maximum values from extemp speaking.

Original Oratory

Description

At the opposite end of the continuum from extemporaneous or impromptu speaking we find original oratory, sometimes shortened to oratory. Even with such an old, traditional term as oratory there are still some differences of opinion as to what original oratory really means. Most people would agree that original oratory is a well prepared speech, written by the speaker himself, and which he has committed to memory. Unlike the extemporaneous speech, the original oration may take a great deal of time in reaching fruition. The good speaker will write and rewrite his speech until it is finally polished. Of course, with this kind of preparation the speaker has a better opportunity to express his ideas with greater precision using carefully chosen and stylistic language. There is, of course more emphasis on delivery in an oration than there is in an extemporaneous speech.

Original oratory is normally persuasive speaking, but differs from the persuasive speaking event as described in this chapter, primarily in its form of preparation and delivery. Many of the nonacademic contests such as the American Legion Oratorical Contest, The Prince of Peace Oratorical Contest, and the Optimist Club Oratorical Contest are examples of original oratory. While in the true sense of the word oratory should include ideas, organization, style, and delivery of the finest calibre, what sometimes happens in speech contests is that there is strong emphasis on delivery, emphasis on the calibre of the ideas presented and very little emphasis on how well the speech is adapted to the specific listeners.

Rationale

Although original oratory flourished in the Lyceum and Chautauqua periods it is still popular in some circles today. Some critics say that it should have remained in the elocutionary days because it serves no real purpose in our modern society. James McCroskey stated in an article comparing modern forensics with the sophistic period of ancient Greece that oratory of today is questionable. "Invention is severely restricted. Style and delivery are paramount. Even in our 'better' oratory contests the speeches are not developed to influence audience's attitudes, but rather are designed to exhibit skill and win an award. . . . The sophistic art of Philostratus is far from dead."[1] Regardless of the complaints there seem to be a number of valid purposes for this contest event with students today.

In the first place, original oratory provides an opportunity for very careful preparation over an extended period of time. Most

---

[1] James McCroskey, "Our Sophistic Heritage: Implications for Modern Forensics." *Pennsylvania High School Speech League Newsletter*, IV, No. 6 (March 1965), 48.

original orations are prepared over a period of weeks or months and are not done in forty-five minutes or even overnight. Because of the extended period of preparation, sentences and phrases can be chosen very precisely to create the best impact on an audience. Style can be on a higher level than is normally used in speaking. Fluency is greatly enhanced and personal involvement in the topic is much greater when it is one of the student's own choosing.

In spite of these attributes nonacademic contests such as the American Legion Oratorical Contest permit certain undesirable features to be included which carry over into the academic contest, and lead educators to wonder about the educational values involved. When a speech is memorized it tends to place a great deal of emphasis on delivery and style, and is very difficult to adapt to a changing audience. Orations sometimes tend to be very stilted and unrealistic—a criticism which has led some people to state that an original oration is nothing more than an essay on its hind feet. It would appear that the original oratory event can be a valuable learning experience for students provided the coach or teacher adequately understands the principles of rhetoric and public address and helps the student to communicate his ideas effectively. Without this proper guidance, oratory contests usually turn out to be exhibitions of elocution.

Persuasive-Informative Speaking

Description

One of the newest innovations in contest speaking today has been the inclusion of persuasive speaking and informative speaking as distinct events. Persuasive speaking and informative speaking are really crosses between extemporaneous speaking and original oratory. In both of these events the student prepares himself to speak extemporaneously (classroom definition). In other words, he prepares a topic of his own choosing, he selects a structure and proceeds to develop the speech materials. He delivers the speech not from a manuscript, but usually from notes. From original oratory it takes the features of self selection of topic and extended period of preparation. From the extemporaneous contest it takes the style of delivery, and the ability to adapt to a specific audience during a speech. It also separates the general purposes of speaking into informative and persuasive so that there is no direct clash within a contest event. Many people have noted that in a contest where both the informative purpose and the persuasive purpose were allowed, persuasive speeches usually won because they seemed to be a little more colorful and exciting. A dichotomy would permit the informative speakers to speak with informative speakers and the persuasive speakers to speak with persuasive speakers.

In the Pennsylvania High School Speech League a few years ago these two events were replacements for the original oratory contest. The rules require not a manuscript, but a typed copy of the speech outline to be presented before the contest.

Rationale

In these particular events a student can become fully prepared on a speech topic without being forced to write it out word for word and commit it to memory. In addition, there appears to be some merit in having a student understand the difference between a purpose to inform and a purpose to persuade. While there are some people who agree with Aristotle that in reality there is only one kind of speech purpose, to persuade, there is some merit in having a student understand that oral book reports and other kinds of speaking assignments where an audience wants to understand something are really informative speeches and demand a different kind of speech preparation than does the persuasive speech. Students normally speak extemporaneously. They are often called upon to give a report or to explain something to someone. Students who participate in the persuasive and the informative speech contest get training which is very closely related to the kind of speaking they do in school or in everyday life.

One weakness of these two events could be in the selection of topics. Students sometimes, especially in the informative speech contest, pick subjects they know very little about and assume they are experts, or on the other extreme pick very trite subjects that they know a great deal about but are not at all interesting or important to the listeners. Properly done, however, these two events can be very worthwhile activities for any forensic program.

Declamation

Description

There are generally three different kinds of declamations, oratorical declamation, humorous declamation and dramatic declamation. Normally the term declamation (some would prefer the term "interpretation") means that a student will select an already prepared document, commit it to memory, and deliver it to an audience. In oratorical declamation the student selects a speech by some other person. In humorous declamation he usually selects a cutting from a play or a novel that is somewhat humorous in nature. In dramatic declamation he selects material which is serious and is a cutting from a play or novel. In humorous and dramatic declamation a student's success at winning is enhanced greatly if his selection includes more than one or two characters.

While these three contest events have a long history, many state leagues are eliminating them from their contest activities.

Rationale

It is difficult for this author to justify oratorical declamation as a speaking event. It does not allow a student to prepare himself to speak on a topic of his own choosing as he would in original oratory, or in persuasive or informative speaking. In fact, he is not required to involve himself in any of the speech preparation stages, such as selecting a subject, determining the purpose, finding ideas, and structuring these ideas in a well designed message. Usually the speeches chosen are by famous men, often delivered scores of years before, and are not suitable for a beginning student, especially a high-school student. Can you imagine a freshman delivering Kennedy's Inaugural Address and being rated high in appropriateness of subject?

Because the student neither chooses the subject of his speech nor prepares the content, but merely memorizes and delivers it, there is a heavy emphasis on the delivery skills. I suppose that if there is any value to this event it would be that students have the opportunity to read and study many speeches of other people, and, therefore, may understand some of the processes involved in preparing speeches. They also have the advantage of reading and understanding the material presented in the speech. In fact, some organizations probably sponsor a tournament primarily to impose information and ideas upon students, with little or no regard for the speaking itself. For example, the WCTU Oratorical Contest is devoted to having students select an oration from a prepared booklet of ten or twelve, all on the evils of alcohol. The students are to select one oration, commit it to memory and deliver it. The hope is that students by reading, memorizing, and delivering the oration will not only be convinced of the evils of alcohol themselves, but in turn will convince other people. Usually in this kind of a contest, speech values are either absent or relegated to a very subsidiary place. A forensics coach would no doubt be hard pressed to justify to school administrators that oratorical declamations have any educational value for a student in this modern society.

There is often confusion with humorous and dramatic declamation because some people think these events are oral interpretation. Other people think these events are acting. In reality they come somewhere between acting and oral interpretation of literature.

Some declamation contests would appear to be solo acting, for in some cases students will kneel, walk around, gesticulate and from all appearances be acting without stage properties or hand properties. Since the selections usually come from a cutting of a one-act or a three-act play, students often have difficulty determining the thin line between declamation and acting. As you will note in a later section, one difference between oral interpretation of literature and declamation is that oral interpretation of literature normally is read and not memorized. There is a serious question that should be raised here about the purpose and value of humorous and dramatic declamations although they seem to have more justification than oratorical declamations. For the student interested in dramatics there is solo acting of one-act and three-act plays. For the student who is primarily interested in reading literature to an audience there is interpretation of literature. But merely to memorize and recite (without adequate bodily freedom) a cutting from a play is misleading, frustrating to the student, and unnecessary.

In summary then, declamations, a number of years ago perhaps, fulfilled a useful function. Their focus today is primarily limited to delivery-centered activities. Their contribution to learning something about communicative speaking leaves much to be desired.

After Dinner—Entertainment Speaking

Description

There are many collegiate and high-school tournaments throughout the states which have some kind of speech to entertain or after-dinner speech. Sometimes these are held at an actual dinner.

At the Joseph F. O'Brien Debaters' Congress at Penn State University there is a feature which is called the gavel girl contest. This contest features several young ladies speaking on an entertaining topic after a banquet. There is a small prize for the best gavel girl, but the real merit of such a program is in the fact that in reality it is a very entertaining situation and a chance for students to become less serious and get involved with a different kind of speaking situation.

Rationale

Since the speech to entertain almost by necessity needs an audience, it provides the speaker with a tremendous opportunity to try to adapt his speaking to the listeners. He gets away from stilted, highly polished speeches and in its place receives valuable training in interaction effects of an audience and a speaker. This event provides one of the few opportunities to attempt to speak with the general purpose to entertain. Most other speech contests deal with informative or persuasive purposes, and are more serious.

Reading Events

Description

Whether they are found in contests or in festivals there are usually three kinds of reading events: prose reading, poetry reading, and dramatic reading, sometimes called dramatic interpretation. Rules in contests or festivals state that oral interpretation of poetry selections must be in poetic form and must have literary merit. In prose reading they should have prose or poetry and may not be taken from a play or from a speech. In dramatic reading or dramatic interpretation the cutting normally is from a play. The primary difference between dramatic reading and dramatic declamation is that the former is read and the latter is memorized.

In contest or festival reading the judges look for selections that not only have literary merit but have some challenge to the reader. It is expected that the selection is suitable for an educational experience, and is particularly suited to the reader. A big husky fellow, for example, would not do particularly well with the selection, *Patterns* by Amy Lowell, nor would a fragile female do well with *The Creation* by James Weldon Johnson.

It is also expected that the student fully understand the selection and be able to communicate ideas and feelings to his listeners and establish the necessary mood. While it is very important for the reader to make good use of delivery skills, the reader should be aware that rhyme and meter should not interfere with the ideas of the poem.

Rationale

There is a running dispute among coaches throughout this country about whether the oral interpretation events should be read or recited from memory. Most of the contest descriptions and rules state that these are oral *reading* events, but in reality the student delivers from memory a selection of prose or poetry. The "reader's" side argues that to be realistic in this modern society of ours one needs to learn to read aloud. In class, students are called upon to read book reports, or to read announcements. At home they often read some stories to younger children, but they are very seldom called upon to memorize passages and recite them to listeners.

A mother or father would normally not think of committing a number of stories to memory and reciting these to the children. It is so much easier to pick up a book and read it aloud. If our goal is to improve the reading ability of our students then they ought to *read*. If we are to improve the delivery skills and fluency of students then we ought to let them commit a selection to memory and recite it.

On the other hand, the "memorized" side contends that a student who selects a bit of prose or poetry and reads this at several contests will eventually have it committed to memory whether he wants to or not, and that it is a difficult task to keep from committing at least a major portion of the passage to memory and even more ridiculous to have him pretend that he is reading by holding a book before him when in reality he is not.

There appears to be conflict of purposes in this dilemma. If the primary goal is to develop reading skill then it seems that oral reading ought to be used in the truest sense of the word. If the primary purpose is merely to create a feeling or have listeners understand what is taking place in a selection then perhaps the best job can be done by highly polishing a performance so that the mood and feeling is paramount in the minds of the listeners. Of course, both of these goals can be achieved in both approaches to the oral interpretation events, but it seems that it should be decided which is primary and concentrate efforts on that. The latter goal of emphasizing feeling and mood would also come close to acting or dramatic or humorous declamation. If reading is the unique feature of oral interpretation, then there should be contests or festivals where a student would read two or three different selections in two or three rounds. Or a student could be required to prepare himself to read a different selection at each festival or contest so that during the course of the school year he might read a dozen or more different selections. Granted, he would not have each selection as polished as if he were to read one during the twelve festivals, but he would have accomplished a lot more in learning about reading and developing his skill in picking up a printed page and assisting his listeners to understand and feel the selection.

In preparing for oral interpretation, the forensics coach should decide which is the primary purpose, to develop reading ability or to convey a feeling to an audience through a highly polished performance. Once he has chosen the primary goal then he should allow his students to participate in those events which foster this goal. It seems quite unethical for a coach to advocate that he is developing the reading ability of his students and yet at the same time he allows them to participate in contests or festivals which encourage the highly polished memorized version of the "oral reading" event.

Discussion

Description

The discussion event can best be described by contrasting the activity with debate. The purpose of discussion is to analyze and solve a problem and the participant enters a discussion to work with others toward a solution. In a debate the participants are advocating a solution which has been imposed on them or a solution which they have derived. The focal point of discussion is inquiry, while that of debate is advocacy. Discussion is a group activity and success is measured in terms of what the group accomplishes as a unit. In a debate more thought is given to attack and defense whereas the discussion process emphasizes suspended judgment and an atmosphere of openness. This does not mean that students are required to cooperate other members "under the table" by agreeing with everything that is entered into the discussion. The same rigors of analysis and tests of evidence that have been discussed earlier in this text apply to discussion. When students are urged to keep an open mind this does not mean that the mind should be open at both ends so that all kinds of ideas sail in and out regardless of their worth or consistency. Discussion is not another term for "pooled ignorance." Each member of the group must be well prepared on the topic if any worthwhile analysis is to take place.

A typical discussion format is designed to get the student to (1) define and locate the problem, (2) analyze the problem, (3) suggest hypotheses or solutions, (4) analyze the solutions, and (5) select and apply a solution. The depth of analysis that takes place in this process will depend largely on the student's knowledge of the problem area and his ability to reason. The discussant must engage in genuine research which includes systematic reading that is guided by analysis.

The criteria of judgment usually applied to the discussion contest include (1) analysis and reasoning, (2) information and evi-

dence, (3) language usage, (4) cooperative thinking, and (5)
delivery. For an excellent composite of the traditional and modern concepts of the discussion process see R. Victor Harnack and
Thorrel B. Fest, *Group Discussion: Theory and Technique*, Appleton-Century-Crofts.

Rationale

Perhaps of all the events in which a student might participate,
discussion is most appropriate in terms of realism. At one time or
another all students will take part in the group problem-solving
process. It is important that students know about the process of
reflective thinking and how to interact in the group setting. This
exercise in cooperative and critical thinking is essential to one
who lives in a democratic society.

Legislative Assembly

Description

The legislative assembly or student congress usually includes
these elements: (1) student research in an area of public policy;
(2) formulation of bills or resolutions proposing some modification of policy or law; (3) formation by caucus of coalitions or
political parties to advance proposed legislation; (4) committee or
conference sessions to consider alternative proposals; (5) a deliberative body with formally elected leaders and other function-
aries; (6) legislative debate featuring the interaction of opposing
political elements and culminating in the passage or defeat of
bills. These elements do not necessarily follow this sequence.
Commonly, plenty of time is allowed to intersperse political caucus and committee discussion between, as well as before, assembly sessions. Time is also provided for individuals or small
groups to revise old bills or write new ones.

Success in legislative assembly experiences is measured several
ways. Sometimes the event is not competitive in the usual sense,
with rewards coming in the form of peer ratings, election to office,
passage of bills advocated, and so forth. In other situations, critic
judges observe the students in action in all the various activities
such as group discussion and legislative debate, and then rate

their performance. Awards are given to those students receiving the highest composite rating of all judges.

Preparation for this event should be very similar to steps taken to prepare for extemp speaking and group discussion as discussed earlier. It will be useful if the students have some knowledge of parliamentary procedure. This can be done by the students themselves if they use one of the programmed texts now available such as Wesley Wiksell, *How To Conduct Meetings*, Harper & Row, or John W. Gray and Richard G. Rea, *Parliamentary Procedure*, Scott, Foresman and Company. It will also be useful if the students have a copy of Henry M. Robert, *Robert's Rules of Order, Revised*, Scott, Foresman and Company, to take to the assembly meetings.

Rationale

The rationale of legislative assembly experience as a part of a forensic program has already been discussed in detail in Chapter 2. Essentially, no claim is made that this is a unique experience in comparison to debate, extemp, and discussion. Rather, student congresses and the like seek to give students first, a taste of real-life deliberation and decision-making, and second, an opportunity to integrate human interactions with the content-oriented emphasis of other forensic activities. In this activity students are given a taste of typically political behavior with all its excitement and "wheeling-dealing" for better or worse. This is not likely to be found in any other forensic activity.

Radio-Television Speaking

Description

Radio speaking contests seek to reconstruct actual broadcast situations, with particular emphasis on news announcing, commercial reading, disk jockey programs, and even on the spot descriptions of important events. For the most part, these contests put emphasis on the ability of a student to prepare and deliver broadcast copy within a limited time, including the reading of difficult material on sight. Students may be given some time to read and mark their scripts, and in the case of newscasts, it is common to give students a five-minute portion of wire-service material which must be edited and prepared by the student into a coherent and interesting newscast. In other cases, students are given a newspaper and told to use facts in it to write a five-minute broadcast in their own style. On-the-spot broadcasting requires the student to pretend he is watching an event such as a fire and describe it.

In a quite different form, some contests require a student or group to produce and tape record a program of any one of a number of varieties including dramatic shows, and the tapes are sent to the judges for decision. This form allows much more variety and realism to the experience, but it is more difficult to control from a competitive point of view.

With the development of inexpensive video-tape recorders, more contests in television speaking are likely to emerge, although such contests have been in existence for more than ten years and already exist in both high school and college tournaments. As schools begin to purchase the video-tape recorders (which cost about $1000), it will be easy to prepare students for television contests. As this happens, it will be necessary to adjust contests to the realities of television broadcasting. It will not be appropriate to take the same formats now used in radio speaking and carry them into television. In the latter medium, emphasis is put on the capacity to integrate within one program a variety of messages and media, including the announcer, film strips, still photos, interviews, music, and so forth. The jobs of the producer and director require attention alongside the writer and speaker. This will probably increase the use of contests featuring the packaging of a program on tape in advance of the judging.

Probably the best way to prepare students for such programs is to send them into actual broadcast situations. It is quite common now for students in high school and college to work in commercial, educational, low-frequency FM, closed-circuit, or other type of broadcasting operation, both radio and television. If the school does not have such a facility, one probably should be started because not only will it be a help in preparing for contests but it will also serve a general educational function.

Rationale

The rationale for radio or television contests is obvious, in the sense that it duplicates an actual communication situation for which students should be prepared. In addition, such experience puts emphasis on communicating to a mass audience which is not found in any other forensic situation, and it focuses attention upon a medium of communication rather than a goal as is the case in debate and most other forensic activities.

TIPS FOR THE COACH

Since the purpose of this book is to assist the *coach* of forensics no extensive treatment of how to speak will be included. Students should be guided to the many fine texts on speaking and to a few books on participating in individual speaking events. This section will attempt to discuss some suggestions for the forensic coach. While some suggestions naturally apply to several events, an attempt will be made to categorize them according to speaking and reading events.

Extemporaneous Speaking

1. *Check the student out in the library.* This suggestion may sound absurd for capable students, but must still be emphasized. The extemp speaker will need to make considerable use of the library facilities and should not be inhibited by lack of knowledge. Even when coaching the best student it is highly worthwhile to have some systematic way of assuring library understanding at the beginning of the forensic year. Often librarians are willing to conduct tours for your speakers, but these are not usually applicable to the needs of the students unless the librarian is given some information about the kinds of materials the student speakers will need.

2. *Start your extemp speaker reading early and regularly.* At the beginning of the school year your extemp speaker should begin to read the various news magazines such as *Time, News-*

week, and *U.S. News and World Report.* In fact, it would be wise for the student to have his own subscription if he can afford one. Then he can mark or cut the articles in any way which appears useful. However, if a student limits his reading to these three magazines he will not be prepared for extemp speaking. He should also regularly read such publications as *Business Week, Atlantic Monthly, Harpers, The Progressive, Saturday Review, Current History, Congressional Digest, The Reporter, Vital Speeches, New York Times,* and *The Wall Street Journal.* As he reads these various publications, he should make use of some filing system, preferably one that he can utilize with maximum efficiency. While he reads, it would also be wise to suggest that he make notes about those articles of possible interest. With notes for a guide and a good filing system for quick reference, the extemp speaker should be able to cope with the information retrieval part of his assignment. Whether the notes can be used in the actual contest will depend on the rules of that contest.

3. *Seek the assistance of teachers in current event areas.* Normally a forensic coach should assume that he is not an expert in all areas of current events. He should consult with teachers in economics, history, problems of democracy, civics, political science, and similar fields to assist him and his students in securing sound information and ideas about extemp topics. This involvement of the teachers in other disciplines has a secondary advantage of arousing their interest and support of the forensic program.

4. *Help the extemp speakers to see the complexities and subtleties involved with most good extemp topics.* Too often students are prone to present overly simplified and shallow material. The suggestion in No. 3 is one way to avoid oversimplification. Another way is to involve students in small group discussions about topics or issues where *inquiry* is "king." This discussion process is one of the most overlooked aspects of preparation for extemp speaking. Too often students begin with assertive speechmaking without adequate perspective. They fail to see the shades of grey. Not only is discussion important at the beginning of the extemp training period, but it is something well worth continuing through the year.

5. *Help your extemp speaker understand purpose and structure.*
Many beginning speakers will not fully realize that speaking
should be purposive. They are essentially speaker-centered or
subject-centered and concerned about the delivery or appearance
of themselves or the specific content of the speech. They need to
be taught to think in terms of the listeners, to become audience-
centered. The purpose can be expressed in several ways. Some
prefer to express the specific purpose in terms of the specific response desired from the listeners. Others think of the concept in
similar terms—residual message, that which is to be left with the
listeners. Whichever way is selected it is necessary to impress
upon the speaker that the audience is of vital concern and that
the purpose of the speech should be determined *before* the speech
is given, and indeed before the speaker prepares himself to speak.

Once the purpose is clearly in mind the speaker can then begin
to provide an organizational frame for the speech. Gerald Phillips
is proposing in a forthcoming college speech text that this step be
given a rather unique treatment.[2] He suggests that before the
student deals with specific bits of information he literally draw a
suitable structure, a verbal PERT diagram. One of the several
patterns he suggests is the distributive pattern which is drawn in
Figure 1. This popular pattern shows Set A being divided into

Set A

Subset B	Subset C
Subset D	Subset E

Figure 1. Distributive Structure

four parts or subsets, B, C, D, and E. Each of the subsets should
be of approximate importance and should be mutually exclusive.

---

[2] Dr. Phillips is presenting this idea in a forthcoming speech-text which he
is co-authoring with Elwood Murray.

When placed together they should give a rather complete picture of the whole set. There is no brief for four subsets; it could be more or fewer. There are, of course, a number of other possible structures for use in organizing speech materials. The chief value in this method of structuring is that the student must do some critical thinking of materials and relationships before he actually speaks. If an extemp speaker cannot diagram a structure he almost assuredly cannot present the materials in a pattern which is meaningful to listeners. This ability to structure is probably the most critical in speech preparation.

6. *Listen to him speak and offer constructive help.* The extemp speaker needs to get as much practice as he possibly can. He should not be permitted to speak before he has adequately prepared himself to speak, but when he is ready, *listen.* A student will not learn much from speaking to a blank wall or to a mirror; he needs a real live audience. It is wise to listen for the first time or two and offer positive reinforcement and encouragement. After this initial period, the coach should begin to offer some constructive suggestions for improvement. These comments should probably be aimed at the content, the idea, or the structure rather than the delivery or choice of words. Delivery can be dealt with later; don't focus on it at this point. When practicing, make use of audio or video tape recorders. These can be tremendously valuable to the student in gaining a perspective more receptive to criticism.

7. *Begin with thoroughly prepared speeches.* There is a tendency when coaching extemp speaking to get the speaker under "game" conditions which includes short preparation time. It seems far more wise to begin the student in a thoroughly prepared extemporaneous speaking situation. Perhaps it will take a week or two to adequately prepare his first speech; perhaps the same time for the next two or three speeches. Eventually he should move to the shorter preparation times, but only after he experiences some opportunity for thorough preparation. How can he learn and have a full appreciation for solid speech preparation unless he goes through extensive training? Likewise in the first few speech attempts there should be no strict time limits. This can be emphasized in the later attempts. It is extremely important

not to emphasize the less important things in the early speaking experiences.

8. *Secure speaking engagements before responsible audiences.* One of the finest ways to sharpen the skills of an extemp speaker is to present him with a realistic audience of mature, responsible persons. This gives him an opportunity to get a response, to adapt to their specific needs, background, and so forth. This still should be a thoroughly prepared speech. The primary lesson to be learned here is how to cope with a real, dynamic audience.

9. *Secure the rules of the contest and the judging criteria.* There is no excuse for the coach not assuming his responsibility for securing the specific rules and regulations for the extemp contest. Rules do differ, and the student takes the brunt of the coach's omissions. It would be a shame for the student to do poorly or to be disqualified because the coach did not inform him correctly.

The judging criteria are also important to secure well in advance of the contest. If the criteria are not acceptable to the coach, then he *should not send the student to participate*. If the criteria agree with the teacher's educational philosophy and goals, then he should make sure his student understands them fully. In fact, if possible the coach should make use of them in practice sessions.

10. *Teach the speaker contest decorum.* This is, of course, not the most important thing to teach the student, but it is essential. While no attempt is made here to exhaust the subject, the following suggestions may be useful for students: (a) always appear on time; (b) don't quibble about topics—take what you draw; (c) don't interfere with others who are preparing; (d) show the speech topic to the judges; (e) place your name or number and perhaps the topic on the blackboard (if one is available); (f) when you have finished speaking sit and listen to the other speakers; (g) request, but do not demand, criticism if the contest allows; (h) never badger a judge; (i) if you use visuals, including the blackboard, remove or erase them before the next speaker begins.

Original Oratory

Some of the previous suggestions for extemporaneous speaking are also applicable to the original oratory speaker. Obviously, any speaker should have an acquaintance with the library. He should also be aware of the rules of the contest although they are not so varied in this particular event. He should also be familiar with and follow the rules of decorum in contest speaking. In addition, the following suggestions are made with a special reference to original oratory.

1. *Original oratory should be original.* Many contests in original oratory should have been won by the coach rather than the student because the coach wrote the oration. The purpose of this event is to help the student learn something about oral composition. He learns best by doing it himself, not when the coach "assists" him, nor when he practices "wholesale borrowing" from other sources.

2. *Encourage the student to select a suitable and worthwhile topic and purpose.* Almost every judging ballot for this event has a category which requests an evaluation on the suitability of the subject. This is a subjective matter, one which cannot be spelled out in clear, concise terms. Balcer and Seabury state that "an appropriate topic is one which will likely challenge the orator and his audience. It reflects good taste and lends itself to a significant and worthy purpose. It can be narrowed so as to be treated adequately in the ten minutes which are usually allotted to each speaker. It is one which the orator can likely keep fresh, new, and up to date."[3] The student should select a topic which has great appeal to him, one in which he has a sincere interest and adequate background. It should be timely and one which will be interesting to an audience. Some of the more recent orations have dealt with such topics as foreign policy, racial problems, education, penal codes, and capital punishment.

Although mentioned in the previous section, the purpose is again very important. Beyond the general purpose choices such as to inform, to persuade, etc., the speaker must choose a specific

---

[3] Charles L. Balcer and Hugh F. Seabury, *Teaching Speech in Today's Secondary Schools* (New York: Holt, Rinehart and Winston, Inc., 1965) 355.

response he desires from his listeners. The oration, which is developed over an extended period of time and given to a number of different audiences, must appeal to a broader and more general audience. The purpose should be designed accordingly.

3. *Help the student relate the purpose to the structure.* With the oration the student has much more time to develop a structure. He perhaps will attempt to use several structures before finally choosing one. For more on structuring see the tips for the extemporaneous speaking event.

4. *Teach the student the difference between spoken and written style.* An important distinction must be learned by the student speaker if his oration is going to be more than just an essay. Many attempts by student orators are more to impress than to communicate (although those orations which communicate can also be impressive). Carroll C. Arnold has offered three attributes of an oral composition in contrast to written composition.

> 1. The prose of a composition for the ear will exhibit an especially energetic struggle for control over the attention of a *particular* set of listeners located in a *particular* set place and time, under a *particular* set of circumstances.
>
> 2. The prose and the actual presentation of an oral composition will contain visible signs of patient accommodation to the reflecting-savoring schedule a particular set of listeners will need to maintain if they are fully to understand what is being said to them.
>
> 3. A well-devised oral composition will be self-evidently true to what the actual speaker can believably express when face to face with the particular audience the speech was planned for. It will be a revelation of thought through language which will remain credible when the *person* of the speaker is finally mingled with the planned thought and language.[4]

The student also needs to know that with an oration the listeners cannot stop and repeat it as they might do with a printed page. The language needs to be instantly intelligible with built-in redundancy as an aid to the listener.

---

[4] Given in a speech to the Summer Speech Institute (August 1966) sponsored by a ESEA Title III grant and conducted by members of the Pennsylvania State University Department of Speech.

5. *Practice the delivery.* Since the oration is planned and written out it is easier to coordinate good delivery with the content. Unlike extemporaneous speaking (where the speaker's subject is not known much in advance) the oration allows ample time for practice. The coach can help here somewhat as one would with an oral interpreter. The speech should be given from memory. Most authorities agree that the speech should sound conversational rather than stuffy, but it is not exactly easy to deliver a speech from memory a number of times before it begins to sound mechanical and not at all conversational. It may be well to have the speakers memorize the basic structure, most of the supporting ideas, but not actual words and sentences. Another way of eliminating this problem is constantly to revise and update the oration. The student should not be afraid to deviate from the original. The judges in the better contests do not keep a copy of the manuscript before them as they listen in order to determine how far one deviates from the text.

Oral Interpretation

While some of the previous suggestions for extemporaneous speaking and original oratory may apply to the oral interpretation events, most will not. The following suggestions are offered to the coach of these events so that he might better prepare his interpreters. A more thorough discussion of oral interpretation for the student can be found in several books on the subject. See the bibliography at the end of the chapter for specific references.

1. *Clarify the oral interpretation event to the student.* An earlier discussion in this chapter stated that there is some confusion and difference of opinion on the oral interpretation events. This can be greatly confusing to the coach; even more to the student. The student should understand that an interpretation event is not an *acting* event but an opportunity to communicate an idea and a mood to listeners. Woolbert and Nelson define interpretation as "an attempt to re-create for an audience, as nearly as possible, real experience as revealed by the author."[5]

---

[5] Charles H. Woolbert and Severina Nelson. *The Art of Interpretative Speech* (New York: Appleton-Century-Crofts, Inc., 1956), 4.

Savage stated that "interpretation should be no different from any other form of oral communication in that the speaker is primarily interested in getting a response from his audience."[6] She goes on to say that "If I . . . can say that I have watched a *performance,* then I have not seen and heard an effective interpreter. He has been more interested in 'acting,' in himself, than in transmitting ideas and feelings to his audience with the prime intent of getting a response from them."[7] A reader reads thoughts and feelings, not words.

2. *Request that your student get some work in literature appreciation.* Most high-school and college students take a course in literature at some time during their schooling. This background is imperative in helping the student analyze and appreciate good literature. If by chance your student reader has no background in literature, request that he take a course or supplementary work.

3. *Help the student choose suitable selections.* The selection of suitable passage for reading is very important in contest or festival work. It is also quite a learning experience for the student (and sometimes for the coach). Usually most judging criteria state that the selection must be suitable and have literary merit. To be suitable the passage should fit the reader and the occasion. The coach should be quite permissive in the initial stages of the selection of literature to be read. It is important to begin with material the student *enjoys* reading and avoid forcing the student to read something he cannot enjoy simply because it is "good" literature. As the student gradually discovers that poorly written material is difficult to communicate he will tend to avoid this in favor of more worthwhile literature. By festival time he should be able to determine what worthwhile literature is and have an appreciation for it. The coach probably has the most difficulty with selections for male students than for female students. Fran Jacobs was prompted to develop a suggested list of prose and poetry selections especially designed for the male reader. This appears at the end of the chapter.

---

[6] Mary Ellen Savage. "Judging Oral Interpretation" *Pennsylvania High School Speech League Newsletter,* I, No. 3, December 1961, 507.
[7] *Ibid.*

Past practice has strongly implied that only the old masters had literary merit. There is a new, fresh approach today which suggests that the contemporary works may also have a great deal of literary value. Much of the modern literature is applicable to the teenager.

4. *The reader should read a number of selections.* The oral reader who works on one or two selections for a year is being deprived of a valuable educational experience. His understanding of selecting, cutting, developing the mood, and communicating are enhanced by a number of varied selections. For the first part of the year a coach would be wise to ask the reader to prepare at least one selection each week. Later in the year he may concentrate more time on a favorite selection; one which may be used for the state festival or national contest. In selecting the variety of material, care should be given to include different periods of prose and poetry and different authors in each period. Hopefully, in addition to learning something about interpreting the material, the reader should have a much better background and appreciation for literature.

5. *Characters in a selection must emerge clearly.* The number of characters in a reading may vary, but usually in a prose selection there are several. Since there is no acting on the part of the reader, nor any costume changes, the voice must play an important role in distinguishing among characters. The listener must have no doubt about the character who is talking or who is the center of attention. Make sure the reader utilizes eye placement, voice quality, bodily poses, gestures, pauses and other techniques of projecting characterizations which can be mastered under your careful guidance.

6. *An introduction is essential.* Most readings seem incomplete without the introduction. In the case of the reading which is a cutting from a much longer passage, the introduction helps the reader get into the mood by clarifying. With a group of readings the introduction helps to tie them together. Even with a fairly short, standard selection the introduction can do quite a bit to motivate and guide the listener. Without an introduction the opening is often abrupt.

7. *Selections should have unity.* When the reader wishes to

read several rather short selections rather than one long one, there should be some unity to the selections. The two most popular ways of grouping selections are the *thematic* approach, and the *author* approach. Sometimes the reader would like to give a flavor of an author. This could indicate his breadth, or narrowness; it could indicate chronological development; or point up a tendency toward a particular subject matter.

The thematic approach gives much latitude to the imagination. Students sometimes enjoy grouping selections around the sports theme, or the outdoors. Other themes such as love, music, famous persons, special days, the sea, death, and education are often used. The student should select a theme such as love and then group several readings on love.

8. *Arrange for practice before real audiences.* In addition to the very valuable practice sessions with the coach, the reader needs to be placed in real audience situations where he can get the feel for audience reactions. Story reading to children can be a frank but rewarding experience. Reading before classmates, women's clubs, and school assemblies provides for varied experience. When possible the coach should accompany the student and give valuable reactions to him which the audience may not be able to provide.

9. *Secure the rules and judging criteria well in advance.* In the area of oral interpretation it is impossible to predict what the rules are likely to be. Some festivals insist on *reading;* some do not allow reading but insist on *memorization.* In prose reading some contests do not permit the reading of an oration or a cutting from a play. Other reading contests insist on dramatic reading. Most contests expect well prepared selections of the student's choosing; some require an impromptu reading; and some have both prepared and impromptu. For the sake of the student and for the instructor's own edification, he should get the rules and judging criteria well in advance of the contest or festival.

10. *Small points may mean a lot.* While not nearly as important as the previously mentioned items, the polish is not complete until some attention is given to appearance. This is not an attempt to give the latest styles in dress, but merely to suggest

that the dress of the reader should not detract from the selection. A girl in a bright red dress with long, dangling beads cannot help but detract from her selection. No "costumes" are necessary, just good taste.

When reading from a manuscript, the reader should obtain a dark-colored, plain, hardback book of medium size. This could be a book on any subject, but preferably one which is no longer usable for content. The manuscript of the reading selection should be pasted on the pages of the book so as to give the appearance that the reader is reading from the book. This technique enables the reader to have the manuscript in much larger type than that provided by the book. Care should be given to avoid any book with detectable print on the outside front and back. When entering a contest or festival, polish is essential.

READINGS FOR ORAL INTERPRETATION

PROSE

My Watch	Mark Twain
The October Game	Ray Bradbury
In Which Eeyore Loses a Tail and Pooh Finds One	A. A. Milne
The Night the Ghost Got In	James Thurber
Eighty Yard Run	Irwin Shaw
The Cask of Amontillado	Edgar Allan Poe
The Tell-Tale Heart	Edgar Allan Poe
The Circus	Mark Twain
The Bet	Anton Chekhov
The Glorious Whitewasher	Mark Twain
The Secret Life of Walter Mitty	James Thurber
The Candy Pull	Mark Twain
These Smith Kids	M. C. Self
The White Rabbit Caper	James Thurber
The Snow Goose	Paul Gallico
The Black Cat	Edgar Allan Poe
The Brothers Karamazov	Fyodor Dostoevski
A Nice Old Fashioned Romance	William Saroyan
The End of Something	Ernest Hemingway
The First Day of School	William Saroyan
The King of the Cats	Stephen Vincent Benet
War and Peace	Leo Tolstoi
Adam's Diary	Mark Twain
The Lottery	Shirley Jackson
The Gay Old Dog	Edna Ferber
The Yellow Bird	Tennessee Williams
Haircut	Ring Lardner
The Devil and Daniel Webster	Stephen Vincent Benet
Call of the Wild	Jack London
Riki-Tiki-Tavi	Rudyard Kipling

POETRY

Captain Stratton's Fancy	John Masefield
The Creation	James Weldon Johnson
A Vagabond Song	Bliss Carman
The Bells	Edgar Allan Poe
Larrie O'Dell	William W. Fink
Messmates	Henry Newboldt
Sea Fever	John Masefield
The Charge of the Light Brigade	Alfred Lord Tennyson
Ships	Margaret Widdemer
Medals and Holes	Lew Sarett
Killers	Carl Sandburg
Ballad of the Goodly Fere	Ezra Pound
Birches	Robert Frost
The Deacon's Masterpiece	Oliver Wendell Holmes
Gunga Din	Rudyard Kipling
Tommy	Rudyard Kipling
The Congo	Vachel Lindsay
General William Booth Enters into Heaven	Vachel Lindsay
The Shooting of Dan McGrew	Robert W. Service
The Cremation of Sam McGee	Robert W. Service
The Hollow Men	T. S. Eliot
Invictus	William Ernest Henley
Lincoln, the Man of the People	Edwin Markham
Annabel Lee	Edgar Allan Poe
Chicago	Carl Sandburg
The Lay of the Last Minstrel	Sir Walter Scott
O Captain! My Captain!	Walt Whitman
Beat! Beat! Drums!	Walt Whitman
Ozymandias	Percy Bysshe Shelley
Out, Out-	Robert Frost
Auto Wreck	Karl Shapiro
To a Mouse	Robert Burns
The Wreck of the Hesperus	Henry Wadsworth Longfellow
Abraham Lincoln Walks at Midnight	Vachel Lindsay
The Yarn of the Nancy Bell	W. S. Gilbert
The Highwayman	Alfred Noyes

SUGGESTED READINGS

Andrews, James. "The American Legion Oratorical Contest: Communication or Exhibition?" *Today's Speech,* VIII, No. 2 (April 1960), 27–29.

Balcer, Charles L., and Hugh F. Seabury. *Teaching Speech in Today's Secondary Schools.* New York: Holt, Rinehart & Winston, 1965.

Buys, William E., and others. *Contest Speaking Manual.* Lincolnwood: National Textbook Corporation, 1964.

Camp. Leon R. "Extemp Speaking," *Forensic,* Series 50, No. 1 (October 1964).

Dedmon, Donald N. "The Extemporaneous Method and Speech Contests." *Central States Speech Journal,* XV, No. 4 (November 1964), 279–84.

Gehring, Mary Louise. "The High School Oration: Fundamentals," *Speech Teacher,* II, No. 2 (March 1953), 101–104.

Hargis, Donald E. "Interpretation as Oral Communication," *Central States Speech Journal,* XI, No. 3 (Spring 1960), 168–73.

Kruger, Arthur N. "The Extemporaneous Speaking Contest," *Speech Teacher,* V, No. 2 (September 1956), 214–22.

Lee, Charlotte I. *Oral Interpretation.* New York: Houghton Mifflin Company, 1965.

McCrery, Lester Lyle. "Educational Aims and Dilemmas of the Extempore Speech Contest," *Western Speech Journal,* XVI, No. 4, 233–38.

Walter, Otis M. *Speaking to Inform and Persuade.* New York: The Macmillan Company, 1966.

Woolbert, Charles H., and Severina E. Nelson. *The Art of Interpretative Speech.* New York: F. S. Crofts & Co., 1945.

CHAPTER 10

Judging Forensic Events

Don F. Faules

A forensics coach told this writer that the only problem that his students had was facing inadequate judges. He complained that most judges were just not capable of judging his students. This coach did not actually want a judgment—he wanted someone to verify the greatness of his students and himself. Perhaps such attitudes could be alleviated by simply removing the judging aspect from forensic activity. However, the removal of judgment would thwart the very purpose of the activity. How does one learn unless he is judged? How does one learn about the decision-making process unless he views the way in which this process operates?

The Purpose of the Judgment

The nondecision debate experiment during the 1920's demonstrated that students did not take the same interest in the activity when a decision was not given. If forensic activities are to be realistic, the fact that we live in a competitive society cannot be ignored. People do make decisions about us, there are winners and losers, and competition lies at the base of the free enterprise system.

Students want to know where they stand in relation to others. They want to know more than who won and who lost. Students who want to learn also have a desire to know the reason for the outcome, because students can only learn and improve by reliable and complete feedback. The forensic activity is in essence a test for the student. Tests serve the function of discriminating between students and instructing students. The stimulus of discrimination ought to motivate a student toward excellence, but the value of the activity should reside in its ability to instruct. If learning does not take place, there is question about retaining the activity in the school system. In order to insure proper instruction there is a need for competent judges and judging systems.

Who Should Judge?

If the primary purpose of the activity is instruction, then those who can instruct should judge. However, there has always been a question about what was being taught and how it should be taught. If we are teaching students to speak to everyday audiences, why not let the layman judge or, better yet, why not let the audience judge? It is likely that the criteria used by a layman judge differs from that of an expert-critic judge. There are some who contend that forensic speaking is a specialized activity and most likely the debater will be facing a specialized audience after he completes his education. Others assert that we may be specializing our students right out of reality. At the present time there is no research evidence that indicates that students cannot make an adjustment to an audience situation. Nevertheless there is constant pressure to evaluate the activity and obtain real audiences.

Those who favor the expert-critic system feel that the expert-critic is one who has had forensic speaking experience, experience as a coach of forensics, and experience as a judge. This type of judge is one who judges on technique and does not make a decision on the basis of personal feelings about the question being debated or the selection of material being presented. He asks himself who did the better debating, speaking, or reading.

It is this writer's position that it is not realistic to expect or want the same type of judging for all forensic activity. The expert-critic had to start judging sometime. If he had been ruled out because of lack of judging experience, it is likely that there would be no expert-critics. Students should be made aware of the differences that may exist between audiences, the layman judges, and the expert-critic. This can be arranged by varied tournament structure and audience activity. It is not enough for the layman judge or the audience to make the right decision. The decision must be made for the right reasons and students must know what they can do to improve their skill. If specialized instruction is desired, there must be reliance on the specialized judge. Specialized judges cannot be obtained for every event without paying a considerable sum of money or curtailing the size of programs. It seems more sensible to turn to the specialized tournament. Many tournament directors make an effort to select quality teams and quality judges. Debaters and coaches must earn the right to attend such tournaments. Some regional tournaments require certain standards for teams and judges. The teams must have competed in a number of quality tournaments and the coach must have judged the current debate resolution in a number of tournaments. Although this system cannot be used in all cases, it must be recognized that not all students are ready for specialized instruction. Tournament structure itself allows for instruction by virtue of the number of rounds in which a student can participate. Elimination rounds are usually judged by a panel of expert-critics which allows for more instruction. The better tournaments reflect considerable competency and consistency on the part of the judges. (See report of the Giffin study in Chapter 12.)

All tournaments cannot be specialized and the director must face the problem of obtaining judges. Many high schools utilize the faculty and students of nearby colleges. When this is not possible, the director must turn to townspeople who are interested and who may have the time. There has been some attempt to instruct judges. This is usually done in one of two ways. Ballots have printed instructions that inform the judges about the activity and how they should judge. Some directors have held instruction meetings for the judges prior to the tournament. Both of these methods present certain problems. How can one instruct a judge in five or ten minutes? For example, the following statement appears on a ballot. "The judges shall vote 'Affirmative' or 'Negative' on the merits of the debate, irrespective of the merits of the question." If someone has not had previous experience with the terminology, this statement calls for some extensive interpretation. Instructions on ballots are best suited for explaining how to fill out the ballot because most instruction beyond this is purely accidental. If such instructions must be given, there should be time to explain them in as much detail as possible. Some schools have held judging clinics for their prospective judges before the tournament started. Judges who can be paid a reasonable fee are normally willing to give up their time for this purpose. Another alternative for obtaining judges is to find individuals who are willing to attend a judging clinic at a nearby university. University speech departments are pleased to carry out such projects. In this way a supply of judges can be created.

The desire to establish judging standards is an admirable one. However, this does not mean that judges can be "standardized." Different judges give different decisions for good reasons because not all judges attach the same importance to each criterion of measurement.

JUDGING DEBATE

Debate is the most complex of the forensic events and makes the greatest demands upon the judge. It is likely that the superior judge of debate will have had experience judging debate, coaching debate, and will have participated in the activity. In addition he will have specialized knowledge of argumentation theory and knowledge of the topic being debated.

What Is Being Judged

Are students judged on their ability to persuade, on the soundness of the arguments that they present, or on their debating skill? We judge students on all of these, because they are indeed difficult to separate. A student persuades us that his arguments are sound and therefore we conclude that he has debating skill. Logic cannot speak for itself and logical and emotional appeals cannot be divided into neat packages. One man's emotion is another man's logic. The general criteria that are used to determine if the speaker has hit his mark are really tools that he may employ to achieve effectiveness. They are analysis, reasoning, evidence, organization, refutation, and delivery. These criteria are not necessarily mutually exclusive, but are intended to give a judge some guidelines to follow in arriving at his decision. This list does not include all the factors that may influence a decision. There are other elements that may influence these criteria. For example, if a student behaves in such a way as to destroy his credibility, the judge may doubt the student's ability and act accordingly.

It is generally agreed that the emphasis in debating is on reasoned discourse and the decision is awarded to the team that did the better debating. Although many student debaters are not exceptional public speakers, it is well to remember that exceptional debaters are superior thinkers and speakers. The goal of the student should be to achieve both.

The Technique of Judging

There is no substitute for a thorough knowledge of argumentation. The following suggestions are offered as reminders of principal considerations. Each judge ought to have a grasp of these fundamentals and a knowledge of the criteria of measurement is necessary. The following questions illustrate the basic definition of the criteria.

(1) *Analysis:* Has the debater found the issues that are critical? Do these issues have the potency to decide whether one accepts or rejects the resolution? Are arguments drawn in such a way as to support these issues and have the most potent arguments been used? Does the student know what he must do to destroy a case or establish one? Has the debater constructed a well-reasoned case with strong support? (See Chapter 5 on Analysis.)

(2) *Reasoning:* Does the debater use cogent thinking? How capable is he of drawing logical inferences from existing data? Does he rely on illustrative material rather than on material that proves? Does he show the capacity to reason for himself?

(3) *Evidence:* What is the quality of the evidence? Is there too much reliance on opinion and not enough on fact? Has the debater looked at the evidence and drawn some inferences of his

own, or has he simply repeated the thoughts of others? Is there an understanding of the tests of evidence? Is the evidence relevant and timely? Is the quantity and quality of evidence sufficient to support the conclusions drawn from the evidence? Is the evidence cumulative and does the evidence come from credible sources? Does the evidence reflect thorough research and preparation? Does the evidence used reflect a student's capacity to select the most potent evidence?

(4) *Refutation:* Does the debater recognize the crucial areas of agreement and disagreement? How effective is the debater in using reasoning and evidence to destroy or weaken an opponent's argument? Can the student demonstrate that what he has used is indeed refutation? In other words, can he show what effect his attack has had or why he has reinforced his own position? Does the student know what he must do to destroy a case or establish one? Does the student exhibit the ability to examine the reasoning of a case as well as the specifics that are used to support it? Is there direct clash on the issues and arguments presented?

(5) *Organization:* Is the student capable of organizing arguments in a cogent manner? Is the organization logical and clear? Are the arguments mutually exclusive? Has the case been organized for maximum effect? Does clear organization prevail throughout the debate? Are internal summaries used to clarify the issues and arguments? Is the refutation systematic and clear?

(6) *Delivery:* Does the delivery enhance the argumentation? Is it intelligible, interesting, and persuasive? Does the debater rely on the materials to do his debating for him? Does the delivery of the material do something for it? Are good public speaking techniques utilized? Does the debater utilize language skills to make the most persuasive argument possible?

Before the judge can make a decision, he must know what was said. It is unlikely that a judge can remember what was said even with the help of two debate teams which are trying to be accurate. This is one of the primary reasons why judges should take notes during a debate. An adequate set of notes also assures the debaters that they have had a hearing. In addition, such notes can be used for instructional purposes. The *case summary* method of taking notes simply outlines the debate from beginning to end. The essence of each argument and its support is placed in outline form during each speech. Some judges use colored pencils or symbol systems to indicate the development of clash between the teams. The *issue summary* method records the major issues of the debate and follows them through each speech. It is impossible to record all that is said and each judge develops his own system of shorthand. It is important to record major issues and the arguments that are used to support those issues. One cannot generally copy all of the data that is used to support each argument, however knowledge of the topic will help the judge to note major sources of information. A complete set of notes helps the judge determine the outcome of the debate. It is at once apparent that judging is a skill that requires concentration.

It is the obligation of the debaters to decide what issues and arguments are significant. This is generally determined in the rebuttal period. The judge is not obligated to defend or promote any debater's argument. Some students say a great deal with the hope that a judge will select the arguments that are most appealing. The judge gives his decision on the basis of what was debated. He may criticize a team for what he believes to be poor analysis, but unless the opposing team demonstrates this it should not determine the decision. In other words, the judge should not debate the debaters. If the judge is competent it is likely that he will see weaknesses that the debaters do not see. He should not make a decision on the basis of how the debate should have gone. If the judge is objective, he will simply ask the question, "What happened?" This does not mean that he will not criticize the teams for what they did not do. He can register his views on the ballot without making an improper decision. There has probably been more than one occasion on which a debater accidentally said a phrase that pleased the bias of a judge. It is not enough for a debater to say "your need is not inherent," "you have not presented a prima facie case," "your causal relationships are not valid," or "your plan does not answer the need." The debater is obligated to explain his conclusions and their importance. The judge should not interpret for the debaters and debaters should not rely on magic phrases.

The decision should be made at the conclusion of the debate. There may be times when a debate is overwhelmingly one-sided. Nevertheless, it is discourteous to mark and seal the ballot before *all* the arguments and evidence is in. In addition, a one-sided debate can change in the last two or three rebuttals. Judges should give a full and *complete* hearing to students who have worked hard to take part in a demanding activity. The judge's behavior has considerable influence on a student's future participation.

What is the basis for a decision? The answer to this question may be largely dependent upon the type of case presented.

(1) *The Stock-Issues Case:* The affirmative is obligated to *win* all the issues. Is there a need for a change from the status quo? Is the proposed plan capable of meeting that need? Would the proposed plan be beneficial? If the affirmative loses any one of these issues they will lose the decision. This does not mean that the affirmative cannot lose a contention and still win. A contention is an argument that is used to support an issue. A team may use two contentions to support one of the issues. Either contention may be strong enough to support that issue.

(2) *The Advantages-Disadvantages Case:* The affirmative is obligated to demonstrate that the advantages of adopting a new policy are indeed advantages and worth the effort of change.

(3) *The Disjunctive Case:* The affirmative must demonstrate that their two contentions are mutually exclusive and that if either contention stands, the new policy should be adopted.

(4) *The Chain-of-Reasoning Case:* The affirmative must establish and defend every contention. If one part of the "chain" is destroyed, the rest is destroyed. If a syllogism is employed, each part of that syllogism must be valid.

(5) *Method-of-Residues Case:* This type of case first shows the need for a change and then proves that solutions other than the proposed policy will fail. The advantages and practicability of the proposal are also established. This is simply a variation of the stock-issues case and carries the same requirements.

(6) *The Counter-Plan:* When the negative agrees with the need presented by the affirmative and proposes a plan of its own, the major question is which plan will best meet the need? The plan proposed by the negative should not be a variation of the same principle advocated by the debate resolution. The plan should be different than the existing system.

The foregoing case structure gives the judge some broad criteria for a decision. Is it possible to have teams evenly balanced on fundamental considerations? Yes, it is possible, and when that happens the judge will turn to more specific criteria. The judge may move from issues to arguments to specific pieces of evidence and then to the criteria on the ballot and decide which team did the better job with the criteria that he deems most important. Which of these criteria are most important? It is popular to favor reasoned discourse, but not all judges agree on what that is. Again, ballots may be standardized, but this does not mean that judges can be standardized. The meaning is not in the criteria, it is in the judge. (See Chapter 12 for ranking of criteria.) It would be quite difficult to assign weights to the criteria because of their lack of standardized interpretation. Agreement is much more likely to occur between judges on the overall effectiveness of a performance than on the individual criteria. The criteria on a ballot serves as a guideline for the judge and as an instructional aid for the student. Generally speaking, judges utilize broad criteria to arrive at their decisions, i.e., who won the real issues? After a judge has determined the general effectiveness of a team, he proceeds to evaluate on specific criteria. It is highly unlikely that a judge will score each individual criterion and then add them up to see who won. The type of debate may also decide which team did the better job of debating. For example in a cross-examination debate the decision may eventually be decided on the basis of which team displayed the better techniques of cross-examination.

For maximum educational value the student should receive oral and written critiques. This is not possible in all situations because of the time element. Therefore it is advisable to have a ballot that provides as much feedback as possible. A good ballot provides quality ratings, rank order of the speakers, a workable and clear set of criteria, space for written comments, a scale that notes the overall quality of the teams, and space to note the decision and the major reason for the decision. Both teams should receive a copy of all comments. It should be kept in mind that no ballot can list all the possible criteria that might be used for a judgment. No ballot contains enough space to make all the comments that might be made about a debate. The judge must be selective and record only the major items. The refinement of the comments will depend upon the refinement of the teams. The following items should be kept in mind when filling out the ballot:

(1) Comments on the ballot should be correlated with the numerical or checking system. For example, if a debater is rated low on the criterion of evidence he wants to know why. The check will tell him little. Did he use too much evidence, too little, evidence that was not relevant, or weak evidence? If one of the criteria was responsible for the outcome of the debate, the comments ought to reflect this. If a team is rated superior on certain criteria, related comments can provide instruction for both teams.

(2) The rating system is designed to indicate to a student where he stands in relationship to superior debaters. It does not necessarily refer to the quality of competition at a given tournament.

(3) The ranking system forces the judge to discriminate between the debaters. They may be tied on quality ratings. The decision of rank can determine the outcome of a tournament and therefore ought to be done carefully.

(4) The major reason for the decision ought to be presented in a clear legible statement.

(5) It takes skill to follow a debate and make comments on a ballot at the same time. It is important that these comments be legible. It is much better to print a few crucial comments than to scrawl many that cannot be read. Judges should keep in mind that someone will have to read the carbon copy. The time factor is important when one considers that the student will not receive the ballot until the conclusion of the tournament. The comments may not make sense to him unless this is kept in mind.

In most cases the judge has an opportunity to make oral comments after the debate. He is usually instructed not to announce his decision. It is wise to make the decision and seal the ballot before these comments are made. In most cases instruction and suggestions can be given to both teams. Many times it is difficult to write as much as one would like about a particular argument or technique. In this case some time for discussion is quite valuable. It is better not to make any comment at all than to discuss trivial matters that play no part in a decision. An oral critique should be used to instruct students toward improvement.

Criticism is not fault-finding. Its purpose is to indicate to a student why one speaker is better than another and why one technique is more productive than another. The nature of the criticism will determine the progress of the student and the educational worth of debate activity. The following general considerations should be kept in mind:

(1) It is possible to give too much criticism. It is likely that the beginning student will make an abundance of errors. Rather than comment on all of these errors, it will profit a student more to know where he must start. What major skills must be mastered first? If a critique is too extensive the student may conclude that he is a failure and has no place in the activity. The fault may lie with the judge and not the student.

(2) Criticism includes positive statements. Most students need encouragement and need to know just what their strong points are. A critique that is filled with negative comments may not motivate at all. In fact, it may tend to have detrimental effects. Positive reinforcement is necessary and the results of positive reinforcement are more predictable.

(3) A lack of criticism or instruction is not in keeping with what is known about learning theory. Knowledge of results is important to learning process. A ballot that contains no comments reflects the ignorance or laziness of the judge.

(4) Criticism is selective in that specific criteria are used to evaluate. A judge's critique ought to reflect an understanding and utilization of those criteria. This does not mean that judges cannot point out factors that may have influenced his view of the criteria.

(5) Judges should avoid comments and remarks concerning trivial matters because students may believe that such comments reflect the basis for a decision. Those students who wish to rationalize the outcome of an event may exaggerate the remarks.

Role of The Judge

The coach who is most generally also the judge, serves in several capacities. In addition to instructing his own students, he is also called upon to instruct the students that he judges. If the coach believes in the educational value of forensic activity for all students, these two roles do not present serious conflicts.

Students expect competent judges who want to give their best effort during the judging process. They expect mature and intelligent criticism from the judge. The judge who is always late, who never has paper and a pencil, who can never seem to fill out a ballot properly, and who suffers from a hangover soon develops the reputation he deserves. The judge who uses his position to display his genius by haranguing students is remembered for his tantrums, not his instruction.

The coach's colleagues expect him to make the same kind of effort that he would expect of others when they judge his students. When a coach does less than this, he is not being fair to his colleagues or to his students. When a host director asks that no decisions be announced before the final results are tabulated, he means just that. It is in bad taste for a coach to divulge his decisions to others or to ask others about their decisions. When a coach discusses the quality of his team or the quality of other teams, he is in essence campaigning for or against students. His comments may bias other judgments and he has indeed left the role of instructor to assume the role of politician.

A major part of a coach's obligations includes the maintainance of professional behavior. The behavior of the coach reflects his standards, the standards of his students, and those of his school. That behavior will also determine the value of forensic activity and its continuity.

The Reception of Judgment

The coaches and students who have learned to receive judgment have also reached mental maturity. There are probably more violations of the reception of judgments than there are bad judgments. The coach or student who is inclined to become emotional over a decision ought to keep the following items in mind:

(1) Judgments made on forensic activity are subjective. We cannot see a ball go through the hoop, or measure the distance between the arrow and the bull's eye. However, research evidence indicates that there is much more agreement between judges than between debaters and judges. Individuals who are to survive in a world that demands persuasion would do well to get accustomed to subjective judgments. The setting that is provided by forensic activities is probably the most idealistic one that a student will ever experience. The student does not even have to obtain a hearing.

(2) It is possible to win a debate and lose a decision. When this happens the student should not berate the judge for the decision, but should look at his own ineptitude for not winning the debate and the decision. Arguments are not obvious, they must persuade the listener. When one believes that he can rely on his logic alone to persuade, he is not in touch with reality. If one assumes that coaches have any influence on their team's cases it is soon observable that there must be many logics.

(3) Coaches who advise their students to ignore the critiques of other judges are violating the very principle that they are attempting to teach. One cannot analyze facts and opinions without examining them. If the coach and his students already have the answers, there is little need to attend forensic tournaments for the purpose of learning. In essence, this type of coach or student is saying that he is willing to display his ability. A student must learn what comments are most helpful to the improvement of his skill. The student should apply the "tests of evidence" to the comments of the judges. This means that when the student receives a particular piece of advice he should ask (a) What are the qualifications of the source? (b) Does the source explain how he arrived at his conclusion? (c) Is the comment critical to

the acceptance or rejection of the resolution? (d) Is the advice typical of the established norms of forensic behavior? (e) Does the advice reflect personal taste or is it a matter of established norms? (f) Is the advice aimed at the level of winning or more concerned with educational values? (g) Have enough judgments been given so that a conclusion can be drawn about a particular item of behavior? and (h) What criteria should be used in accepting or rejecting advice? If the purpose of forensics is to teach students to engage in critical thinking, then the coach must be willing to have the student put these questions to his advice as well as to the advice of judges. When a coach insists that his way is the "correct" way, he has asked the student to forfeit what has been learned about critical thinking. When the coach yields completely to the advice of judges, he shirks his responsibilities as a teacher.

(4) Judges are human and therefore they can be wrong, they can be persuaded, and they can be irritated. Individuals who dwell on wrong decisions are likely never to achieve their potential because of emotional immaturity. In most cases the student is not worrying about injustice or a lack of learning. This is witnessed by the fact that students rarely worry about a decision given to them that they didn't earn. Therefore, when a student is defeated by a weaker opponent and a weaker case he has only himself to thank. Students who believe that they can act any way they please as long as their logic is sound, overlook the fact that credibility is perhaps the single most important factor in persuasion.

(5) Students who rely on the judge to determine what the important arguments are or to clarify the arguments have no right to complain about the decision.

(6) The superior debater or speaker will show consistency in his results. A number of rounds of forensic activity will reflect the skill of the student. Students should not be overly concerned about one individual judgment. The skilled debater knows that cumulative evidence is important. Tournament structure allows for divergence of opinion by virtue of a number of judgments. When these judgments point to one conclusion, it is important that the student do some self-analysis.

(7) Those who are creative must be willing to take risk and the student who takes risk must also be capable of coping with adverse reaction. It is not reasonable for a student to expect automatic acceptance of ideas because they are his. The forensic platform is designed to give the student an opportunity to test his ideas, not impose them. It takes courage to be creative and whether or not an individual has this courage is dependent upon the nature of his reaction to adverse criticism and his willingness to submit his ideas to careful analysis.

(8) A coach should obtain all the facts before he concludes that his team has been misjudged. It is important to use emotional maturity by delaying our response until all the facts are in. Students have been known to leave out a few facts to protect themselves. The coach should not fall into the same practice.

(9) Coaches can do themselves and their students a service by examining the research about the opinions of judges. (The Herbert James study reported in Chapter 12 is a good case in point.) Judges do differ on judgment when there is a question about specific procedures. However, these differences are not great enough to prevent a superior team from achieving success over a period of time.

JUDGING INDIVIDUAL EVENTS

Although individual events are more representative of classroom speech activities, they still present some special problems for the judge. More is expected of the student by virtue of the quality of student selected for these speaking events and the demands of the specific activity. Therefore the judge must be capable of making fine distinctions between students. He must also be capable of giving more than general advice. There is no substitute for specialized knowledge about the activity that one judges. The following discussion contains some considerations that one should keep in mind when judging extemporaneous speaking, original oratory, and oral interpretation.

What is Being Judged

Extemporaneous speaking reflects the ability to exhibit excellence in public speaking although there is a limited amount of time for preparation. Speech composition usually suffers more than delivery. The superior speaker is capable of analyzing data, drawing inferences of his own, and presenting a well organized speech that is couched in effective language. This means that a speaker must do more than repeat what he has read. Judges should be aware of the ideas used in such a speech and the validity of the supporting materials. The criteria of measurement for the extemporaneous speech are the same as those employed in the speech class. Although specific tournament rules usually stipulate the policy on the use of notes, the judge normally does not mind their proper use. Notes are used properly when the student does not rely on them too much and when they do not distract. The interpretation of "proper" is subjective.

What is the difference between oratory and public speaking? Oratory is public speaking that has achieved an art form. In other words the orator reflects perfected skill. Although the criteria of measurement are the same for oratory as for public speaking, the judge has a right to expect more in terms of achievement in oratory. The student also has a right to expect refined criticism.

Oral interpretation is perhaps one of the most difficult areas in which to secure judge agreement. If one placed the definitions of oral interpretation on a continuum he would find that oral interpretation means everything from reading recipes to taking part in a mystical experience. In order to achieve some sort of meaningful view the judge must have a knowledge of what constitutes literary standards, impersonation, acting, suggestion, aesthetic distance, and empathy. Although these terms present problems of definition, knowledge about them will reduce impressionistic criticism.

Judging Procedures

The judge is expected to provide meaningful and accurate feedback for the students and the tournament director. This is accomplished by utilizing a ballot that provides written comments and a numerical system that serves as a discrimination index. Judges determine the relative standing of the contestants by ranking them according to the quality of their performance. The quality of a student's performance is determined by assigning quality ratings or a percentage total.

The quality rating system usually employs a range of points to indicate quality categories. For example, 80 to 100 = excellent; 60 to 80 = good; 40 to 60 = average; 20 to 40 = below average, and 0 to 20 = poor. Quality ratings can also be used by rating each criterion of measurement and then totaling the points. It is important to remember that quality ratings indicate general notions of achievement. Rating scales are not so refined that we can say that someone with a score of 90 is twice as capable as someone with a score of 45.

The percentage total method is another means of indicating the quality of a student's performance. The prescribed range of percentages varies. The judge may be asked to give the highest speaker a percentage of 95 and the lowest a percentage of 50. The other speakers are assigned percentages between the two extremes. One of the problems of such scales is the lack of descriptive categories.

The virtue of the ranking system is that it forces the judge to discriminate between performances. It is not unlikely for ties to occur in the rating or percentage systems. In addition, judges tend to vary in their rating habits. When a number of judges are used for a single round, a comparison of ranks are more meaningful than a comparison of ratings or percentages.

In addition to the critique sheets and ballots provided by the tournament director, the judge should devise a summary sheet for convenience and accuracy. This device helps the judge give systematic appraisals; it also helps him cross-check his final decision. The following summary sheet is only one method of meeting the demands of a contest.

Continuous-Ranking System

Speaker	Rating	Order of ranking after speech					
		1	2	3	4	5	6
Shierloh	45	1	2	3	4	5	6
Hock	80		1	1	2	2	3
Hoffman	80			2	3	3	4
Stiers	95				1	1	1
Chaly	79					4	5
Bainbridge	87						2

Rating System

80–100 Excellent
60– 80 Good
40– 60 Average
20– 40 Below Average
0– 20 Poor

The above summary sheet allows the judge to vote and rank each speaker immediately after his performance. The continuous-ranking system helps the judge avoid errors of recall. This is especially true when there are a number of speakers that are tied on ratings.

When several judges are used in a single round, the final standings are determined by totaling the rankings given by each judge. The following table illustrates this system.

Ranking System Based on Use of Several Judges

Speaker	Ranking			Sum of Rankings	Final Place in Contest
	Judge #1	Judge #2	Judge #3		
McElroy	2	1	3	6	II
Ekers	5	3	5	13	V
Bee	3	6	6	15	VI
Rodgers	4	5	4	13	IV
Fry	6	4	2	12	III
Custis	1	2	1	4	I

It is at once apparent that some system has to be used to break ties in rankings. In the above example speakers Ekers and Rodgers are tied on the basis of summed rankings. Such ties can be decided by (1) determining the number of judges that preferred one speaker over another, or (2) using a "reciprocal system." In this example we can see that Rodgers was favored over Ekers by two of the judges. The "reciprocal" method divides the number of speakers into the assigned rank. The speaker who has the lowest score wins. When this method is used, Ekers receives scores of 0.83, 0.50, and 0.83; Rodgers receives scores of 0.66, 0.66, and 0.83. The totals reveal that Rodgers has the lowest score and is therefore placed ahead of Ekers.

Reliability and Validity of Judgment

Franklin H. Knower[1] made an extensive study of rank-order methods used in speech contests that reveals considerations for obtaining reliability and validity of judgment. This study revealed that:

(1) The mean average deviation in judging speech performance is slightly over one rank position.

(2) The amount of variation is influenced by the number of judges, the type of speaking, and the size of the contest.

(3) Original speaking is ranked with greater reliability than declamation. Extempore speaking is ranked with the greatest reliability.

(4) Judges agree more definitely on the characteristics of speaking they disapprove than they do on the characteristics of speaking they like.

(5) Speakers ranked in the first or last position are ranked with greater reliability than those in the middle positions.

(6) Speakers speaking in the first or last position are more commonly ranked in an intermediate than in a high or low position. Speakers who are assigned the highest final average

---

[1] Franklin H. Knower, "A Study of Rank-Order Methods of Evaluating Performances in Speech Contests," *Journal of Applied Psychology*, XXIV, No. 5 (October 1940), 633–44.

rank by judges most frequently speak in next to the last or
in some other intermediate position.

The validity of a judgment depends largely upon the ability of
the judge to understand what is being judged. This means that the
judge must have knowledge about the criteria that he uses to
arrive at his decision. Agreement between judges on the meaning
of the criteria also increases reliability. Ballots that contain a large
number of exotic criteria are cumbersome and in addition they
tend to distort judgment.

Reliability of judgment can be increased by (1) increasing the
number of performances, (2) increasing the number of judges,
and (3) by using judges that have extensive training in the
particular activity that they are called upon to judge. A good
tournament will generally provide all of the conditions that are
conducive to reliability and validity of judgment. Students generally participate in at least three preliminary rounds of speaking
with different students in each round. If three judges are not used
during the preliminary rounds, the single judge should be an
expert. Final rounds usually have from five to seven judges. Because of possible "order effects," students speak in different assigned positions, or draw a number that gives them their speaking
position by chance.

There is no clear-cut research to determine just how many
speakers a judge can rate or rank before his ability to discriminate
becomes quite arbitrary. However, this writer's experience tells
him that some judges start to experience difficulty after the seventh
speaker. Even with seven speakers the middle positions are difficult to determine.

THE IMPROVEMENT OF JUDGING

Because judging is related to learning it is important to do what
we can to improve on the process. If it is granted that poor judgment is an affliction that everyone possesses on occasion, it is more
likely that judgment will improve.

Judgmental Errors

Conscious bias can occur in the following ways:

(1) *Generosity Bias:* Sometimes judges want to make everyone feel happy. Therefore they just rate everyone as superior. This type of judge might even decide that every participant in the activity must be superior or he would not be there. In addition, he concludes that the coaches of the students will look upon him with favor. In reality students and coaches soon realize that this type of judge does not have the courage to discriminate, and they tend to disregard his judgment.

(2) *Social Pressure Bias:* It is never easy to vote against your friend's students or against students who are supposed to be outstanding. Judges soon learn that coaches and students want them to judge each performance as an independent event. Coaches and students also want an honest judgment and temporary feelings are not as important as future respect.

(3) *Therapeutic Bias:* This type of bias is used when a judge decides to rate someone higher than he deserves for purposes of encouragement. The judge may even vote for a debate team because he has always voted against them. It can also be used in reverse. In other words, a judge decides to teach a student that he does not know everything, so he rates him down so that he will try harder. This is not only dishonest, but it makes for a risky practice. No one can predict just how a student will react. False encouragement may distort a student's view of himself to the point that he thinks he "has it made." A student who is rated down may just decide that it is not worth the effort.

Forensic activity cannot function without coaches who have integrity. The coaches judge their students' competitors and the nature of the judgment can be quite subjective. A coach must remember that his professional standing with his colleagues and all students is the primary measure of what kind of a coach he is.

Unconscious bias is usually reflected on rating scales. The full range of the scale is not used. Judges may be guilty of giving consistently high ratings, low ratings, or ratings that accumulate in the center of the scale. When this happens, students and coaches predict the rating outcome before the debate and tend to ignore the judgment. The purpose of the scale is to compare one student against another. When a judge has never heard a student that was above average, suspicions are aroused. Another form of unconscious bias occurs when a judge perseveres in his judgment regardless of change in behavior. In other words, a judge decides that a student is average at the beginning of the year and persists in this judgment regardless of change. The judge may also commit himself to the idea that a student is superior and persist in this idea. This same notion is reflected by a student in the classroom who says "make a good first impression and your grade is assured." All of us would do well to examine our ratings over a period of time.

Errors of recall can be prevented by keeping a systematic account of what is taking place. Otherwise there is a tendency to give too much weight to a limited part of what has occurred.

Judges sometimes respond to insignificant behavior because (1) there is little understanding about major considerations and (2) it is sometimes easier to rely on a technicality. Debate judges who make a decision on the basis of who exceeds the time limit or who speaks too rapidly are responding to insignificant behavior. That does not mean that the judge should condone such behavior, but it hardly constitutes the basis for a decision.

The Ballot

It was pointed out earlier in this chapter that it is difficult to standardize judges by simply standardizing ballots. However, standardization reduces the differences between judges by focusing attention on well defined criteria and a consistent rating system. An important contribution could be made by the national forensic associations if they would collaborate on standardized ballots for all major forensic events.

Knowledge of Subject Matter

A superior judge not only understands the techniques required of a particular activity but he also has knowledge of the subject matter being used. Judges are unable to give specific criticism about the materials used in debate, oral interpretation, oratory, or extemporaneous speaking unless they have some familiarity with them. Distortions of material do occur. This always poses a problem for a judge because he cannot determine if the distortion was deliberate. Distortions in debate can occur because of student ignorance. When the opposing team fails to see the distortion, this also constitutes ignorance. It seems proper to penalize both teams. At the present time there is no monitoring system to deal with this problem. A judge may question certain evidence but he can seldom make an immediate judgment. Students who distort purposely or otherwise should realize that they may win in the immediate situation, but lose in the long run. If distortion or plagarism is discovered, the student's credibility and the credibility of his school suffers.

Variation of Tournament Structure

Although debate coaches may be used to judge oral interpretation for economic reasons, this is not always conducive to learning. It would seem more realistic to hold separate tournaments for specialized activities that demand a specialized judge. If all activities are held in the same tournament, then an effort should be made to find judges who are trained and interested in the activity that they judge.

Tournaments that are held at the beginning of a season might well emphasize the critique process. This means that time should be permitted for extensive written and oral critiques.

In summing up, students desire judges who are prepared and willing to give their best effort in arriving at an honest judgment. This judgment should provide a learning experience for the student. Judging is a skill and, like most skills, it requires constant self-appraisal. Practice does not necessarily make perfect—in fact it may make permanent. A coach who has judged for twenty years may have judged poorly for twenty years.

Judges have a right to expect students who are capable of receiving judgment and who want to learn. Judging is more than a mechanical process. It requires intelligence and maturity on the part of coach and student. This attitudinal relationship will also determine the maturity and worth of forensic activities.

SUGGESTED READINGS

Books

Braden, Waldo W., ed. *Speech Methods and Resources.* New York: Harper & Brothers, 1961.

Robinson, Karl F., and E. J. Kerikas. *Teaching Speech: Methods and Materials.* New York: David McKay Co. Inc., 1963.

Articles and Periodicals

Boaz, John K., and George Ziegelmueller. "An Audience Debate Tournament," *The Speech Teacher,* XIII (November 1964), 270–76.

Giffin, Kim. "A Study of the Criteria Employed by Tournament Debate Judges," *Speech Monographs,* XXVI (March 1959), 69–71.

Holcomb, M. J. "The Critic-Judge System," *The Quarterly Journal of Speech,* XIX (February 1933), 28–38.

King, Thomas R., and Theodore Clevenger, Jr. "A Comparison of Debate Results Obtained by Participants and Critic Judging," *Southern Speech Journal,* (Spring 1960), 223–32.

Kruger, Arthur N. "The Debate Judge As a Critical Thinker," *Today's Speech,* V (January 1957), 29–31.

Reeves, Mary, and Lynn R. Osborn. "Judges of High School Debate Tournaments: Sources, Criteria, and Orientation," *Speech Teacher,* XIV (January 1965), 59–62.

Sarett, Lew R. "The Expert Judge of Debate," *The Quarterly Journal of Public Speaking,* III (April 1917), 135–39.

CHAPTER 11

Forensic Tournaments

George Ziegelmueller

Forensic tournaments are the dominant medium of extracurricular speech instruction in the United States today. Dual and triangular contests and even some debate leagues existed before 1920, but the first debate tournament was not held until March 14–16, 1923. Since the first tournament at Southwestern College in Winfield, Kansas, the tournament idea has increased greatly in popularity. Today there is hardly a weekend in the school year when there is not some kind of high-school or college speech contest being held somewhere in the country, and on many weekends there are several tournaments taking place in the same area at the same time.

The popularity of forensic tournaments is well justified from the point of view of both administrative efficiency and educational worth. Five specific values of the tournament system may be enumerated. First, tournaments make it possible to provide more intensive training to more students. The average tournament has from three to eight rounds. Thus, in a matter of a few days the tournament can offer more interscholastic experience than could be provided by a full year's schedule of home and home contests. Second, tournaments encourage an emphasis on analysis and research in debate training. Because the tournament system permits working with a single topic throughout the year, rather than requiring the selection of a new topic for each audience, it promotes a greater depth of research and analysis. Third, tournaments permit students to test their knowledge and skills. The opportunity to compete against a variety of schools allows the student to evaluate

his own progress in relationship to other students and to be criticized by many different judges. Fourth, the tournament provides
a high degree of student motivation. The student's desire to excel
in tournament competition tends to encourage more thorough
preparation and more careful performance. Finally, tournaments
are relatively inexpensive. In terms of costs per round, the tournament is a far cheaper means of providing interscholastic forensic
experience than either league or dual contests. Further, the tournament permits students to compete against schools from a wider
geographic area at less cost than would be possible in any other
way.

The tournament system is not, of course, an unmixed blessing.
The competitive atmosphere of the forensic tournament may result
in undesirable attitudes and practices, and the absence of audiences may lead to a lack of concern for persuasiveness. However,
if the coach takes care to develop proper standards in regard to
competitive behavior and persuasiveness and if the tournament
schedule is augmented by a modicum of audience speaking occasions, these problems can be avoided.

Because of the continued popularity of forensic tournaments,
nearly every coach can expect to be called upon to host or to
administer such an event at some point in his career. In order to
be an effective tournament director, the coach must understand
what is involved in hosting, planning, implementing and operating
forensic tournaments.

DECIDING TO HOST A TOURNAMENT

The hosting of a forensic tournament requires a considerable
amount of time and effort. Consequently, before deciding to sponsor a tournament a coach should consider: (1) the possible beneficial effects that hosting a tournament might have on his students
and program, (2) the needs of the forensic community for particular types of tournaments, and (3) the ability of his school and
community to host such an event graciously and efficiently.

Beneficial Effects of Hosting

A forensic tournament can bring increased prestige, publicity, and support to a forensic program, and can provide added educational opportunities to those students who assist in its administration. Because the ability to manage a tournament effectively is often a sign of a strong forensic program, increased professional prestige can result from a well-run tournament. Hosting a tournament may also help in publicizing forensics to the local student body. Non-forensic students can become better acquainted with forensic activities by serving as chairmen-timekeepers or by assisting with other aspects of the tournament. Through this acquaintanceship they may increase their appreciation for and interest in forensics. The sponsorship of a tournament can further benefit a forensic program by encouraging increased support for the activity. The impact on a school or small community of forensic students from twenty or thirty schools can be considerable. The presence of so many visiting students can help focus the attention of the local community on forensics, and the importance of such an event cannot be easily ignored by school administrators. In addition to these benefits to the program, hosting a forensic tournament affords the student staff a valuable learning experience. The planning and management of a tournament can help students develop organizational ability and an appreciation for the importance of details.

Needs of the Forensic Community

Even though the establishment of a new forensic tournament might benefit the hosting institution, such a tournament is not warranted unless some need for it exists within the forensic community. Anyone wishing to host a tournament should, therefore, confer with other coaches and examine existing tournaments in order to determine precisely when additional tournaments might be welcomed and what kinds of tournaments are most needed.

Tournament Date

The selection of a satisfactory tournament date has become an increasingly difficult task for anyone desiring to host a tournament. Courtesy requires a tournament director to try to avoid establishing a new tournament on a date when another tournament in that area has been scheduled. Nevertheless, if two tournaments are essentially different in their emphasis (i.e., one is a novice tournament and the other a varsity tournament) or if the number of entries allowed in either tournament is severely limited, then some overlapping of dates is acceptable and may even be desirable.

The American Forensic Association publishes a fairly complete list of college tournaments for the upcoming school year in the May issue of its *Journal*. Many state high-school forensic organizations publish similar calendars of high-school forensic events. Since most tournaments are held on the same weekend year in and year out, an examination of the most recent calendar of tournaments is helpful in trying to select a tournament date. The tournament date should be set far enough in advance of the actual event (by the middle of February for the *AFA Journal*) in order to permit its inclusion in the calendar of tournaments for the next school year.

Before finally deciding on a particular date for a tournament the coach should consult with school officials and perhaps with community leaders as well, in order to avoid conflicts with other events. Many of the benefits of sponsoring a tournament may fail to be realized if competing events draw attention away from the tournament or deny it sufficient support.

Types of Tournaments

A number of different types of tournaments are available to anyone wishing to sponsor a forensic contest. In general, forensic tournaments are classified according to the level of competition (novice or varsity), the selectivity of entries (open, limited, or invitational), the kinds of contests (debate, oratory, discussion, etc.), the kinds of entries (team or unit), the number and type of rounds, and the presence or absence of audiences.

In order to help assure that students with approximately the same levels of experience and achievement compete against each other, tournaments are frequently designated as either novice or varsity level events. Novice tournaments are intended for beginning students and are usually limited to those in their first year of competition. A student in his junior or senior year of school might still qualify as a novice if he has had no previous experience in forensics. Varsity tournaments are designed for experienced students and are open to those who have had more than one year's experience or who have demonstrated above-average proficiency.

Although most tournaments attempt to attract the best possible schools to their contests, they do not deny entry to any school. Such tournaments as these are known as open tournaments. Other contests, known as limited entry tournaments, restrict participation to certain categories of schools, such as Pi Kappa Delta schools or Eastern Forensic Association schools. A third group of tournaments is invitational. These tournaments send out invitations and accept registrations only from a selected list of schools. Limited facilities or a desire to establish a particular level of competition are factors which result in selective invitations.

There are a considerable number of different events which can be offered at a forensic tournament. Debate, oratory (or persuasive speaking), extemporaneous speaking, impromptu speaking, after-dinner speaking, discussion, humorous reading, and oral interpretation are among the most common. On the college level, debate is overwhelmingly the most popular event, and the vast majority of college tournaments are solely debate tournaments. A limited number of college tournaments provide opportunities to compete in some individual speaking events along with debate, although most states have college speech leagues which sponsor separate oratory and extemporaneous speaking contests. While individual speaking events are much more common at the high-school level, debate is still the most popular tournament event.

Debate tournaments may be designed to allow either unit or team entries. A unit tournament requires the entry of four debaters, two of whom function as an affirmative team and two of whom function as a negative team. The unit tournament is intended to provide intensive experience on one side of a proposition and is used for both novice and varsity debates. A team tournament requires the entry of two-men teams who must be prepared to debate both sides of the proposition. The team tournament is intended to provide maximum educational experience since the students present both affirmative and negative cases. It is usually reserved for more experienced debaters.

There is no uniform or standard number of rounds of competition which must be offered at forensic tournaments. Traditionally, individual speaking contests consist of two or three rounds, but debate competition always involves at least three rounds and frequently includes as many as eight rounds. In addition to these standard, or nonelimination rounds, many tournaments provide a final round or a series of elimination rounds progressing from octa- and quarter-finals to semifinals and finals. These final rounds are designed to let the top individuals or teams compete directly against each other and are normally offered only at the larger and more competitive tournaments. If a debate tournament is a team, rather than a unit, contest, an even number of nonelimination rounds should be held in order to assure that all teams debate an equal number of times on the affirmative and negative sides. Tournament directors usually consider four rounds of debate per day to be an optimum number. This schedule allows for sufficient time between rounds and is not likely to exaggerate the amount of fatigue experienced by students or judges.

Most tournament competition does not take place in front of audiences, but a few tournaments have attempted to provide audiences for at least some rounds. Wayne State University's Debate Days In Detroit tournament, for example, provides each competing school with four rounds of debate before audiences composed of high-school and college students and service-club members. A number of other tournaments attempt to attract substantial campus audiences to final rounds. While it is unrealistic to expect audiences to be present during every tournament round, it would seem to be desirable to provide tournament audiences whenever possible and particularly during final rounds.

Ability to Host

A forensic director should carefully evaluate his school's ability to host a tournament before finally deciding to sponsor such an event. A poorly hosted tournament can significantly detract from the educational value of a forensic contest. When the tournament administrators seem harried and confused and when the mechanics of the tournament do not function smoothly, participating students may become upset and may be unable to concentrate on giving their own best performances. On the other hand, when visiting schools are made to feel welcome, when accommodations and facilities are of high caliber, and when the operation of the tournament proceeds easily and surely, student contestants are more likely to be relaxed and able to profit from the experiences provided by the tournament.

The hosting of a tournament requires adequate administrative support, proper facilities, and an able and willing staff. Administrative support is necessary in order to assure the assistance of other faculty members and to secure cooperation in arranging for rooms and supplies. The facilities needed to host a tournament will depend upon the size and duration of the event, but it is generally wise to tailor the tournament to fit the available facilities rather than to try to stretch facilities beyond comfortable limits. The tournament staff is probably the most important factor in determining a school's ability to manage a tournament. The local forensic group must be large enough to manage a tournament of the size and scope anticipated, and its members must be enthusiastic enough about the tournament to devote their time to its planning and administration. Moreover, the forensic director must be able to give sufficient time to the management of the tournament without seriously neglecting his other responsibilities.

PLANNING THE TOURNAMENT

Once the decision to host a tournament has been made and at least six months to a year before the actual event is to take place, specific planning for the tournament should begin. During this planning period arrangements for tournament facilities and guest accommodations must be made, special tournament features such as banquets and tours should be arranged, tournament finances should be planned, and initial invitations must be sent out.

Facilities and Accommodations

To assure that the desired number and type of facilities and guest accommodations will be available at the time of the tournament, it is essential that arrangements for these be made as early as possible. The ease and graciousness with which a tournament can be hosted depends to a considerable extent upon the facilities and accommodations provided.

Tournament Facilities

The type of tournament facilities needed will normally include contest rooms, administrative rooms, an auditorium, and a lounge or large assembly room. Regular classrooms provide adequate contest facilities for most tournament events. It should be remembered, however, that discussion contests require rooms with movable chairs and that small stages or platforms are desirable for certain interpretation events. The use of offices, storage rooms, or any other rooms which are likely to be crowded, poorly ventilated, or inadequately furnished should be avoided. If possible, contest rooms should all be in the same building or at least in buildings which are near one another. In planning contest facilities it is a good policy to have two or three extra rooms reserved, but left unassigned, in order to guard against conflicting room reservations.

Two or three rooms are usually needed for administration purposes. One of these rooms can be used as headquarters for chairmen-timekeepers and as a place to collect and distribute ballots. This room should be centrally located and large enough to avoid being congested when all the timekeepers report for assignments. A second room may be used as a central administrative office; it should be easily accessible and equipped with a telephone. A third room is needed for the tabulation of results. The tabulation room should be private and free from disturbances in order to protect the secrecy of results and to guard against careless mistakes.

An auditorium will be needed if any kind of opening or closing assembly is planned. It may also be used as the site of a final round in an elimination tournament.

Many tournament directors provide a lounge or large assembly room where contestants and judges can congregate between rounds. A meeting area of this nature permits increased socializing among participants and helps create a freer and more relaxed atmosphere. Ideally, such a room should be large, attractive, and comfortably furnished.

Guest Accommodations

Appropriate accommodations should be arranged for the comfort and convenience of overnight guests. When local hotels and motels are contracted several months in advance of the tournament, they will frequently be willing to offer special rates to tournament participants. If a single good hotel or motel can house all tournament guests, this arrangement is usually to be preferred. The use of a single lodging facility makes it easier to obtain special rates, and it facilitates visiting among participants. When a single hotel is selected, it will normally provide special reservation cards and descriptive brochures. If a number of different lodging facilities must be used, a descriptive list of recommended accommodations should be prepared.

Special Features

Many schools attempt to make their tournaments more attractive by planning special educational or social activities. The most common types of extra-educational features are tours, guest speakers, and seminars. If a tournament is to be held in a community which offers some particularly interesting educational attraction and if participants in the tournament are expected to come from considerable distances, special tours may justifiably be provided. However, such tours require considerable effort to arrange and can create scheduling problems. They should not be offered, therefore, unless the attraction is likely to be of genuine and widespread interest. Seminars and speeches by experts on the debate proposition were in the past fairly popular tournament features. The difficulty of arranging for reliable, truly expert, and articulate speakers and the increased amounts of early season research done by debaters have probably contributed to the decline in popularity of these events. Nevertheless, some tournaments continue to provide seminars and when they are well planned they can be worthwhile. Seminars and speeches by experts are probably most appreciated by high-school and novice debaters and at early season tournaments.

When a forensic tournament extends over more than one day it is customary for the host school to arrange some type of social event for participating students and coaches. However, efforts to provide tickets to local theaters or dances or to arrange special parties for visiting students are seldom received with much enthusiasm. On the other hand, a banquet will probably be well attended and if the food is abundant and tasty and the program brief and entertaining, it will be greatly appreciated. Banquet arrangements should be made several months in advance of the tournament to assure the availability of space and to help with the budgeting of tournament costs. Considerable advance planning is also necessary in order to arrange a suitable banquet program.

Financing the Tournament

At an early point in the planning of a tournament, it is necessary to consider the matter of finances. Most tournaments are financed by charging each school a fee based upon its number of entrants. This system is an equitable one since participating schools are simply asked to pay for the services which are rendered to them. The sponsors of some tournaments have been able to keep entrance fees low or to eliminate them altogether by soliciting outside financial support. Local businesses and well-to-do alumni are often willing to make a contribution to the forensic program in this way.

Whether a tournament is to be financed by entrance fees or by an outside sponsor, it is necessary to prepare an itemized budget of anticipated expenses. This budget will be needed to help set fair entrance fees or to help justify requests for outside financial assistance. In the latter instance, the budget request should probably be accompanied by a description of the type of tournament planned and a list of its educational values. The budget should include such costs as postage, printing, ballots, transportation, trophies, banquet, and refreshments.

A few schools have recently begun to view tournaments as major money-making projects and have set tournament entrance fees at unjustifiably high levels. In effect, these unjustifiable fees force students from the visiting school to contribute to the financial resources of the hosting institution. Such a practice involves serious inequities and inevitably leads to resentment. Although the hosting of a tournament entails a considerable amount of work, it also provides many nonmaterial benefits to the host school. These benefits should be sufficient reward for the work involved.

Initial Invitations

Initial invitations should be mailed out approximately six months before a tournament is scheduled to take place. If the tournament is to be open to all schools, invitations can be sent to as many schools as are likely to be interested. These invitations may be brief but should indicate the name and location of the tournament, its date or dates, the types of events, the number of rounds, special tournament features, and information regarding future tournament mailings. A return form asking schools to indicate their initial interest in the tournament should be included. This form can help in estimating the number of schools likely to attend. If the number of tournament rooms available demands that a maximum limit be established on entries which can be accepted, the initial invitation should indicate this fact and state that entries will be honored on a first-come basis.

Initial invitations to limited entry tournaments often provide more complete data. Information regarding entry fees, the schedule of events, and even housing may be given in addition to the items mentioned above. Invitational tournaments almost always require schools to return a tentative entrance form in order to reserve a place in the tournament.

IMPLEMENTING THE TOURNAMENT

The last two months before a forensic tournament are an increasingly busy time. It is during this period that the tournament must actually be established and implemented. A tournament staff should be organized; awards ought to be decided upon and ordered; final registration forms must be mailed and entrances acknowledged; necessary supplies should be ordered; arrangements for extra judges will need to be made; and a system of contest pairings must be worked out.

Tournament Staff

The size of the staff needed to implement a forensic tournament will, of course, depend upon the size and nature of the particular event, but even a small tournament requires some delegation of responsibilities and division of labor. Careful consideration, therefore, should be given to the selection of an administrative staff and the establishment of an effective committee structure.

Administrative Staff

The forensic coach should head the administrative staff and act as overall supervisor of the tournament. He should provide a firm guiding hand by making his job assignments clear and specific and by continually checking on the work of his staff and committees. He may also assume personal responsibility for such important tasks as the preparation of the tournament schematic and the management of tournament finances. It is essential that the forensic coach, rather than some student, assume this central role, since the coach will normally have greater authority and experience. Moreover, the coach is in a position to adjust his time schedule more easily to the demands of the tournament. In general, experience has demonstrated that tournaments managed solely by students are less likely to be efficiently run than are coach-supervised events.

While students ought not be given the total responsibility for a tournament, selected students can be assigned major administrative roles. A student director and one or two student assistant directors should be named to the administrative staff. These students will need to have a thorough knowledge of the overall tournament organization and must be prepared to assist the director in a variety of different capacities as circumstances may dictate. The student director may be given the specific responsibility of supervising the work of certain committees and of assisting the director in the preparation of schematics and the management of finances. If the tournament is to be an annual one, the assistant director's position should be used to train the next year's student director.

Committee Assignments

Nearly every tournament will require a somewhat different committee structure. However, there are certain fairly standard tasks which usually need to be performed and for which some committee or person must be made responsible. Typical committee assignments include publicity, registration, food, chairmen-timekeepers, and tabulations.

A publicity committee should be appointed to create public awareness of the tournament. Through the use of window displays, posters, newspaper stories, or radio-television announcements this committee can create local interest in the tournament before it occurs. After the tournament, it may inform the general public of contest results through press releases to the wire services and to the winning schools' hometown newspapers.

A registration committee will be needed to handle the details involved in signing visiting schools into the tournament. The members of this committee ought to be attractive, cordial people who will make visitors feel genuinely welcome. Sometime before the first day of the tournament, this committee will need to prepare packets of tournament information to be distributed to each school when it registers.

Some type of food committee is essential for most tournaments. This committee may be placed in charge of tournament banquets, luncheons, or breakfasts, or it may be made responsible for the serving of refreshments at various times throughout the course of the tournament. If the committee must arrange for the serving of a meal, it will need to reserve a dining room, select a menu, determine seating arrangements, and perhaps, plan a brief program. If the committee is concerned with providing refreshments, it will have to reserve an appropriate room, decide on a particular kind of refreshment, arrange for necessary equipment and dishes (a serving table, coffee urn, tea and coffee service, cups and saucers, silverware, napkins, etc.) and provide a staff of people to handle preparations, serving, and clearing.

One of the most important committees is the chairmen-timekeeper committee. The members of this committee must be dedicated and tenacious workers if they are to succeed in providing chairmen for every tournament contest. In order to enlist chairmen-timekeepers, committee members should canvass their own living units and contact responsible people in other living units to do the same. In addition, the help of the speech department staff should be sought in enlisting students from speech classes. Some professors may wish to require students to attend tournament contests as listening assignments. Frequently, speech teachers from the area's high schools will also arrange for some of their students to serve as chairmen-timekeepers. It is usually necessary to enlist more students than will actually be needed to chair contests, since some of those who sign up inevitably fail to appear on the day of the tournament.

A second extremely important committee is the tabulation committee. The work of this committee is often assumed by the tournament administrative staff and should always be closely supervised by the tournament director. This committee is responsible for the round-by-round tabulation of results, for the determination of tournament winners, and for the preparation of individual school folders and a final summary of results. The members of this committee should be maticulously accurate, capable of working under the pressure of time, and closed-mouthed about the results of their work until the winners are publicly announced.

Awards

Tournament awards must be selected and ordered at least two months before the contests in order to allow sufficient time for their delivery. In general, the type of awards selected should be related to the level, size, and prestige of the tournament. If a tournament is small and not widely recognized, large expensive trophies will appear to be extreme and out of place. A large number of trophies is, likewise, inappropriate for all but the biggest national tournaments. The presentation of too many awards or of too large awards only serves to cheapen the significance of all citations.

A trophy does not have to be a large and impressive one to do credit to the awarding school. If it is simple and well designed, rather than flashy, a trophy will reflect the general care and good judgment with which the tournament is administered. Similarly, an award need not be expensive in order to honor the winning school appropriately. A trophy or other award is only a material symbol of a noteworthy achievement and in reality, does little to add to or detract from the accomplishment, itself.

Final Invitations

Final invitations should be mailed two months in advance of the tournament. If the tournament is an invitational one, only those schools which returned tentative registration forms should be sent final invitations. If the tournament is an open contest, all schools which received initial invitations are normally sent final mailings. These final mailings should supply all the information necessary to help schools in planning for their participation; this may include: (1) a cover letter describing the nature of the tournament, (2) a complete schedule of events, (3) housing information, and (4) an entry form.

Cover Letter

The cover letter should describe the special features of the tournament such as banquets, receptions, guest speakers, and participant awards. In addition, it ought to explain the general rules under which the tournament will operate. These rules would cover such matters as student eligibility, judging requirements, the deadline for entering the tournament, and tournament fees. Finally, the cover letter should explain the procedures which will be used in conducting each event. A description of the procedures for debate would include a statement of the proposition, the debate format, the number of rounds, the number of teams per school, and whether teams switch sides. The procedures for individual events would require a description of each type of event and information about time limits, number of participants per school, and number of rounds.

Schedule of Events

A schedule of events must be enclosed with the final invitation so that visiting schools will be able to plan their arrival and departure times. Visitors may also find an advance copy of the schedule helpful in attempting to arrange business or social appointments. When a tournament is held on a large campus, a school map should be included with the schedule to assist visitors in locating parking lots, the tournament headquarters building, and other facilities.

It is important that the schedule of events be carefully planned. It should allot sufficient time for the conducting of contests and ought to allow time between rounds for brief relaxation, for judges' comment, and for travel between rooms or buildings. When a meal must be scheduled between contest rounds, an hour to an hour and a half should be provided. The number and proximity of available eating facilities will determine the exact amount of time needed.

The actual tournament schedules are reproduced below. The first schedule is for a switch-side elimination debate tournament; it provides for six nonelimination rounds of debate plus quarter-finals, semifinals, and final. The second schedule is for an individual event's tournament. It calls for three nonelimination rounds in each of three events—extemporaneous speaking, manuscript speaking, and interpretative reading—and it provides for a combined championship round involving the top three contestants from each event.

Debate Tournament Schedule

Friday

9:00–10:00 A.M.	Registration	Prentis Hall Study Area
10:00 A.M.	General Meeting	Upper DeRoy Auditorium
10:30 A.M.	Round I	State & Prentis Hall
1:00 P.M	Round II	State & Prentis Hall
2:30 P.M.	Round III	State & Prentis Hall
4:00 P.M.	Round IV	State & Prentis Hall

Saturday

7:30–8:30 A.M.	Continental Breakfast	D. D. Henry Lounge, Mackenzie Hall
8:30 A.M.	Round V	State & Prentis Hall
10:00 A.M.	Round VI	State & Prentis Hall
11:45 A.M.	Luncheon	Park Shelton Hotel
1:00 P.M.	Quarter-Final Round	Rms. 10, 17, 21, 27, Prentis Hall
2:30 P.M.	Semifinal Round	Rms. 10, 17, Prentis Hall
4:00 P.M.	Final Round	Upper DeRoy Auditorium

Individual Events Tournament Schedule

Friday

4:00–6:00 P.M.	Registration	DeRoy Lobby
6:30 P.M.	Drawing for Extemporaneous Speaking Topics	DeRoy Lobby
7:00 P.M.	General Assembly for Judges and Participants in Manuscript Speaking and Interpretative Reading	Lower DeRoy Auditorium
7:30 P.M.	Round I Manuscript Speaking	State Hall
	Round I Interpretative Reading	State Hall
7:45 P.M.	Round I Extemporaneous Speaking	State Hall

Saturday

8:00 A.M.	Drawing of Topics for Extemporaneous Speaking	State Hall, Room 127
9:00 A.M.	Round II Manuscript Speaking	State Hall
	Round II Interpretative Reading	State Hall
9:15 A.M.	Round II Extemporaneous Speaking	State Hall
10:15 A.M.	Drawing of Topics for Extemporaneous Speaking	State Hall, Room 127
11:00 A.M.	Round III Manuscript Speaking	State Hall
	Round III Interpretative Reading	State Hall
11:30 A.M.	Round III Extemporaneous Speaking	State Hall
12:30 P.M.	Tournament Luncheon	McGregor Center, Room F
1:30 P.M.	Drawing of Topics for Finalists in Extemporaneous Speaking	McGregor Center, Room F
1:45 P.M.	Championship Round	Lower DeRoy Auditorium
3:30 P.M.	Presentation of Awards	Lower DeRoy Auditorium

Housing Information

Information on housing should be provided if any participants are likely to come into town the night before the tournament or if the tournament will extend over more than one day. When a single good hotel can be used to accommodate all tournament guests, one of its reservation cards and a descriptive brochure should be enclosed with each invitation. When several different hotels or motels must be used, a list of recommended accommodations should be prepared. This list should accurately describe the types of accommodations available, the approximate distance of each from the main tournament building(s), the daily rates, and the addresses to use in writing for reservations.

Entry Forms

The entry form should provide all of the data necessary for the preparation of contest schematics plus any other information which may be needed for inclusion in a tournament program. The name of the entering school, the number of individuals or teams entered in each event, and the number of judges to be supplied or hired are facts which are always needed. In addition, the names of participants and some personal data about them may be requested.

The entry form should always indicate a specific deadline for its return. Normally, this deadline should be set for at least two weeks before the tournament in order to allow sufficient time for the preparation of contest schematics and for the hiring of extra judges. As each entry is received, it should be filed and recorded, and an acknowledgment sent by return mail. The acknowledgment should indicate the name of the school, the number of teams or contestants entered, the events entered, and the number of judges to be provided or hired.

Supplies

Necessary supplies should be ordered well in advance of the tournament. If American Forensic Association ballots are to be used, at least four weeks should be allowed for their delivery. From two to four weeks will be required for the preparation of any commercially printed materials such as program covers or special contest ballots. Many items which are prepared by students or office secretaries can be done at almost any time but should be completed no later than a week before the tournament. This includes judge's instruction sheets, chairmen-timekeeper's instruction sheets, registration forms, time cards, directional posters, and much of the material to be included in a tournament program such as copies of letters of welcome, lists of participating schools, campus maps, and lists of recommended restaurants.

Extra Judges

Most tournaments require participating schools to supply one judge for each unit (or two teams) entered in debate and one judge for every two or three contestants entered in individual speaking events. Because some schools cannot always provide the required number of judges, it is necessary for the tournament host to have available a limited number of extra judges for hire. Possible guest judges should be contacted well in advance of the tournament, informed of the tournament dates, and asked about their potential availability.

Only judges who are clearly qualified should be contacted. Preferably, guest judges should be active forensic people from nearby, nonparticipating high schools or colleges. Former coaches or ex-students who have had considerable experience in the activity they will judge and who have been in recent contact with that activity may also be used. Speech department faculty members who regularly teach public speaking courses may be asked to judge oratory, extemporaneous speaking, and in some instances, novice debates. Oral interpretation and theater faculty members may judge the reading contests. Individuals who have had little or no experience with forensics should not be called upon to judge since their judgments are likely to be less reliable and their critiques less meaningful. If the number of available guest judges is limited, the host school should indicate this fact in its final invitation and should not commit itself to provide judges beyond the qualified supply.

Guest judges should be paid a uniform fee based upon the number of rounds they are asked to judge. This fee should be stated in the final invitation and should be collected at the time of registration.

Contest Schematics

Contest schematics provide an orderly means of pairing contestants and judges and of shifting them from round to round. In order to assure accuracy in their preparation, schematics should be devised several days before a tournament and carefully checked and double checked. An error in the basic schematic can cause great confusion and considerable difficulty on the day of a tournament. Many coaches prepare extra schematics based upon reduced numbers of participants to guard against late withdrawals from the tournament. When last minute changes must be made in the schematic, they can be accomplished with a minimum of confusion if the original schematic was well designed and involved no special problems.

Schematics for Debate

Although a debate tournament schematic may be prepared in a number of different ways, it must meet certain standards in order to assure that the tournament experience will be of maximum educational benefit. All debate schematics should, therefore, adhere to the following principles:

1. No team should be judged by its own coach.
2. No team should be scheduled to meet another team from its own school.
3. No team should meet any other team more than once in the preliminary rounds.

In addition to these principles, certain other standards should generally be met in order to provide a fairer basis for competition.

4. No team should be judged by the same judge more than once.
5. No judge should judge more than one team from the same school.
6. No judge should judge a team which his own team is scheduled to meet.

Because of a small number of tournament entries or because of some other schedule peculiarity, it is sometimes necessary to violate some of these principles in preparing a tournament schematic. The above standards are arranged in order of decreasing significance, so that the ones lowest on the scale may be ignored with the least harmful effects. It is often possible to minimize the effects of any violations of these principles by making adjustments in the schematic. Thus, if a coach must judge a team which his own team is scheduled to meet, it is better for him to judge it on the opposite side of the question or for the two teams to debate each other *before* he judges the one. In this way, the judge will not be able to pass along information about the first team to his own team. Similarly, if a judge must judge two teams from the same school or one team more than once, he should be assigned to hear them on different sides of the proposition. This would provide some protection against a judge being prejudiced against one side of the proposition or against a particular kind of analysis.

In preparing a debate tournament schematic, the concept of concurrent variations should be applied. Thus, each of the elements involved in a schematic (affirmative team, negative team, and judge) should be varied from round to round according to an established and fairly regular pattern. Numbers are normally used instead of school names in working out schematics in order to avoid confusion and to make checking quicker and easier. Two sample schematics are given below. Schematic A (page 304) is for a twenty-school, four-round *unit* tournament, and Schematic B (page 306) for a twelve-school, four-round *team* tournament.

Schematics for *unit debate tournaments* may be prepared by following the procedures utilized in drawing up Schematic A:

Schematic A

Round I				Round II		
Aff.	*Neg.*	*Judge*		*Aff.*	*Neg.*	*Judge*
1	2	7		1	3	10
2	3	8		2	4	11
3	4	9		3	5	12
4	5	10		4	6	13
5	6	11		5	7	14
6	7	12		6	8	15
7	8	13		7	9	16
8	9	14		8	10	17
9	10	15		9	11	18
10	11	16		10	12	19
11	12	17		11	13	20
12	13	18		12	14	1
13	14	19		13	15	2
14	15	20		14	16	3
15	16	1		15	17	4
16	17	2		16	18	5
17	18	3		17	19	6
18	19	4		18	20	7
19	20	5		19	1	8
20	1	6		20	2	9

Round III				Round IV		
Aff.	*Neg.*	*Judge*		*Aff.*	*Neg.*	*Judge*
1	4	12		1	5	14
2	5	13		2	6	15
3	6	14		3	7	16
4	7	15		4	8	17
5	8	16		5	9	18
6	9	17		6	10	19
7	10	18		7	11	20
8	11	19		8	12	1
9	12	20		9	13	2
10	13	1		10	14	3
11	14	2		11	15	4
12	15	3		12	16	5
13	16	4		13	17	6
14	17	5		14	18	7
15	18	6		15	19	8
16	19	7		16	20	9
17	20	8		17	1	10
18	1	9		18	2	11
19	2	10		19	3	12
20	3	11		20	4	13

1. Affirmative team numbers are placed in the left-hand column. They should be arranged in numerical order starting with number one, and the order of the numbers should remain the same from round to round.

2. Negative team numbers are placed in the middle column. They should be arranged in regular numerical order except that the column should begin with number two and proceed downward through number twenty (or whatever the last affirmative number happens to be) and go back to number one. In each succeeding round the column of negative numbers should be rotated from top to bottom so that in Round II number three will be the first number, in Round III number four will appear first and so on.

3. Judges' numbers are placed in the third column. In order to determine what judge number to assign to affirmative team one in Round I, take the number of the negative team that meets affirmative one in the last round and add two to it. Thus, in the sample schematic, affirmative one meets negative five in the last round, so in the first round affirmative one should be assigned judge number seven (five plus two). The other judges' numbers should be assigned in regular numerical order proceeding downward through number twenty (or whatever the last affirmative number happened to be) to number six (or whatever number completes the cycle with the number of the first assigned judge). In Round II, the judges' number cycle is moved upwards three numbers. In the sample schematic, affirmative team one's judge is shifted from judge seven to judge ten (seven plus three), and the other numbers follow in the established order. In Round III and in all succeeding rounds the judges' cycle should be moved upwards two numbers. Again, in the example, affirmative team one's judge is shifted from judge ten in Round II to judge twelve (ten plus two) in Round III and to judge fourteen (twelve plus two) in Round IV.

The procedures outlined above will result in pairings which satisfy all of the established criteria so long as the number of units entered in the tournament is at least five times the number of rounds offered. These procedures may also be applied, with only minor faults, to tournaments in which the number of entries is only three or four times the number of rounds.[1] This schematic should not be used for tournaments with less than three times the number of entries as rounds.[2]

Schematics for *team debate tournaments* may be prepared by following the procedures used in working out Schematic B:

Schematic B

Round I			Round II		
Aff.	*Neg.*	*Judge*	*Aff.*	*Neg.*	*Judge*
1	2	5	4	1	10
3	4	7	6	3	12
5	6	9	8	5	2
7	8	11	11	7	4
9	10	1	12	9	6
11	12	3	2	11	8

Round III			Round IV		
Aff.	*Neg.*	*Judge*	*Aff.*	*Neg.*	*Judge*
1	6	7	8	1	12
3	8	9	10	3	2
5	10	11	12	5	4
7	12	1	2	7	6
9	2	3	4	9	8
11	4	5	6	11	10

1. All of the odd-numbered teams are placed in one column and all of the even-numbered teams are placed in a second column. The odd- and even-numbered teams are assigned to the affirmative and negative sides in alternate rounds. Team tournaments require an even number of rounds in order to assure that all teams debate the affirmative and the negative an equal number of times.

---

[1] While there is no systematic formula which can be used in devising a perfect schematic for a unit tournament with four times as many entries as rounds, it is, nevertheless, possible to work out such a schematic on a trial-and-error basis.

[2] For an example of a schematic which can be used for such small unit tournaments and which contains a minimum number of faults see: Robert Huber, "Debate Tournaments," *Argumentation and Debate,* ed. James McBath (New York: Holt, Rinehart and Winston, Inc., 1963), 340–44.

2. The numbers in the odd-numbered column should be arranged in numerical order and this order should remain fixed throughout the schematic.

3. The numbers in the even-numbered column should be arranged in numerical order for the first round so that team number two will be opposite team number one. In each succeeding round the number opposite team number one should be rotated to the bottom of the even-numbered column. Thus, in Round II, team number four is moved opposite team number one, and team two is rotated to the bottom of the even-numbered column opposite the last odd-numbered team (number eleven in Schematic B). In Round III, team number six is rotated to the top of the column, and number four is moved to the bottom. This same procedure is followed through each of the remaining rounds.

4. Judges' numbers are placed in the third column. Since the schedule is for a team tournament, only half of the available judges will be needed for each round. The system of assigning judges used in Schematic B requires that all the odd-numbered judges judge at the same time and all of the even-numbered judges judge at the same time. The judge for team number one in Round I is selected by going to the two middle rounds of debates (Rounds II and III in Schematic B) and determining the numbers of the teams assigned to meet the team one in those rounds (teams four and six in the sample schematic). The number that comes between those two figures (five) should be used as the judge's number for team one in Round I. The other judges' numbers for Round I should be listed down the column in order through the last odd-numbered judge's number (number eleven in Schematic B) to whatever odd number will complete the cycle with the number of the first assigned judge (number three in Schematic B). The judges for each of the remaining odd-numbered rounds (Round III in Schematic B or Rounds III, V, and VII in a larger tournament) can be determined by moving the judges' number cycle upwards one odd number per round (from five to seven in the sample schematic). The judge for team one in Round II—the first even-numbered round—is selected by going to the last round of debate and determining the number of the team assigned to meet affirmative one in that round (number eight in Schematic

B). The next even number (ten) should be assigned to judge team one in Round II. The other judges' numbers for Round II should be listed down the column in order through the last even-numbered judge's number (number twelve in Schematic B) to whatever even number will complete the cycle with the number of the first assigned judge (number eight in Schematic B). The judges for each of the remaining even-numbered rounds (Round IV in Schematic B or Rounds IV, VI, and VIII in a larger tournament) can be determined by rotating the judges' number cycle upward one *even* number per round (from ten to twelve in the sample schematic).

The procedures outlined above will result in pairings which satisfy all of the established criteria so long as the number of teams entered in the tournament is at least three times the number of rounds offered. These procedures may also be applied, with only minor faults, to tournaments in which the number of entries is two times the number of rounds.

If two teams from a single school are permitted to enter a switch-side tournament, then Schematic A for *unit* tournaments, rather than Schematic B for *team* tournaments, should be used. Instead of designating the two teams of a unit as affirmative and negative, they may be identified as teams 1A and 1B, 2A and 2B, and so on, or the teams in the former negative column may be assigned different numbers from the teams in the former affirmative column (in Schematic A, for example, negative one would become team twenty-one, negative two, team twenty-two, and so on). All teams should debate on opposite sides of the proposition in alternate rounds. Single team entries should be paired with other single entries in order to fit them into the schematic.

The assigning of team numbers to schools may be done in a variety of ways. Sometimes the tournament director randomly assigns numbers to schools in advance of the tournament. This permits the use of school names, rather than numbers in the printed schedule. More frequently, participating schools are permitted to draw their numbers at the time of registration. This method guards against any charges of bias in the preparation of the debate schedule. Two other methods which are occasionally used are the methods of *pre-seeding* and *geographical pairings*.

The purpose of pre-seeding is to protect any team from getting a disproportionately difficult or unusually easy draw. Pre-seeding attempts to achieve this objective by estimating the pre-tournament ability of each team and by placing the teams into appropriate categories. In order to assure that a given team will meet the same number of teams from each category, the number of categories used must be capable of being divided evenly into the number of rounds of debate, and teams from each category must be distributed evenly throughout the schedule. In an eight-round tournament, for example, four categories might be used, and team numbers might be assigned so that every fifth team would be drawn from the same category. In this way every team would meet two of the top-seeded teams, two second-seeded teams, two third-seeded teams, and two bottom-seeded teams. The purpose of geographical pairings is to protect teams from traveling great distances only to meet nearby schools, and to assure each team of an opportunity to compete against other teams from different sections of the country (or state, for high-school tournaments). The system of assigning numbers for geographical pairings is much like that used in pre-seeding. The schools entered in the tournament are each assigned to a geographical category; the number of categories should always be capable of being divided evenly into the number of rounds. Numbers are assigned to schools so that teams from each geographical area will appear regularly throughout the schedule. In a six-round tournament, for example, teams might be assigned to three geographic categories—north, south, and east—so that every fourth number would represent a school from the same section of the country.

Once a system of assigning numbers to teams has been decided upon, a schedule of debates should be prepared from the debate schematic. In addition to indicating the team pairings and judging assignments for each round, this schedule should indicate the time of each round and the location of each debate. This schedule should be carefully checked to assure that the schematic is accurate and to prevent errors in transcription. The schedules should be printed in advance of the tournament and distributed to teams as they register.

A few tournaments do not utilize predetermined tournament schematics, but instead they use a system of *power pairings*. The purpose of power pairings is to minimize the luck of the draw and assure that the tournament winner is a truly topnotch team.[3] The team pairings and judging assignments for the first round or two of a power paired tournament are assigned in a random manner or according to a predetermined schematic. After the first round or two the teams are paired against each other according to their win–loss records, with winners meeting winners and losers meeting losers. Because a considerable amount of time is required between rounds in order to determine the power matchings, this system should probably not be used unless the tournament staff is unusually able and experienced in making tournament pairings. The following instructions may serve as guidelines for arranging power matches:

1. Teams should not meet other teams from their own school nor should they be judged by anyone from their own school.

2. Teams should not be scheduled to meet the same team twice or to have the same judge more than once.

3. As ballots come in they should be carefully checked for accuracy, and if any errors appear to be possible, the decision should be checked with the appropriate judge before proceeding with the power matchings.

4. Wins and losses should be recorded and totaled at the end of each round. If more than one judge per round is used, the number of ballots received should also be recorded and totaled.

5. Teams should be matched by wins and losses and by number of judges' ballots won, if a multiple judge system is used. When there is not an even number of teams having identical records or when it is impossible to pair teams with identical records because they have previously met, the two closest available teams should be paired against each other. Whenever possible, a team that is paired with a higher ranking team in one round should be paired with a lower ranking team in some other round.

6. In a switch-side tournament it is essential that all teams debate the same number of times on the affirmative and negative

---

[3] For a discussion of the advantages and disadvantages of power pairing and pre-seeding see: Austin J. Freeley, *Argumentation and Debate* (San Francisco: Wadsworth Publishing Company, 1961), 334–35.

sides. It is not necessary, however, that every team alternate sides every round.

In addition to a standard six or eight rounds of debate, many tournaments also have elimination rounds. These elimination rounds may begin at the octa- or quarter-final levels if the tournament is very large or at the semifinal or final level. The procedures for selecting teams for elimination rounds and the schematic for pairing them should be determined before the start of the tournament. Teams are generally selected for elimination rounds according to (1) win–loss records, (2) highest rating points, and (3) lowest speaker rankings. If, on the basis of all three of these criteria, two teams are still tied for the last spot in the elimination pairings, the toss of a coin is generally used to determine which team will be assigned the position. Pairings for elimination rounds should be based upon team records in the nonelimination rounds. In order to reward the teams with the best records in the preliminary rounds, they should be paired against the qualifying teams with the poorest records. Therefore, the best team in the preliminary rounds should be paired against the poorest qualifying team, the second best against the second poorest, and so on. The following diagram illustrates a schematic for quarter-final elimination rounds; the Roman numerals represent team rankings at the end of the preliminary rounds.

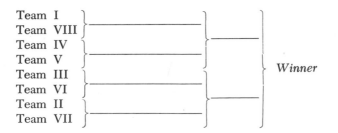

If two teams from the same school qualify for the elimination rounds, they should be bracketed into the schedule according to their rankings, and if the two teams should, thus, be scheduled to debate each other, they should be given the option of debating or of agreeing to have one of the teams advance without a debate. In elimination rounds, the side of the proposition to be debated by a team is normally decided by the toss of a coin. If, however, the two teams have met in the preliminary rounds, they should be assigned to debate on opposite sides in the elimination round.

Schematics for Individual Events Contests. It is somewhat difficult to establish standards and rules for preparing schematics for individual-events tournaments since the forms of these contests are not as uniform as are most debate tournaments. Many individual events contests are designed specifically for one type of event, such as oratory or extemporaneous speaking, while others include a variety of events. Some contests restrict participating schools to a single contestant for each event, while others allow each school to enter several contestants per event. Even the number of judges required for a given number of contestants varies considerably among tournaments. Nevertheless, in spite of these and other variations, certain general suggestions can be made.

In preparing schematics for individual-speaking contests there are four standards which should be met:

1. A contestant should not be judged by a judge from his own school.

2. A contestant should not be required to compete against the same *set* of contestants in more than one round. Contest schematics should be designed to assure maximum regrouping of contestants. This regrouping is necessary in order to guard against all the good contestants being put in one group and being forced to compete directly against each other round after round.

3. The number of contestants assigned to each group should not be less than four nor more than eight. A minimum of four contestants is needed to assure sufficient differentiation in rank orders throughout an entire tournament. A maximum number of eight (or even seven) contestants should be set in order to minimize the effect of speaking order on judges' decisions.

4. In contests, such as oratory and interpretative reading, where contestants use the same materials in each round, judges should not judge the same contestant more than once. In contests, such as extemporaneous speaking or impromptu speaking, where contestants present different materials each round, judges may hear the same contestant twice, although it is not desirable that they do so.

Two sample schematics for pairing contestants in individual speaking contests are given below. Schematic C is for a three-round, twenty-seven–contestant contest. Schematic D is for a three-round, fifteen-contestant contest. In these schematics each number represents a different contestant, and each column of numbers under the capital letters represents a different group of competing contestants. Schematic C assures each contestant of a totally new set of competitors each round. While Schematic D does not do this, it does provide a systematic means of mixing contestants and assures that no two contestants will meet more than twice. Schematic C may be used when there are sixteen contestants or when the number of contestants is above nineteen. Schematic D should be used for all contests in which the number of contestants is less than twenty, except for contests with sixteen contestants.

Schematic C

Round I						Round II					
K	L	M	N	O		K	L	M	N	O	P
1	7	13	18	23		1	2	3	4	5	6
2	8	14	19	24		7	8	9	10	11	12
3	9	15	20	25		13	14	15	16	17	
4	10	16	21	26		18		20	21	22	19
5	11	17	22	27			24	25	26	27	23

Round III					
K	L	M	N	O	P
1	2	3	4	5	6
8	9	10	11	12	7
15	16	17		13	14
21	22	19	18		20
27	23		24	25	26

Schematic D

Round I			Round II			Round III		
K	L	M	K	L	M	K	L	M
1	6	11	1	12	9	1	14	13
2	7	12	6	3	14	12	11	10
3	8	13	11	8	5	9	8	7
4	9	14	2	13	10	6	5	4
5	10	15	7	4	15	3	2	15

In order to prepare a schematic similar to Schematic C, the following procedures should be utilized:

1. The contestants should be divided into four or more groups for the first round. Each group should have the same or nearly the same number of contestants in it. If contestants cannot be distributed evenly through all the groups, extra contestants should first be placed in the groups represented by the left-hand column of numbers. In Schematic C the left-hand columns K and L would each contain six contestants while the other columns would each contain five contestants.

2. Pairings of contestants for Round II are achieved by moving horizontally across the column of numbers used in Round I and by placing all the contestants who are on the same horizontal plane into a new group. In Round I of Schematic C, three, nine, fifteen, twenty, and twenty-five are all in different groups, and since their numbers fall on the same horizontal plane, they are put into the same new group (M) for Round II. When the groups in Round I are not of equal size, it is necessary to have as many groups in Round II as there were contestants in the largest group in Round I. Because two of the groups in Round I of Schematic C contained six contestants, it is necessary to have six, rather than five, groups in Round II and in all succeeding rounds. Once the new groups for Round II are formed through the system of horizontal bracketing, the size of the groups should be equalized as nearly as possible. In the second round, the smallest group will always appear in the last column of numbers. If the last column is short only one contestant, the last contestant in column K should be moved horizontally across the schematic to the last column, (P). If a second contestant is needed to equalize the last group, the second to last contestant in column L should be selected. If a third contestant is needed, the third to last number in column M should be used and so on. As a result of such equalization, columns K, L, and P of Schematic C contain four contestants each and each of the other columns contains five contestants.

3. Pairings of contestants for Round III are arranged by moving diagonally downward across the columns of numbers used in Round II and by placing all the contestant numbers which appear in the same left to right diagonal into a new group.

Thus in Schematic C, one, eight, fifteen, twenty-one, and twenty-seven were all in different groups in Rounds I and II, and since their numbers all fall on the same diagonal, they are placed in the same new group (K) for Round III. Each diagonal should cut all the way across the column from top to bottom. If there are not enough numbers to the right of a diagonal to complete its movement, the diagonal should begin on the left side of the number block (column K) just below that point on the horizontal plane where it was stopped in the last column. Thus, in Schematic C the diagonal grouping that begins with contestant four in column N would include contestant eleven from column O, no contestant from column P, (and moving horizontally back to the left side and then diagonally downward), contestant eighteen from column K, and twenty-four from column L. After the diagonal pairings are completed, the size of the groups should once again be equalized, if necessary.

The procedures utilized in pairing the three rounds of Schematic C can be projected for use in a fourth or fifth round. These same procedures may also be used for a sixth round with thirty-six or more contestants, for a seventh round with forty-nine or more contestants, and for eight rounds with sixty-four or more contestants. Separate schematics must, of course, be prepared for each type of event offered.

For contests in which the number of entrants is too small to utilize Schematic C, Schematic D may be used. The procedures for preparing a schematic similar to Schematic D are explained thus:

1. Contestants should be divided into two or three equal or nearly equal groups. If there are enough contestants to permit three groups of not less than four contestants each, this should be preferred since the larger number of groups will permit more mixing of contestants from round to round. If contestants cannot be evenly distributed among the groups, extra contestants should be placed in the group(s) represented by the left-hand column or columns.

2. Contestant pairings for Round II are achieved by moving horizontally from left to right across the columns of numbers used in Round I. If all the numbers on the first horizontal plane

are not sufficient to constitute a group comparable in size to the first group in Round I, contestants should be taken in order from the second, or even the third, horizontal plane until an adequate group has been formed. The pairings for the second and third groups in Round II should be made in a similar manner, except that they should begin at whatever point the pairings for the preceding group stopped. Thus, in Schematic D, one, six, and eleven fall in the same horizontal plane, but since they do not constitute a group comparable in size to group K in Round I (five contestants) it is necessary to move from left to right across the second horizontal plane and pick up contestants two and seven to complete the first group. The second group for Round II begins with contestant thirteen from the second horizontal plane and moves to the next plane to pick up contestants three, eight, and thirteen; contestant four is drawn from the fourth plane to finish the second group. The remaining contestants constitute the third group.

3. Pairings for the third round are gained by using the same procedures as were utilized in Round II, except that the second-round numbers, rather than the first-round numbers, should be used as the basis for the new groupings.

While Schematics C and D are helpful in pairing contestants for individual events contests, they do not offer any means for assigning judges. Because of the variations in rules and in formats for tournaments with individual events contests, it is impossible to provide a standard system for matching and shifting judges. In tournaments which offer a number of different types of forensic events, the working out of judging assignments is usually not difficult. In these tournaments each judge may be assigned to judge a different type of event every round. However, oral-reading coaches will probably feel more at ease if their judging assignments are confined to humorous reading, declamations, dramatic interpretation, and similar events; likewise, public-speaking coaches are likely to prefer judging extemporaneous speaking, oratory, and impromptu speaking. If men's and women's divisions are held separately, it is usually possible to shift judges between these two divisions. In contests with only a few groups per round it is likely that several judges will not be needed for the early rounds and can be saved for use in later rounds. If two or three judges are to be assigned to each group, it may be necessary to require participating schools to provide extra judges. When only one judge per group is used, it is desirable to instruct him not to give any contestant (in a six-to-eight contestant contest) a rank below 4 or 5. This procedure tends to prevent any single erratic judge from eliminating a contestant, since a three-round ranking of 1–1–4 might still advance a contestant to the finals.

Once contestant pairings and judging assignments are worked out, a schedule for each individual speaking event should be prepared. This schedule should reveal the names or code numbers of all the contestants in each group for each round and the names or numbers of the judges for each group and round. It should also indicate the times of the rounds and the contest rooms. In scheduling extemporaneous speaking, an hour's preparation time should be allowed speakers between the time of their drawing of topics and the start of the contest. The room where extemp topics can be drawn should be clearly designated. This schedule does not normally indicate the order of speaking, although it may do so. The speaking order is usually determined by drawing lots just before the contest.

OPERATING THE TOURNAMENT

If a tournament has been carefully planned and implemented, the actual operation of the event should not be difficult. The operation of a tournament involves the registration and orientation of tournament participants, the management of chairmen-timekeepers' activities, the handling of emergency situations, and the tabulation and publication of results.

Registration and Orientation

The registration of participating schools should proceed smoothly, quickly, and graciously. Adequate advance preparation is necessary, however, to guarantee that this will occur. Registration packets should be prepared for each school a day or two before the tournament. These packets should include copies of the tournament program, maps of the campus, debate and individual events schedules (if these are not included in the program), and name tags. Enough of these items should be included in the packets so that every contestant and judge will receive one of each of them. If schools' and contestants' names are not used in the schedules, then each school should also be given a sheet of paper with its code number or numbers on it.

In order to assist visiting schools in locating the registration area, it is desirable to have large signs prepared which can be used to direct them to the proper place. On the day of the tournament these signs should be posted at conspicuous spots throughout the immediate vicinity of the registration desk.

Then tournament fees are to be collected at registration, a cash box and receipt books will be needed. If receipts are partially made out in advance of the tournament, the registration process will move along more rapidly on the day of the tournament. A sufficient supply of money should be on hand for making change, since visiting coaches often pay their registration fees with large denomination bills.

Simple refreshments of coffee and doughnuts or of punch and cookies may be served during the registration period. Such refreshments may encourage friendly socializing among participating schools and may help to keep contestants relaxed and less impatient while waiting for the competition to get under way.

It is generally necessary to plan a brief opening assembly. The meeting room for this assembly should be large enough to accommodate all the tournament participants comfortably, and if possible, it should be located near the registration desk. The assembly should begin on time with a few, brief words of welcome from the tournament director or from some departmental or university official. If any last minute changes in schedules, rooms, or procedures are necessary, they should be explained following the welcoming remarks. In addition, some explanation of how to locate tournament facilities ought to be given to help orient visiting contestants and judges. The assembly should end in sufficient time to allow participants to get to their first rounds on time and without hurrying.

Chairmen-Timekeepers

The chairmen-timekeepers' assignments should have been confirmed several days before the tournament, and written instructions ought to have been given to them. These instructions should have included a reminder to bring a watch with a second hand, some suggestions regarding appropriate clothing, and information on where and when to report. It is generally wise to have timekeepers report for duty forty-five minutes before the start of the first round. This allows time for a short briefing session and still makes it possible for the timekeepers to get to their first rounds on schedule. At the briefing session a sheet of final detailed instructions should be distributed, and one of the members of the chairmen-timekeepers' committee should go over this sheet with the timekeepers. (A sample chairmen-timekeepers' instruction sheet follows.) The importance of being friendly and of being on time should be particularly stressed and questions from the timekeepers should be encouraged. After the briefing session, the chairmen-timekeepers should each be given a set of time cards and a ballot and assigned to chair a specific contest. At the end of each round the chairmen-timekeepers should return their ballots to the timekeepers' office and receive new ballots and new assignments.

Instructions for Chairmen-Timekeepers

1. At the timekeepers' desk pick up your timekeeping assignment and room number, a judge's ballot, and a set of time cards.
2. Proceed to your assigned room. Be there at least five minutes before the round is scheduled to begin.
3. Introduce yourself to the judge and contestants as they arrive. Remember that your friendliness and helpfulness can contribute much to a good impression of a school.
4. Ask the contestants to write their names and speaking order, and their school's name or code number on the blackboard. This will help the judge in filling out his ballot.
5. Give the ballot to the judge when he enters.
6. Take a seat near the front of the room where you can be seen easily.

7. As soon as all the contestants are in the room and the judge has completed filling out his ballot, indicate to the first speaker that he may begin.
8. Each of the speeches should proceed in order. The order of speeches and the time for each speech are as follows:

> 10 minutes—1st Affirmative constructive
> 10 minutes—1st Negative constructive
> 10 minutes—2nd Affirmative constructive
> 10 minutes—2nd Negative constructive
> 5 minutes—1st Negative rebuttal
> 5 minutes—1st Affirmative rebuttal
> 5 minutes—2nd Negative rebuttal
> 5 minutes—2nd Affirmative rebuttal

IN CASE OF PROBLEMS CALL
TOURNAMENT HEADQUARTERS: 123-4567

One member of the chairmen-timekeepers' committee should keep track of the ballots as they are returned so that he will know what specific ballots remain out and when all of them have been returned. A second member of the committee ought to be responsible for the distribution of the new ballots and assignments. As soon as all the ballots from a round are in, they should be taken directly to the tabulation room.

Preparations for Emergencies

Unexpected and unwanted eventualities are frequently associated with the operation of forensic tournaments. However, these emergency situations will cause less disruption and less concern if preparations for dealing with them are made in advance. One of the most serious emergencies which is likely to occur on the day of a tournament is the failure of one or more schools to register as expected. Such a situation inevitably demands last-minute schedule changes. In order to make these changes quickly and accurately, the tournament director must be free from other responsibilities and must understand the system used in preparing the original tournament schematics. A competent assistant should be on hand to check the changes as the tournament director makes them. If only minor changes are required, they can probably be announced at the general assembly, and corrections can be made on existing schedules. If, on the other hand, there are a number of late withdrawals and extensive changes are necessary, an entirely new schedule may need to be printed. A stenographer, a typewriter, and some kind of duplication equipment should be kept available in anticipation of such a situation.

Forensic squad members (and if possible, their friends) should be asked to stand by to fill in for chairmen-timekeepers who fail to appear, and a list of the telephone numbers of extra judges should be ready to guard against problems caused by sick or irresponsible judges. A list of extra rooms should also be available in case assigned rooms are locked or occupied by other groups.

The telephone number of the tournament headquarters office should be included in the program and in the chairmen-timekeepers' instruction sheet. Answers to many difficulties can be provided by the headquarters staff, since they are usually in the best position to decide what to do, when to do it, and whom to contact. For example, the tournament staff would be most likely to know what to do in an emergency situation.

Tabulation and Publication of Results

The tabulation of results is an important and time-consuming task. In order to expedite tabulations on the day of the contests, it is wise to prepare large master tabulation sheets before the tournament begins. Two master tabulation sheets will be needed for debate. One sheet should be prepared for recording team win–loss records and team rating points. A second sheet is necessary for tabulating individual debaters' speaker rating points and contestant rankings. Individual speaking contests will require separate master schedule sheets for each type of event. These sheets should provide spaces for recording each contestant's rating points and rankings.

On the day of the tournament, results should be recorded on the master tabulation sheets at the end of each round. If the tournament involves both debate and individual speaking contests, separate tabulation crews should be assigned to each of these major categories of events. After the results of each round have been recorded they should be double checked to make sure that no errors in transcription have occurred. Each school's ballots should be placed into the appropriate school folder. Only after each round's ballots have been recorded, checked, and filed should the next round's ballots be opened. During the early rounds of the tournament, a stenographer should begin typing the master dittos and stencils which will be used for printing copies of the final tournament results. Once the results for a round have been recorded on the master tabulating sheets and checked, the secretary may copy that round's results onto the ditto masters or stencils. If a tournament extends over more than one day, all the ballots from each day's contests should be tabulated before the start of the next day's activities. Running totals of rankings and speaker ratings should be kept to help expedite final tabulations. Before selecting tournament winners the ballots and tabulated scores of each of the top contenders ought to be checked a final time to avoid any possible mistakes. The secretary should have an assistant ready to start printing stencils or dittos as soon as the final results have been decided so that participants may receive copies of the tournament results at the closing assembly.

Winners in individual-events contests are usually determined on the basis of the contestants' *rank order*. A contestant's ranking is based upon the judge's evaluation of him in relationship to other contestants. Since a rank of 1 is best, the contestant with the lowest total rankings should be declared the winner. If two or more contestants have the same total rankings, the methods of reranking, ratings, or reciprocals may be used to break ties. *Reranking* requires that a tied contestant's rankings for each round be paired against the round-by-round rankings of the other contestant. Each of the contestants is given a new rank of 1 or 2 depending upon whose original ranking was lower. Thus, if contestant A had original rankings of 1–4–1 and contestant B had original rankings of 2–2–2, contestant A would win with a reranked score of 1–2–1 as opposed to B's 2–1–2. The method of speaker *ratings* requires judges to give each contestant a qualitative score which is usually based upon a thirty-to-fifty-point scale. This method allows the judge to indicate the degree of difference between contestants. Thus, a judge may rank three contestants in order–1, 2, 3–but he may give the first contestant fifty points, the second contestant forty-eight points, and the third contestant only thirty-five points. When this method is used to break ties, the contestant with the highest total rating points throughout all the rounds of the tournament is declared the winner. The method of *reciprocals* utilizes the original-speaker rankings, but turns them into fractions by placing the number 1 over each ranking. The fractions are, then, added together and the contestant with the highest total score wins.

Winners in nonelimination debate tournaments are determined on the basis of win–loss records. If two or more teams have the same win–loss records, total team rating points are usually used to break ties. Speaker rankings are used as a second method of breaking ties. In elimination debate tournaments the winners are, of course, decided on the basis of the sudden-death playoff.

TOURNAMENT TIMETABLE

The decision to host a tournament should be made from six months to a year before the anticipated date of the event.

1. The decision to host a tournament should be based upon a consideration of its possible beneficial effects on students and the forensic program.
2. The needs of the forensic community for particular types of tournaments at specific times in the school year should be considered.
3. The ability of the school and the community to host a tournament graciously and efficiently ought to be considered.

Planning for a tournament should begin at least six months before the actual event.

1. Tournament facilities and housing accommodations should be arranged for at an early date.
   a. Contest rooms, tournament administrative offices, and assembly rooms will be needed in order to operate the tournament.
   b. Hotels and motels should be surveyed to determine the availability of housing accommodations and to negotiate special tournament rates.

2. Special tournament features such as guest speakers, seminars, or tours require considerable advanced planning.
3. Matters of finance will influence many later decisions.
   a. Tournaments may be financed by means of outside sponsorship or by tournament entry fees.
   b. A tentative tournament budget should be prepared.
4. Initial invitations should be sent out six months before the tournament.

The actual implementation of the tournament should start two months before it is scheduled to take place.

1. The tournament staff must be established.
   Tournament awards should be decided upon and ordered far enough in advance to assure their delivery before the tournament date.
3. Final invitations consisting of a descriptive cover letter, a schedule of events, an entry form, and housing information should be mailed two months before the tournament.
4. Supplies should be ordered well in advance.
   a. AFA debate ballots may require up to four weeks for delivery.
   b. Commercially printed materials normally require from two to four weeks for delivery.
5. A list of possible guest judges should be prepared several weeks before the tournament.
6. Contest schematics ought to be prepared several days in advance of the tournament.
   a. Some tournament directors prepare extra schematics based on reduced numbers of participants to guard against late withdrawals from the tournament.
   b. If the original schematic is well designed, last-minute changes can usually be made with a minimum of effort.

The actual operation of the tournament should not be difficult if adequate preparations were made.

1. Tournaments usually begin with the registration of participants and with brief orientation sessions.
2. Chairmen-timekeepers should be instructed to report for a briefing session at least forty-five minutes before the first round of competition.

3. Emergency situations should be anticipated and planned for.
4. Results should be tabulated throughout the tournament to assure the rapid announcement of winners.

SUGGESTED READINGS

Freely, Austin J. *Argumentation and Debate.* San Francisco: Wadsworth Publishing Company, 1961, 325–42.

Huber, Robert. "Debate Tournaments," *Argumentation and Debate,* ed. James H. McBath. New York: Holt, Rinehart, & Winston, Inc., 1963, 331–49.

McBurney, James H., James M. O'Neill, and Glen Mills. *Argumentation and Debate.* New York: The Macmillan Company, 1951, 299–303.

CHAPTER 12

Current Practices and Attitudes in Debate

Edward L. McGlone

EMPIRICAL STUDIES OF DEBATE

To the debater, the term "statistics" usually means numerical proof, or—more precisely—evidence consisting of numerically represented collections of instances. To the novice debater, statistics may seem to be the ultimate kind of evidence—the facts. But before long he discovers that there are conflicting statistics on just about any issue. Thus, it is not unusual for a debater or a debate coach to distrust statistics entirely. Perhaps this partially accounts for the failure of authors to include principles derived from empirical research in texts on argumentation and debate.

It is not the purpose of this author to argue that empirical research offers the only meaningful way to study debate. Nevertheless, this chapter proceeds from the assumption that statistical studies and statistics about debate provide useful information about norms, standards, and practices in debate. It is acknowledged that this may be a difficult premise for many debaters and debate coaches to accept; and so this first section attempts to provide a defense of that assumption by discussing the nature of empirical research.

The Survey and Experiment as Research Methods

The usual understanding of the term "statistics" involves one branch of empirical research—the survey. In this sense, statistics are counts or measurements of things which can be quantified. Surveys about debate, for example, might include a count of the number of schools and colleges which have debate programs, and separate counts of the novice debaters, varsity debaters, and debate coaches. They might include such measurements as the College Board examination scores of debaters, the miles traveled on debate trips, and the percentages of wins and losses of certain teams or schools.

However, statistics can refer to a discipline as well as to surveys. Just as algebra and geometry are branches of mathematics, so is statistics. In this sense, the term refers to a tool for the analysis of data in experiments. Statistics helps the researcher to analyze and interpret the counts and measurements which he may have collected in a survey. It is obvious that the data collected in a survey may be incomplete. Application of statistical tests to the data can suggest to the researcher how confident he should be that his data is representative of the complete picture. Often, the results of a survey may suggest that certain accepted principles are not true; indeed a survey of attitudes about debate could seem to indicate that a particular new strategy of presenting a case is desirable. It is in the process of verifying these suppositions and predictions that the experiment and statistics have the greatest application. A researcher can draw a sample and experiment with the new principles and strategies; and again statistics provides a method of analyzing the significance of his findings.

In debate, an experiment might reveal whether authoritative evidence is significantly more effective than specific instances. It could suggest whether college debaters with high-school experience turn out to be more effective than those with no experience. An experiment might provide evidence about the development of critical thinking ability of debaters in comparison to non-debaters. In all these cases, the application of statistical tests to data can tell the experimenter about the significance of his findings and the confidence he may have in drawing conclusions.

The two kinds of empirical studies discussed use statistics in two very different senses. In the case of the survey, statistics *are numerical facts;* in the case of the experiment, statistics *is* a *body of methods* for making inferences about numerical data. The use of statistics in the latter sense provides insurance against the misuse of statistics in the former sense. Empirical studies of debate can provide useful information about debating and debaters whenever proper methodological safeguards are employed and whenever sensible interpretations are made of the results of such studies.

Interpreting Empirical Studies of Debate

Accepting the results of empirical studies of debate uncritically leads to confusion and self-deception. Rejecting the results of such studies indiscriminately leads to ignorance. Somewhere between these extremes lies the position of the discerning reader or student, who may not be a statistician or even a researcher, but who can apply these simple rules for interpreting empirical studies:

1. *Use common sense.* This seemingly superficial principle has special relevance to the problem of interpreting empirical studies in general, and studies of debate in particular. If advertisements and political claims are accepted blindly by laymen, debate coaches and debaters attribute it to indolence in thinking on the part of the "masses." Yet, claims offered by professors in support of new theories in professional journals are often accepted by debaters and coaches as readily as claims made by football players for hair tonic in newspapers and magazines. Most of the confusion and ignorance about research findings would be cleared up if the reader would simply apply the rules for judging evidence in a debate in his evaluation of empirical studies. Indeed, with one exception, this list of rules for interpreting empirical studies is just a summary of the rules for judging evidence found in another chapter of this book.

2. *Ask the question "Are the results of the study consistent?"* Are they internally consistent? Are they consistent with other research? Few articles fail to contain at least a partial bibliography of other relating articles. If the reader plans to invest some time

and effort in applying the research findings, he can certainly use some of that time and effort to study other findings.

3. *Consider the source.* The most prolific writers about debate are not necessarily active participants in the activity. Coaches and debaters may be hypercritical about debate judges; it is not unreasonable for them to exercise some judgment about who is qualified to write about debate. This is critical for evaluating the reports of experiments about debate. Behavioral experiments require the identification and control of all the variables which may influence the outcome of the experiment. If the experimenter has little knowledge of the variables of debate, he may fail to control them in his experiment. Also consider the publication in which the research appears. A significant study is rarely sent to a house organ for first publication. It is much more likely to be submitted to *Speech Monographs, Speech Teacher,* the *Quarterly Journal of Speech,* the *Journal of the American Forensic Association,* or one of the regional speech journals first. This is not to say that something is wrong with an article if it appears in the *Rostrum* or the *Speaker-Gavel.* However, such publications are not the primary sources of the published research about debate.

4. *Be wary of the language used in reporting the research.* Usually experimenters limit their conclusions to the data; but it is very easy to generalize beyond the findings. A case in point; one experimenter studied debate case construction among the high-school debaters in Ohio. He found that the "advantages" approach on the affirmative was considered ineffective and even unethical in many instances. His conclusions applied to Ohio high-school debating, but it is very easy to infer that these conclusions should be applied to high-school debating and perhaps to debating in general. One can expect differences in geographical areas and even from one school to another. Hold the experimenter and yourself to generalizations justified by the data.

5. *Evaluate the sampling procedure of the experiment.* Television coverage of the presidential elections has done a good deal to increase the credibility of findings of empirical research. Viewers are able to observe computerized research in action in the prediction of winners in national political races on the basis of small returns. Predicting the behavior of populations from analy-

sis of very small samples is possible; but the key to its accuracy is sampling. The most sophisticated statistician with the most complicated computers cannot do a decent job of generalizing to populations unless his samples are representative of those populations. Most of the experimentation concerning debate does not involve sampling procedures adequate for generalizing to debate throughout the country. Availability seems to have replaced sampling as a procedure for getting subjects for an experiment. If a researcher wants to experiment with debaters, he uses the ones who happen to debate for his school—as many as he can get. The large debate tournament offers a partial solution to this problem; but still, it is difficult to argue that the debaters at a given tournament are representative of the national population of debaters. The student of empirical studies in debate must make a judgment about the nature of the sample used before he can interpret experiments and surveys meaningfully.

These are the things a reader of empirical research reports must keep in mind. Following these simple guidelines should allow a debate coach to make the most of the volumes of research available on debaters and debating. Within this research lie solutions and answers to many of the problems and questions a debate coach must face. The rest of this chapter deals with a number of empirical studies of the more significant areas of concern.

RESEARCH ABOUT DEBATERS

Few debate coaches have ever failed to ask themselves, "What kind of student makes a good debater?" Most coaches assume that debate affects debaters favorably in terms of developing thinking and organizational skills; more often than not, these same coaches are worried about the effects of overzealous competition on the personalities of debaters. Much research has been conducted to investigate the makeup of the debater. This section deals with the findings of that research.

Perhaps the greatest number of consistent conclusions among all empirical studies of debate is to be found in the area of personality correlates with skill in debate. This subject has been investigated by various researchers since the thirties with many of the same findings. A fairly recent study of Kansas high-school and college debaters[1] is typical of such studies. The researchers wanted to study the personality characteristics of successful debaters, and so they needed some way to measure personality characteristics as well as some "successful debaters" to compare with non-debaters. As an instrument to measure personality characteristics, they selected the Edwards Personal Preference Schedule, a personality inventory not unlike the types used by psychologists and counselors in advising high-school and college students on personal, rather than career, problems. To obtain experimental groups, they defined "success in debate" as the winning of some debate tournament; and, for every "successful debater," they selected a non-debater of the same sex, age, general ability, grade point average, and general popularity. This procedure is questionable: the principles of experimental design require that any matching on variables be accomplished before the assignment of subjects to experimental groups (in this case—debaters and non-debaters.) The widespread use of such matching procedures has done much to discredit the results of such studies. After this, Hetlinger and Hildreth subjected both the debaters and the non-debaters to the Edwards Personal Preference Schedule, and analyzed the differences with statistical tests.

In general they found that successful debaters are different from non-debaters in the following ways:

(1) Debaters have a greater need than non-debaters to be recognized as a success by doing things better than others. (Achievement.)

(2) Debaters have fewer feelings of inferiority than non-debaters. They are less willing than non-debaters to accept criticism and blame. (Abasement.)

(3) Debaters have a fondness for leadership that non-debaters do not have in the same degree. They desire control and influence over others. (Dominance.)

(4) Successful debaters seem to value friendship less than non-

---

[1] Duane F. Hetlinger and Richard Hildreth, "Personality Characteristics of Debaters," *Quarterly Journal of Speech*, XLVII (December 1961), 398.

debaters. In any case they tend not to seek out cooperation and friendship of others. (Affiliation.)

(5) Debaters like competition. They like to meet and to defeat opposition forcefully. Non-debaters have this tendency in much less degree. (Aggression.)

(6) Finally, debaters feel less of a need to assist and care for others than non-debaters. (Nurture.)

To be sure, these differences were not observed between all groups of debaters and non-debaters. In fact, they were not consistent between the sexes of comparable groups of debaters. Successful women college debaters and non-debaters differed in the need for autonomy, the desire to assert one's independence, with the female debaters having this need in much greater degree. Successful male college debaters were discovered to need change in routine and to follow current fads and fashions less than college female debaters. High-school debaters seemed to have less need for organization and planning before making decisions than high-school students who were not debaters. Also, there were fewer differences in the characteristics listed above between successful high-school debaters and non-debaters.

Does the Hetlinger and Hildreth study suggest that to build a debate program a debate coach should go look for students who are aggressive, dominating, high achievers who refuse criticism and friendship? Of course, it does not. It does suggest that debaters tend to have these personality characteristics. These tendencies are not necessarily bad. While the test does not establish a causal relation between debate and these characteristics, it does suggest that debate and such personalities have some relationship. The largest question left unanswered by this study is whether such personality tendencies are undesirable. The problems of matching discussed above and the importance of this unanswered question create much doubt about the value of most studies of this kind.

Another study[2] suggests that some very desirable personality characteristics are associated with debaters. This study involved

---

[2] R. R. Allen, "The Effects of Interpersonal and Concept Compatibility on the Encoding Behavior and Achievement of Debate Teams," *Central States Speech Journal*, XIV (February 1963), 23.

only college debaters at the University of Wisconsin; and it defined "success" in terms of high ratings and winning debates. The effort here was to compare low-rated debaters with high-rated debaters in terms of interpersonal and concept compatibility. The researcher discovered that the abilities of teams to work well together and to achieve a common understanding of concepts and issues both correlated with success in debate. This suggests to the coach that his teams ought to be paired not only in terms of debate ability, but also in terms of their ability to get along with and to understand each other.

The effect of debate training on student skills is the subject of inquiry for much empirical research. The problem with most of the studies is that there seems to be no way to attribute any differences between debaters and non-debaters to debate training itself. Debaters are more intelligent than average students; they have more organizational ability; they seem to be more critical thinkers: nevertheless, it may be that students with those attributes are the ones who go out for debate. No claim can be made for these skills resulting from training in debate. One study[3] compared the improvement of critical thinking as measured by the Watson-Glazer test of debaters with that of non-debaters. The results were consistent with those of two older studies[4, 5] in showing that debaters outrank non-debaters significantly in critical thinking ability. Nevertheless, this simply may indicate that the kind of person who goes out for debate or who enrolls in an argumentation class has a greater proficiency for improving in this ability than others. Also, most of these studies used the questionable matching procedures described above. Some statisticians would contend that utilization of this procedure by itself makes the research worthless. Further research in this area has revealed that successful debaters (success-winning) are more proficient in both critical thinking and organizational ability than less successful debaters.[6] This too is

---

[3] Ted R. Jackson, "Effects of Intercollegiate Debating on Critical Thinking Ability," paper read before the 1966 Conference of the Central States Speech Association, Chicago, Illinois, April 16, 1966.

[4] Winston L. Brembeck, "The Effects of a Course in Argumentation on Critical Thinking Ability," *Speech Monographs*, XVI (1949), 177–89.

[5] William S. Howell, "The Effects of High School Debating on Critical Thinking," *Speech Monographs*, X (1943), 96–103.

[6] "Some Characteristics of the College Debater," (Research Report), *Central States Speech Journal*, XV (November 1964), 293.

subject to the "chicken-or-the-egg" argument—that able people turn out to be good debaters. Regardless of the confusion about the effects of debate training, it is a safe conclusion that debaters are able students for the most part, and that debaters seem to be able to profit from debate training.

A final effect of debate training on students which has been researched widely involves changes in attitude toward the proposition resulting from debating on a particular side. A recent study of sixty-eight high-school debaters in Kansas[7] revealed a relationship between success on a particular side and attitude change in the direction of that side. The experimenter suggested that this phenomenon can be attributed to some need on the part of a debater to adopt the position inherent in the side on which he has the greatest success. Of course, it may be that a debater has more success after or during this attitude change. In any case, this is not a very startling finding.

It would seem that the measurement of a debater in terms of personality and abilities is far from complete. For the most part, replications of older studies make up the bulk of the current research in this area. Although one researcher[8] has reported some success in the area of developing a new measurement instrument for examining debater vs. non-debater capabilities, several questions go unanswered: How does debate affect a student's personality development? Can only bright students profit from debate training? Is debate training superior to other pedagogical methods for teaching organization, critical thinking, and so forth?

SURVEYS ABOUT COACHES AND TOURNAMENTS

While most of the research mentioned so far in this chapter is prescriptive in the sense that the researchers put forward principles which can be implemented in a forensics program, the studies reported in this section may be labelled descriptive research. A

---

[7] Terry A. Welden, "A Congruity Prediction of Attitude Change from Debate Win–Loss Record," *Journal of the American Forensic Association*, III (May 1966), 48–52.

[8] Don F. Faules, "The Measurement of Refutation Skill," paper read before the 1966 Conference of the Central States Speech Association, Chicago, Illinois, April 16, 1966.

number of recent surveys have had the goal of trying to describe the typical debate coach. There are so many variables involved in coaching that it is difficult to quantify them to the extent of actually achieving this goal with a survey. An even greater weakness inherent to such research derives from the relative unimportance of typicality to any competitive activity like debate. While standards concerning practices must be discovered in order for them to be maintained, it is highly unlikely that knowledge of the average coach's background should affect any other coach's preparation for his job. (Similar research concerning the typical debate tournament may be of more practical value, and this is also reported in this section.) It may have its greatest value for the undergraduate who wants to insure that his *vita* sheet will not place him at a competitive disadvantage should he seek a debate-coaching job.

Nevertheless, these studies are interesting. Together with the tournament surveys, they can provide information to the director of a small program concerning national activities and standards; but, for the most part, their value to the reader depends upon whatever fascination he may have for finding out how he compares to his colleagues.

One survey of forensics directors at 156 colleges and universities[9] produced the following information. Most directors of forensic programs hold the rank of assistant professor or higher in a speech department. Most were debaters as undergraduates, and most majored in speech as both undergraduates and graduates. Few have ever coached debate in high school, but the median amount of experience in coaching is six years. Also, nearly 45 per cent have earned the doctorate degree, and most of the rest are working on Ph.D.'s. A similar study[10] involving both college coaches and high-school sponsors of National Forensics League chapters gave much the same information. In addition, the Klopf and Rives study of college and high-school coaches allows the following comparisons:

[9] Donald J. Cameron, "Backgrounds of Forensic Directors," *Journal of the American Forensic Association*, I (May 1964), 59–61.
[10] Donald Klopf and Stanley Rives, "Characteristics of High School and College Forensics Directors," *Journal of the American Forensic Association*, II (January 1965), 33–37.

(1) Neither high-school nor college coaches permit students to have much of a role in administering the forensics program; but high schools allow this practice to a much greater extent.

(2) Most programs—both high school and college—have only one faculty coach; but college coaches usually receive some load reduction (the average is two hours) for the activity, while this is rarely the case for high-school coaches.

(3) Both high-school and college directors have taught about the same amount of time (high-school average—10.4 years; college average—11.6 years; and both have been directors for an average of about 7.5 years. However, about a third of the college directors and an even larger percentage of high-school directors are in their first five years of teaching.

(4) Nearly half of the high-school directors and nearly 70 per cent of the college directors have salaries of more than $7000 a year. Over 40 per cent of the college directors earn more than $9000 a year.

(5) Both college directors and high-school directors claim to spend about the same number of hours per week in their forensics duties (college average—18.7 hours; high-school average—18.1 hours). Both groups assign the largest number of hours to tournament activities, the next largest to coaching, and the least number to administration.

This same study involved material reported in another source[11] concerning the reasons for the high turnover rate among college and high-school coaches. A big weakness in this study lies in its failure to survey coaches who had actually quit. Nevertheless, the speech department heads, directors of forensics, and NFL chapter sponsors provided a list of the most common complaints about the coach's job, regardless of whether it reveals much about why coaches leave their jobs. Among college coaches the most frequently cited reasons for quitting involved time (34% of the respondents mentioned this as one of the four primary causes); overwork and fatigue (27%), travel (26%), other academic duties and interests (23%), and disinterest (21%). The high-school

---

[11] Stanley Rives and Donald Klopf, "Debate Coaches: Why They Quit," *Central States Speech Journal*, XVI (February 1965), 38–40.

coaches were more in agreement about time (49%) and overwork and fatigue (44%) than the college coaches; and they
ranked several other reasons for quitting higher than the college
coaches: poor compensation (44%) and nonrecognition and support (32%). Another interesting result of this survey was that 15%
of the college respondents listed the demands of teaching and
research as a reason for quitting, while it was not listed at all by
high-school respondents; and 7% of the high-school coaches listed
either problems with other coaches or poor results as reasons for
leaving the job, neither of which was listed by a college coach.

Finally, the institution of the college debate tournament was
described in a study of 210 tournaments held during 1962–63.[12]
It was discovered that the majority of these tournaments were
restricted, either according to membership in an organization,
such as a debate fraternity (36%), or to invitation (24%). The
Midwest had the largest percentage (45%) of open or unrestricted
tournaments. Most of the tournaments had only one division of
competition: in the East, 72% of the tournaments made no distinction according to experience; in the South, the figure was 56%; in
the Midwest, 47%; and in the Far West, 33%. The Far West had
the largest percentage of two division tournaments with junior-
senior or novice-varsity consisting of 44% of the total number and
men-women tournaments consisting of 11%. Sixteen per cent of
the Midwest's tournaments were novice-only affairs, the highest
percentage of the four areas. Also, 70 per cent of the 210 college
tournaments were limited to debate, while only 2 per cent limited
competition to individual events. Debate has already seen the
demise of the tournament which separated male and female
competitors. This survey suggests that segregation according to
ability may also be on the way out. Its findings also support the
thesis that the importance of debate as a tournament activity far
exceeds that of individual events.

The study further reveals that college debate has embraced the
orthodox format almost as completely as the NFL high-school
tournaments have adopted the cross-examination format. For the
1962–63 season, only 17 per cent of the college tournaments used
any other format either in conjunction with or instead of the

---

[12] Donald W. Klopf, "Practices in Intercollegiate Speech Tournaments,"
Journal of the American Forensic Association, I (May 1964), 48–52.

standard 10–5 style. Switch-sides debating was preferred by a sizable margin over four-man teams with 82 per cent of the tournaments providing for this procedure either by itself (69%) or in combination with four-man divisions (13%). The written critique and the combination of written and oral critiques were the most commonly used types of evaluation. The use of quality ratings along with win–loss results was in effect in nearly 70 per cent of the tournaments polled, while win–loss results alone were used in an additional 20 per cent. While there were some regional differences in these items, they were insignificant in comparison to the relative agreement of college tournaments in use of formats and determination of results.

All this data about coaches and tournaments tends to suggest that debate has become as national and standard an activity as the athletic extracurricular activities. Coaches and tournaments are very similar from school to school and from region to region. While there may be some argument from time to time about whether debate is an academic profession, there certainly can be no doubt that it has developed all the formality of a profession.

ATTITUDES ABOUT JUDGES AND JUDGING

One empirical study which could be done might deal with the amount of time spent by debaters and coaches arguing about decisions and judges. Probably no person who has been on a debate trip as a debater, coach, judge, or observer, has completed the journey without either participating in or listening to at least one heated discussion about the eccentricities of particular judges in awarding adverse decisions. Some judges seem never to vote *for* any team; but allegedly they listen only for overly rapid deliveries and errors in pronunciation, carefully noting the amount of time speakers take to lay out their evidence cards, so they can carefully weigh the number of technical errors for each team to determine who loses the debate. While in all probability judges do not deserve a fraction of the abuse which has been heaped upon them, some undoubtedly are better judges than others; and it is certain that different judges use differing standards in evaluating debates. This section deals with research relevant to three aspects of this problem.

Backgrounds and Qualifications of Judges

Several surveys have included questions concerning the selection of judges for tournaments. Two relatively extensive projects involved a part of the survey of procedures in 210 collegiate debate tournaments mentioned on page 337,[13] and a study of the practices of thirty-six state high-school speech leagues in employing judges.[14] Comparison of the two surveys reveals differences between the procedures for selecting judges of high-school and college debate. Every one of the college debate tournaments surveyed used speech instructors or debate coaches as judges, but eight of the thirty-six responding state high-school leagues did not use high-school coaches at all in their official tournaments. This would seem to indicate that college coaches have fewer misgivings about the capabilities of their colleagues in giving fair, competent decisions than do their high-school counterparts.

The survey of high-school organizations revealed a number of differences among the states in hiring judges. Only one of the thirty-six states reported using only high-school coaches as judges. No state relied on laymen for more than half of their judging, while thirteen states did not use laymen as judges at all. Finally six states used only college faculty as judges, and all but two states used some college personnel for judging. One could conclude that the high-school organizations have high regard for college faculty as debate judges, but very low regard for other persons not connected with high-school debate. In fact, it would seem that in some areas the high schools consider college faculty to be more objective or more qualified as judges than high-school debate coaches themselves.

The college survey produced quite different results. As it has been noted, every tournament made use of coaches as judges. Of the 210 tournaments included in the study, thirty-three per cent

---

13 *Ibid.*

14 Mary Reeves and Lynn R. Osborn, "Judges of High School Debate Tournaments: Sources, Criteria and Orientation," *Speech Teacher*, XIV (January 1965), 59.

involved only speech faculty and coaches as judges. An additional twenty-six per cent of the tournaments had these as well as other college faculty as judges. Thirty-two per cent of the tournaments had laymen in some combination with other judges; and student critics were used with other judges in twenty-eight per cent of the tournaments. While it would seem that college tournament directors consider coaches to be the best judges of debate, it also appears that they are quite willing to go to diverse sources for judges when there is an inadequate supply of coaches.

Criteria Used in Judging Debates

One researcher[15] hypothesized that judges should use certain criteria in awarding decisions because these criteria were related to educational values; then he set out to test his hypothesis. His study of judges at one of the fine intercollegiate debate tournaments in the Midwest concluded that judges not only use these criteria in judging debates, but that they are aware of these standards for evaluation in and out of debates. The trouble with this kind of study is that when people are given such a list of factors to respond to, either during a debate or outside one, they typically give consideration which might be lacking otherwise. The physical presence of a list provides great power for suggestion. Nevertheless, a by-product of this somewhat misleading study was the production of a ranking according to importance of the traditional quality ratings in debate. Thus the study does provide some information about the way a judge claims his mind works. Following is the list of factors in the order of their ranking by judges at the tournament surveyed:

(1) selection of logically defensible arguments (case)
(2) support of arguments with information (evidence)
(3) perception of irrelevant or irrational arguments (refutation)
(4) ability to analyze the topic-area (analysis)
(5) ability to speak well (delivery)
(6) ability to organize ideas into a structured whole (organization)

---

[15] Kim Giffin, "A Study of the Criteria Employed by Tournament Debate Judges," *Speech Monographs,* XXVI (March 1959), 69–71.

(7) phrasing of concepts clearly and concisely (language)

The list itself may be questioned because of its reasonably discrete items. Who can separate the "selection of logically defensible arguments" from the "ability to analyze the topic-area"? It would seem that the latter is a prerequisite for the former. Also, the problem of separating the last three concepts in this form of wording is difficult.

A methodological safeguard against some of the problems in the above experiment lies in the technique of factor analysis. With this method of statistical analysis, a very large number of criteria can be rated rather than ranked by each judge in each debate; and treatment of the data will produce a few significant factors made up of groups of the criteria which the judges seem to use together as "dimensions" of debate effectiveness. Also, these factors can be correlated with overall effectiveness to discover their relative importance to the judge's final decisions. A couple of studies of high-school debate judging by the same researchers[16, 17] have produced consistent results.

The more recent experiment involved the judging at three high-school debate tournaments in Wisconsin. It was discovered that in the 138 debates at the tournaments, four major factors appeared to account for the judges' behavior in evaluating the debates. The dominant factor could be labeled "argument." The analysis revealed that this dimension seems to consist of such specifics as relevancy of evidence, logic, validity of evidence, pertinency, reasoning, supporting material, analysis, concreteness, and organization. Thus, judges do evaluate debates according to argument, but argument consists of the items listed above. The next most significant factor was called "delivery-persuasiveness" and consisted of facial expression, eye contact, spontaneity, use of motive appeals, interestingness, and persuasiveness. The third factor was also a delivery-related dimension of evaluation which the researchers labeled "vocal correctness." This factor consisted of articulation, vocal quality, pitch, grammar, and pronunciation. A

---

[16] Frederick Williams and Sally Ann Webb, "Factors in Debate Evaluation: a Pilot Study," *Central States Speech Journal*, XV (May 1964), 126.

[17] Frederick Williams, Sally Ann Webb and Ruth Anne Clark, "Dimensions of Evaluating in High School Debate," *Central States Speech Journal*, XVII (February 1966), 15–21.

final identifiable factor which judges use in evaluating debates was called "apparent character." This dimension consisted of sportsmanship, courtesy, and ethics. It was discovered that while judges do make evaluations in this dimension, they are separate from the evaluation of general effectiveness in the debate.

The results of the study have profound implications for students of the debate evaluation, if indeed there are any such students. One would hope that a debate ballot would include among its quality ratings some measure of the significant factors used by a judge in evaluating a debate. Yet the six categories on the standard ballots (analysis, reasoning, evidence, refutation, organization, and delivery) would certainly be inadequate for revealing the actual evaluations made by the judges who participated in the Williams, Webb, and Clark study. A weakness in this study lies in the researchers' failure to correlate evaluations associated with the four factors with the actual decisions in the debates; but one would not expect the results to be significantly different from the correlations with general effectiveness.

Variability Among Judges

If there were no variability among judges, it might be possible to program a computer to award decisions; and human error in judging could be eliminated. Nevertheless, most people probably would agree that differences in opinion about what team is the winner of a debate is necessary and even desirable as long as there are differences among debaters and debate coaches. While little evidence is available to indicate whether certain decisions are "wrong" ones, a good deal of research indicates that decisions may be affected by a number of specific characteristics associated with judges. One of the most often noted variables affecting judges' decisions and evaluations is the judges' differing associations with debate.

In the previous study[18] the data was divided according to three types of judges: high-school debate coaches, other high-school faculty, and university graduate students. Although the makeup for the factors was slightly different for each judge type, the

---

[18] *Ibid.*

general dimensions of argument and delivery-persuasiveness as described previously, were the most significant factors used by all three groups in evaluating debates. Apparent character was a relevant factor for all judge-types; but it did not correlate significantly with overall effectiveness for any of the groups of judges. The most significant difference occurred in the dimension of vocal correctness. While this was a main factor for the non-coach faculty and the graduate students, it was not a dimension of evaluation used by the debate coaches. It would seem that only the coaches in this study treated both the correctness and the effectiveness of delivery as a single entity.

A correlation between differences in judging and differences in debate background has been observed in other studies. While the Wisconsin study involved many different debates, a study in Hawaii[19] used only one taped debate which was "judged" by college and high-school debate coaches, other faculty without training in either speech or debate, laymen outside the teaching profession, and experienced debaters. It was discovered that there were no significant differences among the four groups in the awarding of the decision, nor were there any significant differences in the quality ratings between the coaches and the experienced debaters. Coaches and other faculty did disagree in the evaluation of reasoning and evidence, refutation, and organization in the debate. Coaches and laymen had significantly different judgments concerning refutation and delivery. It makes sense that coaches and debaters evaluate debates similarly. It seems reasonable that coaches judge according to different criteria than laymen and other faculty. Nevertheless, if all groups reach the same decision with virtual unanimity, other differences between individual criteria may become less significant.

A third study involving only judges at a Southern tournament in 1964 and 1965[20] also supports the notion that a judge's background does not affect his decision. It was discovered that both high-school and college coaches in both years agreed for the most

---

19 Donald Klopf, Dianna Evans, and Sister Mary Linus DeLozier, "Comparative Studies of Students, Laymen and Faculty Members as Judges of Speech Contests," *Speech Teacher*, XIV (November 1965), 314–18.

20 James C. McCroskey and Leon R. Camp, "Judging Criteria and Judges' Bias in Debate," *Journal of the American Forensic Association*, III (May 1966), 59–62.

part on the rank order of criteria for judging debates. Unfortunately, the study involved the same criteria used in the Giffin study. The same problem of "leading" the judges in their selection of criteria is evident. Also, the researchers failed to attempt to correlate the rankings with decisions. Nevertheless, the significant agreement between high-school and college coaches is noteworthy.

Two studies involved projects designed to pick out "bad" judges. Their authors do not admit to this goal as such; one discusses the "maverick" or "independent thinker," and the other never gives the culprit any label. The former[21] contains the allegation that a maverick can be identified by the frequency with which he participates in split decisions. Indeed, study of a tournament such as the National Debate Tournament, in which there are three judges in every round, might provide data for such analyses. Nevertheless, in this study, the data were derived from a tournament in which there were two judges per round. If a judge participated in at least four split decisions in six rounds, he won the title "maverick." The researchers argued that such identifications could lead to the possible certification of mavericks. This is quite an extreme recommendation to follow such a small-scale study.

The second study[22] may have been attempted as a diverting exercise, but its results turned out to be quite serious. This researcher studied the ballots at a midwestern debate tournament in order to discover whether judges awarded decisions consistently to the most successful teams. By a number of criteria, the experimenter was able to identify nine out of a total of 192 decisions as suspect. It should be noted at this point that one conclusion which might be drawn is that debate judging at this tournament was quite consistent. Of these nine deviant decisions, six involved judges voting for teams from their own states; and another had a judge voting for debaters he had formerly coached. While the experimenter's conclusions are quite restrained, the suggestion is clear that such factors can account for "bad" decisions.

---

[21] Otto F. Bauer and C. William Colburn, "The Maverick Judge," *Journal of the American Forensic Association*, III (January 1966), 22–25.

[22] Roger Hufford, "Toward Improved Tournament Judging," *Journal of the American Forensic Association*, II (September 1965), 120–25.

Of course, there are kinds of bias which are inescapable, even if they are not very important. Just as people in general are not very good critics of their own behavior, debaters are not very good judges of their own debates—two studies have revealed that debaters rate themselves higher than nonparticipants do.[23, 24] This does not detract from their ability to judge other debates as discussed above. A related kind of biased behavior is that which a judge may exhibit when he sees his own beliefs about the proposition ignored or challenged. Research indicates that this is a rare occurrence.[25, 26] The allegation that judges have "favorite sides" seems to be more closely related to matters of preference in debate strategy than to any prejudice against the merits of the affirmative or negative side of a debate resolution.

All this research may be considered as exploratory. As it has been noted, some of the studies could be repeated with slightly different procedures; and the results might be considerably different. Certainly, geographical differences might confound some of the limited conclusions which have been drawn from these research efforts. Nevertheless, it seems reasonable that while judges may be selected for differing reasons at different tournaments, and while there may be different standards used by different judges, few of these differences are significant enough to warrant the carping and complaining about judges which probably will always occur. What is justified is more research efforts to discover the dimensions of evaluation which are being used by judges so that reformers and defenders of current judging practices can find common ground for argument.

---

[23] Larry L. Barker, "A Comparative Analysis of Debater-Judge Ratings," *Journal of the American Forensic Association*, II (January 1965), 17–20.

[24] Thomas King and Theodore Clevenger, "A Comparison of Debate Results Obtained by Participant and Critic Judging," *Southern Speech Journal*, XXV (Spring 1960), 223–32.

[25] Robert L. Scott, "The Objectivity of Debate Judges," *The Gavel*, XXXVII (November 1954), 14–15.

[26] McCroskey and Camp, *loc. cit.*

ATTITUDES ABOUT DEBATE PRACTICES

Not too many years ago, an adequate discussion of attitudes about debate practices in a book similar to this might require a full chapter on the subject of the advisability of switch-sides debating. It seems that the hot controversy about the ethics and the educational benefits of switch-sides debating has finally subsided. A recent survey of nearly three hundred college members of the American Forensic Association and about two hundred National Forensic League chapter sponsors[27] revealed that over 90 per cent of both groups consider the requiring of students to debate both sides of the proposition to be both ethical and good debate procedure. Nevertheless, there are a number of "burning issues" concerning the ethics and advisability of certain debate practices on which there is much difference of opinion. This section includes reports of some of the more significant attitude studies about these practices.

Ethical Debating

The major problem with most of the studies of attitudes about ethical practices is that they fail to attempt to discover factors which might be related to certain attitudes. Most of the studies have been merely public opinion polls on different lists of practices. It might be hypothesized that coaches from different areas have different conceptions of what is ethical and what is not. Some have suggested that the age of a coach has something to do with his judgments concerning ethics. Perhaps even more interesting would be a study of the extent to which the persons surveyed maintain their own standards of ethical conduct. It would seem that a number of the researchers have collected data which would allow them to test hypotheses about these issues. If they have conducted such experiments, the results have not been made available. Nevertheless, the published studies do reveal wide disagreement about the propriety of a number of debate practices.

One of the most extensive studies of attitudes about debate

[27] Donald Klopf and James C. McCroskey, "Debating Both Sides Ethical? Controversy Pau!" *Central States Speech Journal,* (February 1964), 36.

practices involved the same survey which provided the denounce-
ment of switch-sides debating as an issue of ethics mentioned
above.[28] The results of this study were reported in an attempt to
categorize some forty different practices as either ethical and good
procedure, ethical and bad procedure, of questionable ethics, and
unethical. Such a scheme of evaluation is at best confusing, but
the large number of college coaches polled make the research
worth examining. The researchers found virtually unanimous
agreement among those polled concerning three obviously unethical practices: fabricating evidence, judging debates on the
basis of personal opinions, and awarding decisions because of
friendship. On more than a dozen obviously ethical practices, the
researchers also discovered massive agreement. It is unfortunate
that the respondents were not allowed to label some practices as
being inappropriate to the labels "ethical" and "unethical," because a number of the practices obviously fall into that category
too. Nevertheless, the following practices showed the most disagreement among coaches concerning their ethics. Each number
refers to the percentage of coaches surveyed who considered the
practice to be either of questionable ethics or unethical.

1. Introducing a new issue in the rebuttal (70%)
2. Using sarcasm (43%)
3. Failing to identify sources of information (39%)
4. The affirmative waiting to answer important issues until the
   final rebuttal (68%)
5. The negative waiting to present a counterplan until the second constructive (49%)
6. The witness taking unnecessary time in answering questions
   in cross-exam (61%)
7. Asking tricky or leading questions in cross-exam (39%)
8. The witness conferring with colleague in cross-exam before
   asking or answering a question (61%)
9. The judge not writing comments on ballots if space is provided (36%)
10. The judge refusing to give an oral critique if time is avail-
    able and the tournament rules permit such critiques (34%)
11. Bombarding the opposition with a series of oral questions all

---

[28] Donald Klopf and James McCroskey, "Ethical Practices in Debate," *Journal of the American Forensic Association*, I (January 1964), 13–16.

of which obviously cannot be answered in the allotted time
(40%)
12. Using personal letters as evidence (34%)
13. Debating the debate after the debate with the judge or
opponents (47%)

At this point the reader probably is surprised to learn that there
is so much disagreement about the ethics of some one or more
of these practices. Remember that this list excludes the practices
ranked as unethical by the largest numbers of the 244 members
of the AFA who responded in the survey.

In another study of attitudes about ethical practices,[29] researchers at Kansas University attempted to measure debaters' evaluations of certain practices, the estimation of occurrence of these
practices, and their judgment of the wisdom of these practices.
The researchers selected ten "questionable" practices and surveyed debaters at twenty-four randomly selected colleges and
universities throughout the nation. Instead of asking the debaters
surveyed to categorize practices as ethical or unethical, the researchers asked the respondents to react to the practices by using
a number of seven-point scales which supposedly represented
degrees of judgment about a practice according to different
criteria. (The researchers used six different scales to measure a
debater's degree of rejection of a practice, two scales to measure
his beliefs about the frequency of each practice's occurrence, and
one scale to measure his judgment of the wisdom of a practice.)
The researchers discovered that the debaters rejected these practices as unethical: manufacturing evidence, violating the intention
of a quotation, changing the source of a quotation, misrepresenting the significance of an item of proof, misrepresenting the competence of the source, and attempting to distract a speaking
opponent. Practices receiving a judgment of neutral or ethical
included employing a "trick" case, misquoting opponents, appealing to known prejudices of the judge, and case-scouting. Of the
practices considered unethical, only two—misrepresenting the
significance of an item of proof and violating the intention of a
quotation—were considered usual or quite usual in occurrence by

---

[29] Carl E. Larson and Kim Giffin, "Ethical Considerations in the Attitudes
and Practices of College Debaters," *Journal of the American Forensic Association,* I (September 1964), 86–90.

the debaters. None of the unethical practices was judged as expedient or wise by the debaters. The researchers did discover that less-experienced debaters tended to rate the list of practices as a whole as more unethical and less expedient than did more experienced debaters.

A number of conclusions might be drawn from this study. Debaters do have standards of ethical conduct, and they say that they follow them. They do not consider unethical practices to be expedient, and they accuse their peers of relatively few transgressions of these standards. It should be noted that these were not the conclusions of the researchers (lest this author be accused of unethical debating). In a subsequent study reported in the same article, these researchers attempted to evaluate the practices of debaters at a midwestern tournament in the use of evidence. While this author could find in their reported data little to indicate frequent unethical practices, the researchers' conclusions imply the opposite. Nevertheless, their final conclusion calls for further inquiry into the ethics of college debating; and further inquiry would seem desirable, if only to produce more information about the attitudes concerning unethical practices than now exists.

Perhaps more than any other research, these studies provide principles which can be implemented into a debate program. Even with the wide disagreement about ethical practices a coach can warn his debaters about practices which he may consider ethical, but which may be judged as transgressions. Adopting standards of conduct which cannot be questioned is simply good audience analysis in this case. Hopefully, revealing the attitudes of coaches and debaters will affect the attitudes of those who are deviant in their own evaluations. The result may be that campaigns will be conducted to change attitudes and to raise or change the standards for evaluating ethical behavior. In any case, it seems critical for common standards to be discovered and published to protect the integrity of debating as an academic activity.

Strategies, Tactics, and Rules

Relevant to the problem of ethics is a discussion of how to win debates. Not much research has been carried out concerning winning strategies and tactics. Indeed textbook authors almost always treat the subject on a microcosmic level; and they rarely draw on any principles other than those which have been handed down from Classical rhetoricians. It seems fanciful to argue that coaches and debaters should not be concerned with winning since the decision debate is the criterion measure of success in the activity. This is not to say that improvement and practice in speaking along with other educational goals are not important to debate. It is just that the instrument used to attain the educational goals is the decision debate. Surely improvement in argumentation is related to greater success in winning debates; if debate as an academic activity can be justified, it ought to be causally related. The studies reported here then should be treated as sources of information for improving debaters' performances.

Dresser examined the use of evidence in ten final rounds of the National Debate Tournament at West Point.[30] His findings have profound implications for textbook writers as well as debaters and coaches. He discovered that the standards for evaluating evidence and using evidence, as well as the mere processes for identifying evidence, which are suggested in debate texts were not consistent with the standards and processes used by "championship" debaters. There are many possible explanations for this result: textbook writers are inaccurate or impractical in giving advice about the use of evidence; national championship college debaters are not very effective in using evidence; perhaps the transcripts used were not adequate representations of the actual debates themselves. This author feels that none of these conclusions are fully justified, but perhaps part of each is true. Typically, final rounds at the West Point tournament involved two battle-weary teams. Teams may be exhausted; and this fatigue manifests itself in sloppy debating. Furthermore, debating at the West Point tournament was a hybrid of the activity of debate itself because so much of the subject matter was accepted at that time of the year that debaters used a sort of shorthand in citing evidence and refuting arguments with very brief references. Finally, textbook writers go into such detail in conceptualizing evidence and tests of evidence that it is impractical to verbalize all the standards in

---

[30] William R. Dresser, "The Use of Evidence in Ten Championship Debates," *Journal of the American Forensic Association*, I (September 1964), 101–6.

an actual debate. To give the benefit of the doubt to the text authors, it can be said that their advice is useful in developing the kind of thinking habits which will enable a debater to analyze evidence quickly in his own mind before he makes the oral argument. All this is not to suggest that the Dresser study is not applicable to the subject of rules and strategies. One of his most significant discoveries was that, in spite of the many confounding variables evident, "good" debaters tend to be conscientious about qualifying sources used as evidence. This may be one of the good habits developed through debate training.

A study of Michigan high school debate programs[31] suggested some more immediately applicable advice for improving debate practices. This researcher surveyed both coaches and debaters attending a high-school forensics institute at Michigan State University on twenty practices. Comparison of the two groups of responses revealed that coaches thought they gave more criticism, evaluation and supervision to their debaters than perhaps they really did. In any case, the debaters felt that the amount was not so great as the coaches thought. On the other hand, the use of some good debate practices, such as extempore delivery and audience debate programs, evidenced themselves among the responses. The limited nature of the sample makes this a survey from which it is difficult to generalize; but it would seem that debaters and coaches agree on the worth of a number of debate practices.

Perhaps the most revealing study of successful debate practices available among the empirical studies of debate involved a relatively small survey of fifty-seven college debate coaches' attitudes about judging refutation.[32] Within the limitations of the study and the extent of the polling, it provides a fascinating picture of the standards used by judges in awarding decisions. To the extent that these preferences of judges can be translated into debate tactics, this study may be of great practical value to the coach in preparing his teams to win debates. The results of the James study are summarized below:

---

[31] Gordon L. Thomas, "A Survey of Debate Practices in Michigan High Schools," *Central States Speech Journal*, XVI (May 1965), 129–35.
[32] Herbert L. James, "Standards for Judging Refutation," *The Register*, IX (Spring 1961), 21–25.

1. Judges are strongly influenced by the order in which arguments are introduced.
   a. A significant minority (39%) would penalize the affirmative for introducing their plan in the closing seconds of the second affirmative constructive.
   b. An overwhelming majority (96%) would penalize the affirmative for introducing provisions of their plan in the first affirmative rebuttal.
   c. The first affirmative rebuttal speaker is expected to refute negative objections to plan. Many judges would penalize the affirmative for failing to do this. Most judges would not vote against an affirmative team for failing to refute plan evils in the first affirmative rebuttal, though a minority (16%) would.
   d. A vast majority (82%) would penalize an affirmative team for withholding until the final rebuttal speech a refutation to one or more vital issues.
   e. A majority (54%) would not accept a contested definition of terms in the second negative constructive speech.
   f. A majority (66%) expect a counter-plan to be introduced in the first negative constructive.
   g. A majority of judges would accept the introduction of plan evils in the first negative rebuttal.

2. Factors extrinsic to the debaters; utterances influence a judge's evaluation of refutation.
   a. A significant minority compensate for a "loaded" issue.
   b. A majority permit their evaluation of evidence to influence judgment.
   c. A majority permit their evaluation of reasoning to influence their judgment.

3. Direct refutation is the most vital method of refutation.
   a. A majority of judges attach more weight to direct refutation than to constructive negative cases; however a vast majority favor a negative approach which combines the two.
   b. A majority of judges coach their teams to use direct refutation in the second negative constructive; however most would not penalize the negative for devoting the entire second negative to plan evils.

4. Skill in refutation is affected by a variety of factors which follow no set pattern.
   a. If an argument can be refuted without the use of counter

evidence, a vast majority of judges would not penalize a team for the lack of evidence.

b. While a minority (18%) awarded issues on the strength of superior evidence and reasoning alone, all judges are influenced in their evaluation of a speaker's skill in refutation by organization and delivery (style and selection are also factors).

5. Judges will *not* vote against an affirmative team for failing to make out a *prima facie* case *unless* the negative discovers this deficiency.

6. A majority of judges will vote against an affirmative team which loses *any one* of the stock issues—need, workability of plan or plan evils; however, a significant minority will permit an affirmative to lose one of the stock issues.

Finally, the practice of spending money on debate is worth consideration. A survey of more than 500 high-school forensic budgets in 1965[33] showed wide differences in the amount spent on activities from school to school. Seven per cent of the programs had no budget; an additional 42 per cent of the programs had budgets of $600 or less; 36 per cent had budgets in the range $601 to $1200; only 15 per cent had budgets larger than $1200. The average budget was reported to be $696. An extensive survey of college forensics budgets in 1964[34] revealed a range from $100 to $12,000 among the 210 colleges and universities reporting. Seventeen schools had budgets of $5000 or more; forty-four additional had budgets of at least $3000; another one hundred and twenty-five had budgets of $1000 or more. This great variation in both surveys in part reflects differences in size of school, size of squad, and number of activities other than debate in a given program; but it is difficult to find any meaningful patterns associated with these variables. Perhaps more than anything else, the varying sizes of budgets result from the administrations' or coaches' varying beliefs in the worth of tournament debating. The beginning debate coach should be aware of the sources of moneys for debate budgets: 52 per cent of the schools reporting in the college survey received all or part of their funds directly from the college administration; 40

[33] Klopf and Rives, *loc. cit.*
[34] Nicholas M. Cripe, "Intercollegiate Forensic Budget Survey," *Journal of the American Forensic Association*, I (May 1964), 53–58.

per cent received their money from student activity fees; the rest of the money came from endowments and alumni grants. Altogether, the 210 colleges and universities spent more than a half million dollars on debate in 1963–64.

Perhaps the greatest justification for research about debate ethics, practices, and rules, comes from the tremendous financial investment made in the activity. Even at the high-school level, where expensive travel is not so much of a necessity, large amounts of money are allocated for students to participate in the activity. If there are low ethical standards, this money is certainly wasted; if there are no common standards of practice, at the very least, the money could be better spent on other student activities.

SUGGESTIONS FOR FURTHER RESEARCH

More and more the college teacher—and consequently the college debate coach—is expected to make the conduct of research part of his professional and occupational responsibilities. While this is less true in the high schools, the research requirements for advanced degrees offer the high-school debate coach the opportunity to seek further formal education and more information about debate attitudes and pratices at the same time. A number of the articles referred to in this chapter are revisions of theses for the authors' advanced degrees. The journals mentioned constitute evidence of the large number of outlets for publishing empirical research about debate. A director of forensics should feel an obligation not only to be aware of the relevant research which is being done, but to participate in the research efforts of his field.

It has been noted that many questions about the effects of debate training on debaters are unanswered. Some of the problems as well as the tentative conclusions of the research to date are included in an early section of this chapter. What kind of student can profit the most from debate training? Do any undesirable personality characteristics result from debating? Will debate training improve a student's ability to reason, to organize, to speak fluently? Another large area of research is far from complete: judging. To what extent does the background of a judge influence a decision? Are certain ballots better than others for allowing a judge to make and to reveal his decision? Finally, can any more be done to isolate the criteria which judges actually use in making decisions; and should these criteria be revised? A discussion of the unanswered questions in the area of the ethics of debate alone might fill a good-sized volume. Some of the more important questions have already been mentioned above. This author has commented on the lack of research about the strategies of debate. What are the winning techniques that a coach can teach his debaters? What revisions in the textbooks on debate and argumentation ought to be made to bring their advice in line with the realities of tournament debating? It should be evident that some of the practices which are thought to be most useful in winning debates are those which may be considered unethical by some judges. This inconsistency has resulted in part from a lack of codification of rules for debate. Aside from the National Forensic League's procedural rules and the varying standards proposed by such authors as Musgrave[35] and Newman,[36] there seems to be no written code of conduct for debaters. A whole new area of research is opened by this fact. Debaters and coaches should be surveyed about their attitudes concerning the NFL or Newman rules. Perhaps there is an informal code operating effectively. Experiments and surveys might be designed to find out.

The first section of this chapter contains a discussion of some of the limitations and restrictions on empirical research. Much of the research to date has been discredited because of ignorance or violation of these limitations and restrictions. Yet the methodological requirements for any good research are stringent. A coach who is anxious to do research about debate will not find the rules for the conduct of experiments and other empirical studies difficult to find or to use. Departments of Education and Psychology—and many Departments of Speech—usually have a number of experienced researchers who can provide sufficient advice and direction. There is certainly no shortage of areas and subjects in debate in which

---

[35] George Musgrave, *Competitive Debate: Rules and Techniques,* (3rd ed.; New York: H. W. Wilson Company, 1957).

[36] Robert P. Newman, *The Pittsburgh Code for Academic Debate,* (Pittsburgh: University of Pittsburgh Press, 1962).

research is needed. The novice director of forensics may discover that researching debate offers a most rewarding way to close some of the gaps in his preparation and to contribute to the general knowledge of his colleagues at the same time.

SUGGESTED READINGS

Bormann, Ernest G. *Theory and Research in The Communicative Arts.* New York: Holt, Rinehart & Winston, Inc., 1965.

Kerlinger, Fred N. *Foundations of Behavioral Research.* New York: Holt, Rinehart & Winston, Inc., 1966.

Miller, George A. *Language and Communication.* New York: McGraw-Hill Book Company, 1951.

Van Dalen, Deobold B. *Understanding Educational Research.* New York: McGraw-Hill Book Company, 1966.

Wallis, W. Allen, and Harry V. Roberts. *Statistics, a New Approach.* Glencoe Illinois Free Press, 1958.

Index